Modern
Scottish
Writers

Liz

Lochhead's

Voices

edited by
Robert Crawford
and
Anne Varty

Edinburgh University Press

© Edinburgh University Press, 1993

Edinburgh University Press Ltd
22 George Square, Edinburgh

Typeset in Linotron Garamond 3 by
Photoprint, Torquay, and
printed in Great Britain by
Hartnolls Ltd, Bodmin

A CIP record for this book is available
from the British Library.

ISBN 0 7486 0447 2

The publisher gratefully acknowledges subsidy from
the Scottish Arts Council towards
the publication of this volume.

Contents

Preface

In several senses this is a pioneering book. It is the first substantial study of Liz Lochhead's work. It is one of the few books devoted to the work of a Scottish woman writer, and one of an even smaller number of volumes which attend to Scottish drama in any detail. Given the lack of critical writing in all these areas, and given the contemporary nature of its subject matter, *Liz Lochhead's Voices* aims to offer readers starting-points, information and stimulation, rather than magisterial conclusions. The book offers both broad and detailed coverage of Lochhead's work. It supplies a variety of contexts – from biographical to Bakhtinian, from feminist ideology to theatre history – in which her work may be read, viewed, heard and relished. This book is committed enough to contain value-judgments and adverse criticism; it contains, as it should, some disagreements. Yet its contributors are united in recognizing Lochhead's sparky fidelity to living speech. For reasons of accessibility and availability, we have chosen to concentrate on Lochhead's published volumes, but we have deliberately included material on broadcasts and performances as well. Lochhead's work demands hearing, not just reading and watching. As poet, performer and dramatist, Lochhead attends to the nuances of the spoken word in ways which are constantly arresting. Most of all, what this book aims to do is to help those who encounter her work to tune in as accurately as they can to Liz Lochhead's living and enlivening voices.

The editors would like to thank Liz Lochhead for patiently answering several interviewers' questions, for clarifying some factual points, and for allowing quotation from various published and unpublished works as detailed in the text of this book. For permission to quote we would also like to thank the publishers of the copyright works detailed in this volume's list of abbreviations and in the endnotes to the chapters.

Particular thanks are due to Polygon, to Methuen and to Penguin, Lochhead's principal publishers.

We would also like to thank especially those who have helped to assemble the dispersed material of Lochhead's work in the theatre: Heather Baird, Morag Neil, Gerry Mulgrew (Communicado), Ashley Bramwell (Dukes, Lancaster), John Carnegie, Joyce Deans, Malcolm Duffin (Contact Theatre Co.), Jane Ellis (Traverse), Alex Heatherington (Tron), Marilyn Imrie (BBC), Emma M. O'Ferrall (Kaleidoscope), Siobhan Redmond, Denise Winford (Dundee Rep.).

R. C., University of St Andrews
A. V., Royal Holloway, University of London

Abbreviations

The following abbreviations of works by Liz Lochhead are used throughout this book:

BM   *Bagpipe Muzak* (Harmondsworth: Penguin, 1991)

DF   *Dreaming Frankenstein & Collected Poems* (Edinburgh: Polygon, 1984)

GS   *The Grimm Sisters* (London: Next Editions in association with Faber and Faber, 1981)

I   *Islands* (Glasgow: Print Studio Press, 1978)

LL(1)   *Liz Lochhead* (Glasgow and London: National Book League, 1978)

LL(2)   *Liz Lochhead* (Glasgow and London: National Book League, 1986)

MFS   *Memo for Spring* (Edinburgh: Reprographia, 1972)

MQD   *'Mary Queen of Scots Got Her Head Chopped Off' and 'Dracula'* (Harmondsworth: Penguin, 1989)

Nicholson   'Knucklebones of Irony', interview with Colin Nicholson in his book, *Poem, Purpose and Place: Shaping Identity in Contemporary Scottish Verse* (Edinburgh: Polygon, 1992), 203–23

PW   *Blood and Ice*, in Michelene Wandor, ed., *Plays by Women, Volume Four* (London: Methuen, 1985), 81–118

T   *Tartuffe: A Translation into Scots from the Original by Molière* (Edinburgh and Glasgow: Polygon and Third Eye Centre, 1985)

TCNC   *True Confessions & New Clichés* (Edinburgh: Polygon, 1985)

Verse   interview with Emily Todd, *Verse*, 8.3/9.1 (Winter/Spring 1992), 83–95

One

Liz Lochhead: Speaking in her Own Voice

Alison Smith

For a writer so clearly concerned with versions of the self and with interpretations of identity, Liz Lochhead has so far written very little that is overtly about her *own* self. 'If you asked me to write something autobiographical,' she says, 'I would find it incredibly difficult. People always think of me as an autobiographical kind of poet.' This is an assumption which she finds 'flattering', suggesting that she achieves a level of authenticity of the personal in the voices and the lives she creates in her poetry and drama. But she stresses about her work, 'I'm not nearly as autobiographical as people think. It's a lot of fiction, personae, personifying.'[1]

This chapter is an attempt to present a version of Liz Lochhead's own life so far, largely through her own words. She has written only one substantial piece of directly autobiographical prose, the short essay, 'A Protestant Girlhood', published in 1977.[2] It is an intelligent recreation of her childhood and teenage years, displaying her ability to be at once discerningly objective and sympathetically subjective; strong and witty in its presentation of the atmosphere of a time, an essay that makes you hope that at some point she'll write more autobiography. I use it centrally in the first part of this chapter. My other sources for Lochhead's own voice are the interview with Lochhead by Emily B. Todd (*Verse*) and an unpublished interview by me carried out in September 1992.

'I was born', she writes, 'at the bleak end of 1947. . . . There were a lot of us born then, most of us to parents just as recently demobbed, just as newly optimistic and no better housed than my father and mother were.'[3] Elizabeth Anne Lochhead, or Elsie, as she was known as a child, was born on Boxing Day in Motherwell and spent the first four years of her life crammed with her mother and father into spare rooms in the houses of both sets of grandparents. 'This incredible overcrowding, that's what my early life was like.' Lochhead vividly and actually remembers

being part of the Bulge, the population explosion after the war that made
for long queues for housing, tribes of children on the council estate, and
huge classes, sometimes over fifty children to a class, from primary school
through to secondary.

Lochhead's mother and father both came from industrial Lanarkshire,
and both served in the army through the war years. They married in 1944
and returned to the 'dull country' Lochhead describes in one of her more
plainly autobiographical poems, 'After the War'. In 1952 the family
moved to Newarthill and the new life, the 'square green lawn and a
twelve-inch tele':

> a brand-new council four-apartment in the small mining village of
> Newarthill. A couple of miners' rows, the school, the pub, the
> Tallies' Cafe, the Post Office and the Co-operative. . . . I went
> with my mother to do the place up before we moved in. I could feel
> her excitement. Eight years married and a house at last. We
> approached along newly laid out paths. What would soon be careful
> turfed lawns and neat rose-borders were great banks and churns of
> clay. The rooms seemed big and empty and hollow-sounding. Full
> of space.[4]

Newarthill was on the edge of countryside and the moors while still an
'industrially scarred' landscape, one which would surely form Lochhead's
notion of an industrial pastoral found in many of the poems of her first
collection, *Memo for Spring*.

Lochhead describes her parents and her roots as 'posh working class —
my father wore a shirt and tie to work' (he was a local government clerk),
'but he'd never have described himself as middle class'. She was brought
up in the Church of Scotland and though her parents deplored religious
bigotry, such bigotry was part of the landscape and a religious split was
accepted as part of daily life. She remembers her grandfather, always ill
with silicosis contracted in his time down the mines, berating Roman
Catholicism, furious still at the strike-breaking Irish Catholics brought
over at the time of the General Strike. There were different coloured tin
huts in the village for Catholics and Protestants. 'The area was very
divided. Catholics and Protestants lived, in many ways, quite separate
lives because of the separate schooling. . . . Our village was sort of
Protestant and the next village down was largely Catholic' (*Verse*, 83). In
interview, Lochhead speaks out angrily against segregated schools and
the 'different tribes' they create, and she remembers too 'the mysterious
attraction of the different coloured uniform'.

Newarthill Primary School, with its teachers and its 'club-footed
piano', is wittily and fully remembered in 'A Protestant Girlhood'. Here,
and in poems like 'In the Dreamschool', 'The Teachers' and 'The Prize',

Lochhead pictures school as a nightmare place, where 'everything was a competition' and 'your place in this civilization . . . was fixed by weeks of tests'. Primary school, though, was a paradoxical place, one where you also learned wonderful things, like how to tell trees by their leaves, or breeds of swan. Lochhead was, she remembers, best at 'composition'; 'sometimes they even got Read Out . . . I loved Composition. I knew what they wanted you to write.'[5]

Though school is later the stuff of nightmare in her work, she stresses she loved it, 'because I was brainy', she says, though emphasising that she was never top, never *too* brainy. Except at English: 'I was always the best at English.' Perhaps the nightmare quality comes from somewhere or something else? 'I loved school, but I didn't much like being a kid.' Having lived so much of her infancy with adults and old people, she had found it difficult to adapt to a society made up of other children, both when they moved to Newarthill and at school. Furthermore, it wasn't an easy time to be young: if you ask her to sum up her childhood, the word she chooses is 'anxious'. 'The thing I can remember most about childhood is enormous anxiety about atomic war'; fearful nights under the covers in bed, not telling her parents of her fear 'so as not to upset them'; childhood was a time of crises, of newspaper headlines, 'real cold war anxiety. So I didn't really enjoy childhood, although it got better all the time.'

As a child, she loved listening to the radio, which, when she was very small and living with in-laws, was invariably a speaker attached to the main set downstairs. If anyone switched channels, the Lochhead family had no choice but to listen to whatever was playing. 'I loved the radio, radio plays particularly', voices in air, disembodied language. She didn't write when she was a child, 'not for fun', only if pressed to do something. Instead she painted and drew 'all the time'. And she 'read voraciously', a mixture of pony books, boarding school books and classics like *Wuthering Heights* and *The Mill on the Floss*. 'I didn't read them thinking I was reading anything special – it was just among the things you read' (*Verse*, 83). Before she was able to read for herself, her parents read her *Tanglewood Tales*, Nathaniel Hawthorne's versions of Greek myths rewritten for children, and she clearly remembers the tale of Europa, the innocent child in 'The Dragon's Teeth' who is beguiled by a beautiful bull and carried away on its back, never seen again. Her mother was a great storyteller and could be persuaded to tell 'true-life romance' stories of the exciting, romantic things that happened to her in wartime, 'like her coming home from work, finding a new dress across the bed that somebody had saved up their coupons for'. Lochhead remembers how, when she was small, 'these Greek myths and stories about your parents' life in the war got all mixed up together, all as dramatic as each other' – a notion of the mythological and dramatic quality of ordinariness forming early in her life.

Being one of the six or so brightest in the class of forty five at Newarthill Primary, she effortlessly passed the entrance qualifications to Dalziel High School in Motherwell and there became one of the three out of that six to be taking the 'five-year Academic Course', with Latin and Greek. Here, as at Newarthill, she quickly learned the correct voice and manipulated it in her school composition, 'My Favourite Season':

> Autumn. Compare the falling leaves to ballerinas pirouetting to the ground. Get in the words golden-ochre and russet. And not least of my pleasures when autumn spreads its golden wings around us is a good book and tea by the fire and toasted muffins and jam while the wind and rain blusters on the window pane: I don't think I'd ever tasted toasted muffins and jam in my life but they sounded right. English enough . . . it was not a lie, exactly. Just that it had never occurred to me, nothing in my Education had ever led me to believe that anything among my own real life ordinary things had the right to be written down. . . . I knew what they wanted you to write.[6]

From an early stage she had the innate ability to manipulate, even to ape a demanded style, choose the voice for the occasion.

Looking back, she remembers Dalziel High as 'completely unsexist', with the same education (or Education) for girls as for boys. In fact, girls were 'proxy boys complete with ties and blazers, you just wore a skirt instead of trousers. The thing about it – there was nothing that actually allowed you to express your *femaleness*'.

In those Brodie terms of what everybody was famous for at school, she quickly became famous for 'being arty, acting. I always got the starring part, and I always won the essay prizes.' She remembers acting in an A. A. Milne play in her first year; she recalls later landing the part of rich, mad, enigmatic Mrs Snell in Bridie's *The Amazed Evangelist* and knowing, as she stood behind the scenery, that by speaking in a quiet voice she could bewitch the listening audience. 'But as far as school was concerned, I was also famous for being completely crap at sport and maths. You wanted to get your O-level maths for going to university – but I didn't want to go to university anyway. I wanted to go to art school.'

This was something she had decided by the age of fifteen; she already drew and painted all the time, and the decision promised a kind of freedom. She persuaded the Rector of Dalziel High 'after my third visit to his office', to let her drop Greek and take art and eventually he gave way, 'washed his hands of me, said it was my own lookout'. The Rector had wanted her to go to university to study English. 'It was art which caused the rift', she wrote later, 'between you and your schooling. Before that, the report cards glowed.'[7]

But it was the mid-Sixties, a time of liberation and there can't have been many more self-consciously exciting places to go to than art school. Lochhead entered Glasgow School of Art in 1965 ('it *was* exciting, but it wasn't the wild sixties that everybody remembers, because they took ages to get to Glasgow! It was the late sixties before you had the middle sixties really') and remembers her time there with affection. Art school was the place she met and made many of the friends she still has, the place of the usual initiations, 'falling in love, getting drunk' and, particularly in the first two years, she says, working very hard.

Lochhead feels now, however, that she suffered a 'failure of nerve' as far as her drawing and painting were concerned, 'I lost the place, I lost faith in it, got all mixed up.' This, she says, was mostly to do with current artistic trend, the fashion for 'hard-edged painting, abstract painting'. She found she was interested in abstract art, but that she didn't at all enjoy *doing* it. 'I think if I'd been at art school ten years later, the time of the new narrative painters, it would have been different.' Her own work was mainly figurative; although 'towards the end they were getting abstract, they always came from *things*'. There's a poem in *Memo for Spring* called 'Notes on the Inadequacy of a Sketch' – Lochhead says now that she did feel that for her, visual art was inadequate, that there was more she could say and do in writing:

> Once I got a bit of facility with my drawing, I didn't know what I wanted to *do* with it. The kind of drawings and paintings that I felt were the right kind to do didn't give me, personally, satisfaction, because they didn't have a narrative. I'm not really interested in abstractions. Maybe if I'd not been a writer I might have had to come to terms with that. I've often wondered whether or not, if I'd gone to university, I might have become a *painter* – I think I might've! Painting might have been what I *did*, the way that at the end of art school, writing was what I did.

Writing now doesn't make her want to paint, however, but it does make her want to work with the visual. Perhaps one of the reasons she writes so much drama is related to her early work with the visual arts. Writing plays, she says, 'feels like making pictures'; it comes from that initial interest in the figurative rather than the abstract, interest in a necessary narrative, 'and there's always been a narrative streak in my poems too'.

Suddenly at art school, then, Lochhead found she was writing poems (her very first poem, 'The Visit', which can be found in *Memo for Spring*, was written when she was at art school). 'Certainly about halfway through art school my real love switched to writing' (*Verse*, 84).

Painting had been a personal liberation before she matriculated at Glasgow School of Art, now it was 'your work'; it took breaking the pattern of being the girl good at the right voices in English at school and going to art school, to allow writing to be a liberation and to allow the poet to emerge and be able to choose her own voices and personae for what she wrote.

Lochhead began going along to an informal, small creative writing workshop held by Stephen Mulrine, who taught in the Art School's Liberal Arts Department. Over half of the poems in *Memo for Spring* had been written by 1970 when she graduated with a Diploma in Art; in fact part of her final Diploma exam had been the submission of an illustrated thesis — a book of poems (typed up by Lochhead's mother) and drawings by Lochhead, many of the poems that would make up the first collection in 1972. This original book still exists, she says, 'in bits'.

Mulrine's workshop, which she attended two or three times, acted initially 'in lieu of a literary education' (*Verse*, 84), and she found his attention to her poetry extremely useful, invaluable help with first structures and first criticism. After art school she went to an extra mural writers' workshop run by the critic and poet, Philip Hobsbaum, which met on Sunday nights and allocated a night each to one or sometimes two writers, providing somewhere their work could be aired and discussed. Lochhead attended Hobsbaum's group once or twice, as she comically says now, partly in the self-conscious knowledge that she would be 'discovered', seeking out other writers, and because she had read and liked Hobsbaum's poetry and wanted to know what the poet would make of her own work. She became Hobsbaum's 'discovery' of that particular year — Jim Kelman was the 'discovery' of the following year. 'He took me seriously as a writer, which was nice. And the following year he took Jim very seriously as a writer.'

Discovery was swift. In 1971, Lochhead won the Radio Scotland poetry prize with two poems, 'Revelation' and 'Poem for Other Poor Fools'. In 1972 she read with Norman MacCaig at a one-day poetry festival in Edinburgh, 'Poem 72', and later in the year her first collection, *Memo for Spring*, was published. She began reading poetry all over Scotland and to move in a circle of new, young, talented Scottish writers. The night of the poetry prize, she finally met Alasdair Gray, whom she knew to see on the street as the 'famous genius' who had preceded her at Glasgow School of Art. They became very good friends, and Lochhead particularly points out that Gray gave her 'the most practical help. The Arts Council had given him a grant or an award and with some of the money he bought me the present of having my poems all typed up on stencils. He always helps other artists, Alasdair.' Tom

Leonard she met later, when they were reading together at the end of 1972. And she remembers being interested in, and mildly jealous at art school of Tom McGrath's exclusive-seeming group of writers, who called themselves 'The Other People'. 'I used to think, "my poems are as good as theirs." Though I don't know how they were meant to know that – osmosis, I suppose!' Then in the early seventies she found herself sitting at McGrath's kitchen table, invited round for the evening, listening to Alan Spence read out his poems. 'Everything took off suddenly. It was fabulous.'

The publication of *Memo for Spring* came about as a result of Hobsbaum's workshops, the Radio Scotland prize, the short reading at 'Poem 72' and Gray's present of the stencilled poems. The publisher, Gordon Wright, approached Lochhead and asked whether she had a collection ready. She was able to send the poems Gray had had typed up. 'And he wrote back and said, "I've got a grant from the Arts Council – it'll be out in six weeks."' Wright chose the title, which Lochhead says she didn't particularly like, feeling it was too 'pretty', lacking the irony she would have wanted.

After *Memo for Spring*, the short pamphlet, *Islands*, was the next book, published in 1978 by the Print Studio's own press in Glasgow. The Print Studio Press was a writers' co-operative, publishing writers such as Kelman, Gray, Leonard, Spence and Lochhead in editions of six hundred copies of each pamphlet. *Islands* had been prompted by a stay on Skye, where 'it rained and rained, so I wrote lots of poems,' and Lochhead remembers finding the Gaeldom 'very foreign', a stimulus for the poems. (Lochhead often goes to stay in the north-west of Scotland now; she and her husband Tom Logan have a caravan on the west coast, and love to visit there.)

In the years between these publications, Lochhead had been doing a lot of part-time teaching in secondary schools, in Bristol and in schools round Glasgow and Cumbernauld. Often she was 'the most reluctant member of the art department' (*TCNC*, 1). 'I hate teaching in schools. I don't like schools', she says, although anyone who's seen her talk to a class will know she must have been a talented teacher, instantly engaging students. Though she enjoys teaching writing in week-long residences or creative writing placements, she stresses, 'I can only teach very fitfully. And I really don't like Scottish secondary schools, the exams, the smell and the feel of them. I even have to overcome that to go into schools and do readings.'

Lochhead taught first in Bristol in 1972, also travelling to Turkey and back the following year. These moves were made with her partner, Tarık Okyay, who had been a graduate student in Bristol; they left for Turkey intending to live there, but were forced to return because Okyay was unwell with what turned out, much later, to be cancer. Lochhead cites Okyay as a 'great influence', whose encouragement to her to write, whose wide knowledge and love of architecture, film and theatre she remembers with much feeling. The big decision made to go and live 'somewhere other than Glasgow' in the early seventies, especially 'attempting to live somewhere *really* far away', culminated in painful anticlimax on her return to Scotland in 1973, and she remembers the mid-seventies as a bleak period in her life.

In 1978, when the chance came to take a year off teaching and go to Canada on the Scottish Arts Council first Scottish/Canadian Writers' Exchange, she was more than happy to take it. The exchange (the writer who came to Scotland was Graham Gibson, the novelist and husband of Margaret Atwood) took her to Glendon College, Toronto, a small independent College of Liberal Arts attached to York University. Here she was free to attend what classes she liked and people would come to show her their writing. There was also plenty of time to work on her own writing; most of *The Grimm Sisters* was completed there and many other poems written, some of which are in *Dreaming Frankenstein & Collected Poems*. She also began a version of *Blood and Ice*, her first stage play. Canada was a relief, a personal rejuvenation at thirty; more, she recalls the sense that this was serious time, real time to devote to writing, 'whereas I'd done things for fun before'. After living there for a year, she visited and stayed in New York, returning to Scotland at the beginning of 1980.

The years following this return were filled not just with the writing of poetry – *The Grimm Sisters* was published in 1981 – but with the very busy schedule of various writer-in-residence posts (work which she says she enjoys greatly) and a dizzying amount of theatre work, both writing and performance. Lochhead, herself, feels there is a substantial split between her poetry and her performance pieces and drama, what she calls the difference between the 'black book', *True Confessions and New Clichés*, the collection of monologues and performance pieces published with a black cover in 1985, and the 'white book', *Dreaming Frankenstein & Collected Poems*, with its white cover, published the year before.

> That interest in performance . . . seemed slightly to split away from an interest in writing . . . it feels to me that I write two quite different things . . . I feel as though they are written by two different people. (*Verse*, 86)

In conversation, she comments, 'the plays and the poems are probably more alike than I think they are. But a poem's more complete, more compact, intensified.' In the *Verse* interview, she elaborates:

plays are for something . . . for a deadline. A play is something that doesn't exist when you have written it. It only exists when it begins to be performed. Whereas a poem . . . even if it's lying under the bed, there is it; it's a thing. . . . that's what satisfies me the most about poetry, that it is not for anything whatsoever and that you don't really do it to order. (*Verse*, 87)

Lochhead's career in theatre, however, one rich in revue work, original drama and inspired adaptation of history and literature, began in poetry, with a poetry reading that became performance-conscious. In 1978 she collaborated with writer/performer Marcella Evaristi and musician Esther Allan, to produce *Sugar and Spite*, a run of poetry performance at the Traverse in Edinburgh. Having realised early, when giving her first readings, that a writer reading work to an audience at a traditional poetry reading has a responsibility to do it so that it can be heard, so that it can be felt and so that it won't send the audience to sleep, with *Sugar and Spite* she faced something a little different, what she calls her 'first attempt at doing anything specifically for out-loud performance' (*TCNC*, 1). To the usual notion of a poetry reading, Evaristi, Allan and Lochhead added a structure, costumes, props, music; they decided to learn the poems, rather than read them off the page. Lochhead remembers naturally finding that many poems, poems other than overt dramatic monologue, didn't adapt well to being performed in this way and so she and Evaristi found themselves writing new work specifically for performance. (*Sugar and Spite* was also where Lochhead developed what's now her unique performance trademark of rhythmic rap-like speech; since neither she nor Evaristi could sing very well, they 'spoke' poems to musical accompaniment.)

After Canada and back in Scotland as writer-in-residence at Duncan of Jordanstone College of Art in Dundee, Lochhead had put together a second show, *Goodstyle* (1980), a history of art revue 'written and pinched and compiled', also directed by her, with a 'cast of thousands'. This she found highly enjoyable, and for the moment having 'burned her fingers' at serious drama, with a 'disastrous premature version of *Blood and Ice* in Coventry', she relaxed into revue, and the years that followed produced *True Confessions* (1981), the revue which in one sketch introduced the character of Verena, who would graduate to the tragicomic *Quelques Fleurs* in 1991, *Tickly Mince* (1982), *The Pie of Damocles* (1983), then later, *Nippy Sweeties: The Complete Alternative History of the World Part 1* (1986). Lochhead herself performed in *True Confessions* and *Nippy Sweeties; Tickly Mince* and *The Pie of Damocles* offered the enjoyment of collaborating on the writing with Tom Leonard, Alasdair Gray and Jim Kelman (Kelman on *The Pie* only). A collaboration with Wildcat Theatre

Company followed in 1983, producing *A Bunch of Fives*, and in the same year Lochhead also worked on *Red Hot Shoes*, a mixture of fairy-tale and dance with Peter Royston of Scottish Ballet as choreographer.

Meanwhile Lochhead was writer-in-residence at the Tattenhall Centre in Cheshire and had been writing drama. *Blood and Ice*, her version of Mary Shelley's life, finally opened at the Traverse to success in 1982. *Disgusting Objects*, a script about schoolgirls encountering sexism for the first time, was Lochhead's script for the Scottish Youth Theatre annual summer school in 1983, and an hour-long play she had written for Borderline Theatre Company, *Shanghaied*, focused on four children evacuated from Glasgow in the war years and the changing power-relationship between them. This, written after a week spent working with the actors, was her first attempt, and an enjoyable one, at devising a script after improvisation. Lochhead is not always happy with the notion of devised drama, however, and found little satisfaction later working on *Jock Tamson's Bairns*, the devised piece commissioned to celebrate Glasgow's year as European City of Culture in 1990.[8] For this piece she prefers the title of 'scribe' rather than writer: 'it was always a performance piece, and I don't really like performance art myself, it's the same as how I felt about abstract painting at the Art School. It's not what I'm interested in doing.'

In contrast, *Dracula* (1985), her stark, complex version of Stoker's classic, is one of the plays she remembers working on with most fondness. 'From the minute of beginning to work on it, I just loved it. A huge task, a big sprawling Victorian novel to adapt', it became one of the plays she is most pleased with. The highly successful, raucous, Scots version of *Tartuffe* followed *Dracula*; Lochhead had seen a version of *The Miser* in which the central character had been played as a Scot and had remarked to the director of *Dracula* that a whole Scots Molière might be workable: 'what I saw in the play [was] social gradations . . . and Scots is a fascinating language for multiplicity of register' (*Verse*, 93). She thinks of *Tartuffe* now, however, as 'just a translation . . . purely linguistic fun', where *Dracula* was a 'personal' version and vision. (Later, in 1989, she would adapt another Molière play, *Les Precieuses Ridicules*, into Glaswegian, and call it *Patter Merchants*.)

Mary Queen of Scots Got Her Head Chopped Off, produced by Communicado in 1987 at the Lyceum Studio in Edinburgh, was one of the most difficult plays to write, she says, but the one she sees as her favourite, and thinks is her best work – 'first it was the worst. I mean, I was the most panic-stricken, kept putting off the actual writing doing research, research, more research on it.' In fact the writing of it left her unwell after it, in an acute state of exhaustion. Her way of working has been one that encourages anticlimax in the recent very busy years: 'I work in a pressurised way, then I flop, then I work. It's not a very healthy way to work, to overtire yourself.' It's difficult, though, she says, not to '*have* to put your whole self' into some projects; easy enough if you're adapting *Tartuffe* and having 'linguistic fun', impossible to escape the consequences of *Dracula* or *Mary* even in your dreams. '*Dracula* was like some sort of Jungian therapy or something. That's not why I was doing it, but I felt great when I'd finished it, gone to all those dark places and come through their woods. It was complete, very all-consuming, and so was *Mary*.'

Now, looking back, she is particularly pleased with both *Mary* and *Dracula*, especially because she senses that they go some way to healing the split she feels lies between the performance work and the poetry; she sees these plays as her closest to 'long poems'.

Most recently Lochhead has translated and adapted the York Cycle of medieval mystery plays for the York Festival of 1992, with a huge cast of amateurs 'and one professional Jesus'. For this she changed the 1950 translation quite radically, adapting the language into northern middle English, 'something like a spoken version of the language of the ballads'. And for the last four years she has been working on a project with the Royal Shakespeare Company, a play entitled *Damages*, due for production in 1993. It takes the real-life incident (the same story adapted by Lillian Hellman into her play *The Children's Hour*) where an accusation of unnatural practices is made against a governess and a teacher at a girls' school in Edinburgh last century, by one of the girls attending the school. In this, she examines notions of colonialism between Scotland, England and the Caribbean as well as notions of class, as a line of white upper class judges on the bench are forced to take the word of a black child (illegitimate, albeit related to aristocracy) to decide the fate of two middle class white women. The play promises to be fiery.

Of course, Lochhead has also written film, radio and television scripts, and her play, *Quelques Fleurs*, which she performs, the tale of Verena, the 'suburban monster' whom Lochhead clearly loves, has just been adapted for radio. Lochhead herself says she loves performing:

> there I was at school, this arty wee girl who was supposed to be good at acting and writing, and I went to art school, deliberately set off to do this other thing that I wanted to do, and I end up acting and writing! Performing's easy, you perform as yourself, but acting is a complete thing you do on stage from the moment you come on. Acting's like becoming other people.

This 'becoming other people', creating convincing and authentic personae or voices, is after all what her work for the last twenty years has concerned itself with.

There has certainly been recent pressure, from both publishers and the public, for writers to appear, to be available, to perform their work as part of the promotion of the work. Lochhead enjoys this aspect, 'performance is what I do, I can do readings, appearances, very easily.' But even on these terms, a lot is expected of Lochhead in the media's version of her as 'the literary Miss Scotland, feted by the media, courted by the chattering classes, praised by fellow scribes and idolised by schoolgirls'.[9] 'That', she says, 'is enough to depress anybody', her approach is characteristically straightforward, levelheaded:

> I don't really like that sort of notion of myself as having a public persona that's separate from me. You can very easily become a token Scottish voice on the radio, and a token woman for that too. Where it bothers me I just stop doing it, and other times I just ignore it, it's not really what you're doing anyway.

A recent press article laid emphasis on Lochhead as being strangely split, the bright comic public persona who suddenly reveals a peculiarly dark, introspective 'other' side.[10] Lochhead herself is always keen to deny or break a limiting category. If a journalist insists she's bright and funny, a kind of tartan Victoria Wood, then she'll equivocate, be something else, be the opposite – she'll unbox herself from the assumptions of the media, or of people who dare to assume she's one thing, not the other.

'I'd love to write short fiction', says the poet and playwright, 'I have already written a couple of short stories, it's my favourite thing to read.' She cites Grace Paley, Raymond Carver and Alice Munro as among the fiction writers she likes best. Among poets, she likes to read MacCaig, she admires Edwin Morgan's ease with variety of form, she remembers being influenced by American poets, the Black Mountain poets, Whitman, Ginsberg and the Beat poets – 'it made poetry about breathing, about talking' (*Verse*, 91). She comments that Robert Garioch is 'probably more of an influence than anyone else' in his use of voice, his satirical mischief. And good argumentative close friendships with Kelman, Gray and Leonard have been a big part of her life as a writer.

As for writing autobiography, as she says, all of her voices – whether it's Mary Queen of Scots, Mary Shelley, Verena, or the teller of tales in *The Grimm Sisters* – come from the self after all. 'I mean, how could *Dracula* be autobiographical? But it is, it was very psychologically about the way I felt about things at that time. It all comes out of the self. I don't see the point in not admitting that.' She denies that her poetry is confessional, knows it's all too easy to see it as this, with its authentic presentation of very personal voices. To see it as such, she says, is to simplify the identity. Twenty years of poetry and drama by Liz Lochhead go all out against such simplification.

CHRONOLOGY

1947	Elizabeth Anne Lochhead born, 26 December, Motherwell. First child of John Lochhead and Margaret Forrest.
1947–52	Lives at 13 The Broadway, Craigneuk, Wishaw, and 12 Hosier Street, Carluke.
1952	Moves to 13 Tillanburn Road, Newarthill.
1953–60	Attends Newarthill Primary School.
1957	Birth of only sister, Janice.
1960–5	Attends Dalziel High School, Motherwell.
1965–70	Attends Glasgow School of Art, studying drawing and painting. Diploma in Art, 1970.
1970	First visit to the States, for three or four months travelling and working.
1971	Wins BBC Radio Scotland poetry prize with 'Revelation' and 'Poem for Other Poor Fools'.
1971–2	Teaches art at Bishopbriggs High School, Glasgow.
1972	Reads with Norman MacCaig at Poem '72 in February. *Memo for Spring* published in May. Works on a "poem voice-over" for a screenplay, *Now and Then*; Alasdair Gray works on paintings for the same (the film was never completed). Moves to Bristol, teaching art at Winterbourne, South Gloucestershire.
1972–3	Wins Scottish Arts Council award for *Memo for Spring*.
1973	Goes to Turkey to live, with Tarık Okyay, and returns alone due to his ill health.
1974	Travels extensively in Turkey with the temporarily recovered Tarık Okyay (who later dies in 1981, aged 39).
1973–6	Teaches art at Bannerman High School, Baillieston.
1976–8	Teaches art at Cumbernauld High School.
1978	Writes and performs *Sugar and Spite* at the Traverse, Edinburgh, with Marcella Evaristi and Esther Allan in May. *Islands* published in September. Takes up the first Scottish Arts Council Scottish/Canadian Writers' Exchange Fellowship, to Glendon College, Toronto, in September. Stays in Toronto for over a year, and subsequently moves to New York.
1980	Returns to Scotland in January to take up Writer-in-Residence post at Duncan of Jordanstone College of Art, Dundee. Writes, 'cobbles together' and directs *Goodstyle*, Christmas revue. Later this show is brought to Glasgow

School of Art. This year and the next, lengthy periods in
New York, where she almost goes to live.

1981   *The Grimm Sisters* published in January. *Mary and the Monster*,
an 'embryonic, unsuccessful first draft' of *Blood and Ice*,
performed in Coventry in February. Writes and performs
True Confessions with Siobhan Redmond and Esther Allan at
the Tron Theatre Club, Glasgow, in August, and again in
the New Year.

1982   Writes for *Tickly Mince*, with Tom Leonard and Alasdair
Gray, performed by Merryhell Theatre Co. in Glasgow in the
spring. Writes *Disgusting Objects* for the Scottish Youth
Theatre Summer School. *Blood and Ice*, her first full-length
play, is premiered at the Traverse in the Edinburgh Festival
Fringe in August. *Tickly Mince* and *True Confessions* both
revived at the Fringe.

1982–4 Writer-in-Residence at the Tattenhall Centre near Chester,
in Cheshire, a residential centre for local schools.

1983   Collaborates on *A Bunch of Fives* for Wildcat Theatre
Company, with Dave MacLennan, Dave Anderson, Tom
Leonard and Sean Hardie. Writes for *The Pie of Damocles* for
Merryhell Theatre Co., with Tom Leonard, Alasdair Gray
and Jim Kelman, performed at the Fringe, and after in
Glasgow at the Third Eye Centre. Writes *Shanghaied*
performed by Borderline Theatre Company in the autumn,
and writes *Red Hot Shoes*, choreographed by Peter Royston,
for the Tron Christmas Show, 'a pantomime for grown-ups',
from Snow White.

1984   *Dreaming Frankenstein & Collected Poems* published in May.
Writes *Same Difference* for Wildcat, performed at Mayfest
with tour following. *Shanghaied* revived by Borderline for
Mayfest. Works with Scottish Youth Theatre on a summer
production. First TV play, *Sweet Nothings*, shown by BBC1 in
their 'End of the Line' season of new drama (written 1982–3).

1985   *Dracula* performed at the Royal Lyceum, Edinburgh, in
March. Adaptation of Molière's *Tartuffe*, commissioned by
the Lyceum. *True Confessions and New Clichés* published in
July.

1985–7 Writer-in-Residence at the University of Edinburgh.

1986   *Tartuffe* performed at the Lyceum in January, and in Glasgow
for Mayfest. *Tartuffe* published by Polygon/Third Eye.
Writes and performs in *Nippy Sweeties: The Complete Alternative History of the World Part* 1 with Elaine C. Smith and

Angie Drew, both at Mayfest and later at the Fringe. *Fancy You Minding That*, her first radio play (written 1985) broadcast by Radio 4 in the autumn.

1987   *Tartuffe* revived at the Lyceum in the summer. *Mary Queen of Scots Got Her Head Chopped Off* performed by Communicado at the Royal Lyceum Studio at the Fringe and is awarded a *Scotsman* Fringe First. Marries Tom Logan in September.

1988–9 Writer-in-Residence at the Royal Shakespeare Company under bursary scheme and commission from Thames Television. Working on *Damages* under this scheme, to date.

1988   *Mary Queen of Scots* revived at the Lyceum, followed by tour. Writes *The Big Picture* for Dundee Repertory Theatre, performed in Dundee in March/April, and in Glasgow for Mayfest.

1988–91 Working on *Rough Trade* feature film screenplay, unmade to date.

1989   Writes *Them Through the Wall* with Agnes Owens for Cumbernauld Theatre Company. Writes *Patter Merchants*, an adaptation of Molière's *Les Precieuses Ridicules*, for Winged Horse Theatre Company, performed at the Fringe in August, followed by tour. Work as writer/scribe on devised piece, *Jock Tamson's Bairns*, with Gerard Mulgrew and Communicado, commissioned for performance in the opening festivities of Glasgow, European City of Culture 1990. *Mary Queen of Scots* and *Dracula* published in single volume by Penguin.

1990   *Jock Tamson's Bairns* performed at the Tramway, Glasgow, in January. Radio version of *Blood and Ice* broadcast on Radio 4. Writes new first half-rhyming setting for Rimsky-Korsakov's *Mozart and Salieri* for the Royal Scottish Academy of Music and Drama. Small acting part in Timothy Neat's and John Berger's film *Play Me Something*. Writes *Quelques Fleurs*.

1991   Rewrites and performs *Quelques Fleurs*, with Stuart Hepburn also performing, at Assembly Rooms for the Fringe, revived at the Traverse at Christmas. *Bagpipe Muzak* published in September.

1992   *Quelques Fleurs* revived for Mayfest at the Tron. Translates and adapts medieval mystery plays, *The York Cycle*, performed in June/July at the Theatre Royal for the York Festival. Writes *The Story of "Frankenstein"* for Yorkshire Television, transmitted Autumn '92. *Quelques Fleurs* broadcast by Radio 4 at Christmas. Working on a half-hour pilot

for BBC TV, *Rosaleen's Baby*, featuring Elaine C. Smith.
Adapting Shakespeare's *The Tempest* for the Unicorn Chil-
dren's Theatre, and writing final adjustments to *Damages*, to
submit to the RSC in 1993. Constant revival of plays – the
1993 season alone promises three separate new professional
productions in Scotland: *Mary Queen of Scots* (Perth Repertory
Theatre, Sept/Oct); *Tartuffe* (Dundee Rep); *The Big Picture*
(The Brunton, Musselburgh). *Three Scottish Poets* (MacCaig,
Morgan and Lochhead) published November 1992 by
Canongate Classics.

NOTES

1 From an unpublished interview with Liz Lochhead by Alison Smith, 4
September 1992. All unsourced comments from Lochhead in this
chapter will be from this interview.
2 In Trevor Royle, ed., *Jock Tamson's Bairns* (London: Hamish
Hamilton, 1977), 112–25.
3 Royle, op. cit., 112.
4 Ibid., 115.
5 Ibid., 117–8.
6 Ibid., 121.
7 Ibid., 123.
8 Where writers such as Kelman and Leonard were outspokenly
dismissive and controversial about Glasgow's year as City of Culture,
Lochhead is refreshingly equivocal. 'I mean, obviously these things are
just marketing ploys and hype, but they didn't seem to me to be
intrinsically wicked. I thought it'd be interesting to see what Glasgow
was like afterwards, and whether the money would disappear. It was
being done for cynical reasons, certainly, but I enjoyed a lot of the
things I saw that year, and I do think the more European and
multicultural Glasgow becomes, the better for all its citizens, even
the most dispossessed. To me it's simply not a case of either-or, as in
either have festivals or fix the dampness in Easterhouse. That's quite
an unhelpful way to look at it.'
9 Ajay Close, 'Almost Miss Scotland', *Spectrum, Scotland on Sunday*, 8
September 1991, 33–4.
10 Ibid.

Two

Liz Lochhead and the Ungentle Art of Clyping

Dorothy Porter McMillan

The telling and retelling of stories may well be the central project of contemporary women's writing. The construction or reclamation of a women's tradition shapes or brings to light hidden or neglected stories. And the retelling of traditional stories or myths has become one of the significant strategies of female and feminist creativity. In prose narrative there are numerous exponents of the art of deconstructive tale-telling from a variety of cultural backgrounds – from Canada (Margaret Atwood), from Ireland (Maeve Binchy), and from England Sarah Maitland and the grand priestess of the twisted tale, Angela Carter, while in Scotland Alison Kennedy's recent 'Cap o' Rushes'[1] pulls in fairy story to investigate marital collapse. In poetry the list might run from the barbed nursery rhymes of Stevie Smith, through the feminist *Transformations* of Anne Sexton, Judith Kazantis's *The Wicked Queen* to Liz Lochhead who most explicitly utilises the tricks and tropes of revisionary story in *The Grimm Sisters*, *Dreaming Frankenstein* and in her plays *Blood and Ice* and *Dracula*. Lochhead is wholly self-conscious about her story-telling vocation – or rather, as she puts it, her work. She thus characterises the function of both story and teller as useful rather than merely decorative:

> No one could say the stories were useless
> for as the tongue clacked
> five or forty fingers stitched
> corn was grated from the husk
> patchwork was pieced
> or the darning done.
> · · ·
>
> To tell the stories was her work.
> It was like spinning,

gathering thin air to the singlest strongest
thread.

('Storyteller', *GS*; *DF*, 70)[2]

Again in 'In the Cutting Room' (*DF*, 34), the story-telling activity is
paralleled with the editing of film to make a picture fit to be viewed,
and both acts comment on the shapes of love:

> Under the light of the
> anglepoise I am
> (beauty & the beast) at my business
> of putting new twists
> to old stories.
>
> Working together & we seem
> to love each other (but
> that too is an old story)

Yet the very self-consciousness, the deliberateness of the twisted tale has
been felt to constrict rather than liberate the potential of women's
writing. Jan Montefiore, while recognizing Lochhead's witty miscegen-
ations in both language and story (she exploits the resonances of orality
and splices fairy-tales with each other and with classical myth), still
feels that 'even Liz Lochhead does not escape the determinist
implications of interpretative storytelling'.[3] Then, 'who shall 'scape
whipping?' Certainly not the framer of this question. Of course,
Montefiore's worry derives from her sense that women have truck with
inherited tradition at their peril because they are thus complicit with
the very misrepresentations of female experience that they are supposed
to be deconstructing. We might note in passing that similar problems
almost always arise for the satirist, guiltily implicated in a love of what
is excoriated. And Lochhead, particularly in her performance pieces, is
characterisable as a social satirist: it may turn out that there is more in
common between the conditions of production of her serious poems and
her lighter pieces than is usually granted. In 'The Complete Alternative
History of the World, Part One' (*BM*, 12), Eve is provided with an
exuberant denial of male-ascribed roles:

> I'm not Jezebel
> And I'm not Delilah
> I'm not Mary Magdalen
> Or the Virgin Mary either.
> . . .
>
> Not Medusa, not Medea
> And, though my tongue may be salty,

> I'm not the Delphic sybil –
> Or Sybil Fawlty.
> . . .
>
> No, I'm not your Little Woman
> Not your Better Half
> I'm not your Nudge, your Snigger
> Or your Belly Laugh.

The verse rattles vigorously through half a hundred stereotypes until the energy of rejection is indistinguishable from the poet's joy that there is so much to reject.

But more general worries about women telling stories loom larger than this and shadow the tale-telling impulse that fuels most of Lochhead's poetry, whether or not it is explicitly revisionary. Because the story-teller is also otherwise nameable as a tell-tale and one of the still raging debates about not merely female propriety, which we can probably thumb our noses at, but female solidarity, is about what I should like to style 'clyping', and Lochhead, also the poet of the Scottish school playground, will know what I mean. The verb 'clype' in Scotland means to gossip or more firmly to be a tell-tale; a 'clype' or a 'clypie' is a gossip or tell-tale, often malicious, and the word is most often applied to women. Significantly, it derives from the Old English *cleopan*: to name or to call. I still wince at one of the most painful moments of my childhood which occurred when a slightly older boy called me a 'wee clype' because I had (without malicious intent) revealed the whereabouts of my girl cousin to her mother who wanted her to go home for lunch. It was no use to protest that I meant well, I thought she wanted her lunch and so on; I stood accused and stigmatised, I had broken solidarity and I was diminished by the act – I was 'a wee clype'. The much more serious revelation of the secret hiding places of women, however much feminists allege its necessity, remains equivocal. It still needs defending against the lurking strictures of earlier women writers against the revelation of the self and others.

The novelist Mrs Craik wrote in 1861 that, 'The intricacies of female nature are incomprehensible except to a woman; and any biographer of real womanly feeling, if ever she discovered, would never dream of publishing them.'[4] Eighty years later, Catherine Carswell is made uncomfortable by the love poems of the Brontës and Christina Rossetti, and the confessions of the feminist icon, Marie Bashkirtseff and of Sophie Tolstoi. 'Is there', she asks, 'a marked, an essential disparity between men and women? The woman because she is a woman, must as artist suppress what the man as artist or as man is entitled to reveal.'[5]

Well, of course, we may say that much water has flowed under the
gender bridge since then, yet it seems to me that Lochhead's own
procedures reveal that there is still a case to be answered. Her poetry
derives its characteristic tensions from the problem 'to clype or to
conceal'.

In a recent interview with Colin Nicholson Lochhead defends her
treatment of women by laying claim to the very sisterhood that Dinah
Mulock Craik adduced to demand silence: 'I'm very ambivalent about
women; they're people with problems too. I get at them because I am
one. I'm allowed to' (Nicholson, 204). That this is perhaps a little
defensive might be validated from Mary Shelley's dealings with her half-
sister 'millstone', Claire Clairmont in *Blood and Ice*. Mary Shelley
defends her revelation to Claire of the vicious and scurrilous references
to her in one of Byron's letters: 'You have to be cruel to be kind.' 'No,
Mary,' Shelley replies, 'you have to be kind to be kind.'[6] In a play which
mostly undermines Shelley's positions, this reproof jumps out with
surprising force. Mary has momentarily released that monster within,
that Lochhead believes we all harbour. The motivation of her clyping is
suspect, whatever the beneficial effects.

Between the twin poles of revelation and concealment Liz Lochhead's
poetry oscillates. Women are sluts with ashcans full of 'stubbed
lipsticks' and 'lipsticked butts', 'matted nests of hair' lurk in the
'hedgehog spikes' of brushes: they pop pills and cherish their own
masochistic self-offerings to men, they are selfish lovers and bad
mothers and they don't grow old gracefully (variously, especially in the
poems of *The Grimm Sisters* and *Dreaming Frankenstein*). True sisterhood
may turn out to depend paradoxically on betrayal. But betrayal has two
faces to be caught in Lochhead's ubiquitous mirrors. Clyping women
may be witches, disgustingly gorging themselves on the lying tales of
former loves ('Last Supper', *GS*; *DF*, 93), or poets of the self engaged on
an enterprise of creative rebirth ('Mirror's Song', *DF*, 67).

The punishment of the clype, the cruel to be kind betrayer of
sisterhood, might well be expulsion from the group, which would
deprive the writer of the material for her tales. In the first place
Lochhead's insistent openness about her own self through the location of
experience in actual place and time validates the claim 'I'm allowed'.
Even ostracism, however, would not disempower the poet because
women may be known through other women, hence through the self (it
is a premise of the poetry that there are at least some consistent
identifiable female behaviours), and women are also involuntary clypes
about themselves. Thus Brueghel's painting of Dulle Griet (Mad Meg)
is demystified, its story told, when the poem's speaker identifies with

the subject, admitting her own embarrassing desperation after her lover's desertion:

> Oh I am wild-eyed, unkempt, hellbent, a harridan.
> My sharp tongue will shrivel any man.
> Should our paths cross
> I'll embarrass you with public tears, accuse you with my loss.
>
> ('Harridan', *GS*; *DF*, 75)

The early poems of *Memo for Spring* are fed by the involuntary exposures, the vulnerabilities of teenage girls with fishnet stocking snares ('Cloakroom', *MFS*; *DF*, 151), women displaced in hospital ('Homilies From Hospital', *MFS*; *DF*, 153), girls caught with skirts up, themselves sideshows in the very carnival they attend ('Carnival', *MFS*; *DF*, 149), or a grandmother on whose athritic hands, endlessly knitting clothes her grandchildren will never wear, is written the painful story of her selfless life ('For My Grandmother Knitting', *MFS*; *DF*, 137).

Unsurprisingly, given Lochhead's often remarked manipulation of narrative registers, language itself is seen by her as sharing with its user the role of clype. In the colloquial Scottish idioms which she so often uses to test the false coin of more elevated discourse Lochhead also finds stories embedded in cliché and often exposable by pun. Interviewed by Rebecca Wilson she says:

> I think my principal love is language itself. When I can't write it's because I can't find the right language. It's not the ideas. Any ideas I've got come already clothed in language . . . I find language very funny anyway . . . the whole act of framing untidy old experience in language is inherently funny. . . . If something doesn't have irony in it for me it wouldn't be alive. The kind of amazement I have is often in simple language, how much of a giveaway it is.[7]

Many of Lochhead's subjects then are written by the words they speak. Her own role as tell-tale becomes in one sense unavoidable because language will not keep its own secrets, the attitudes and frailties encoded in it must out, she is midwife to a natural process. As early as *Memo for Spring*, Lochhead is preoccupied with what language gives away. In 'Homilies from Hospital' she describes how the patients who 'are up to it' arrange the flowers:

> There's not much to it to tell the truth
> it's just a matter of the fresh ones
> arranging them as best you can and
> picking out the dead ones
> then disposing of them in the polythene sack in the slunge

which smells a bit.
This is only natural.

(*DF*, 154)

The serious implications in the automatic, usually meaningless, conversation punctuator, 'to tell the truth', are teased out to link the art of flower arranging with the unsentimental patching up and discarding processes of the hospital, and both with the construction of poetry. 'This is only natural' gives itself away as our clichéd refusal to face up to the smelly intimations of disease and death that must be embedded in any invocation of the natural. In *Islands* Lochhead again uses notions of the 'given away' to comment more explicitly on her writing's relation to the natural:

walking by the sea
we find clean bones
cork floats tiny
coral branches
green glass   cockleshells
driftwood   a broken
copper sprinkler rose gone green
and botched and oxidised
smooth pebbles mermaid purses
things to pick.
a collage on the windowledge.
I'd like
an art that could somehow marry
the washed-up manmade
and the wholly natural
make a change
('Inner', III, *I*; *DF*, 115)

The pun on 'washed-up' confirms a poetry that takes its materials from what has been discarded and by cleaning them reveals their beauty; the pun on 'wholly', of course, sanctifies the processes of art. I suspect a pun in 'manmade' as well and 'marry' resonates beyond the merely conventional, and 'make a change' is an injunction to the self as much as characterisation of the art. The lines turn out to be the very art that is desired, not simply because they lay open the loveliness of a 'copper sprinkler rose' (and note how 'rose' too gives away its floral origins) 'gone green' in a natural process of degeneration which is made to seem like a process of regeneration; but also because the holy natural art of Liz Lochhead makes 'washed-up manmade' cliché give away its secrets.

Thus what is natural in language itself becomes identified with the poet who uses it and with the female subjects (including, of course, herself) that she gives away. 'A Giveaway' (*DF*, 42), six years later, crystalises these connections. The poet is telling her lover how she has handled the poem about her relationship with him: 'I cancelled out the lines that most let on/ I loved you'. Here the refusal to confess becomes confession. Claims to truth in love and art are equally suspect:

> The tripe that's talked at times, honestly −
> about truth and not altering a word,
> being faithful to what you felt, whatever
> that is, the 'First Thought's Felicity',
> I have to laugh . . . the truth!

The artful placing of 'whatever that is' undermines both the notion of faithfulness and the claim to understand the quality of feeling. The constructedness and the revisionary processes of poetry parallel those of love. Despite the ruthless use of black biro the verse set in the bedroom still clypes through the obliterations: the fragments that defeat the excisionary art are tellingly, 'hay/ fever sneeze spill and kiss'.

> Never could cancel with a single stroke!
> Oh maybe it is a giveaway but don't
> please be naive enough to think I'd mind
> your knowing what I might invent of what I feel.
> Poets don't bare their souls, they bare their skill.
> God, all this
> long apprenticeship and still
> I can't handle it, can't
> make anything much of it, that's my shame.
> It's not an easy theme.
> But finally I've scrubbed it, faced it, I know
> the whole bloody stanza was wonky from the word go.

The determination to deny that writing is confession is itself a giveaway. The lover's ability to identify the invented feelings implies his knowledge of the real. As she with casual but clearly assumed insouciance dismisses poem and lover, 'scrubbing' her poem out and herself clean, her contention that 'Poets don't bare their souls, they bare their skill' is both demonstrated by the art of the verse and simultaneously exposed as a bare-faced lie.

The poem ends with its beginning and the beginning of the relationship: 'the word go'. But 'go' insofar as it also dismisses the lover, closes a phase of life and presages a new opening, a new 'word go'. The ungentle art of clyping shares these contradictory pressures towards recapitulation in the telling of the old story, and openness in its ground clearing preparation for the new. As the involuntary giveaways of language are to be celebrated not regretted, so the vulnerability of the exposed female subject may turn out to be the very source of female power. Exposure then becomes the preserver, not the destroyer, of the secret places of the private life. The act of giving away then comes to figure a retained plenitude.

It is unsurprising then to find an increasing tendency in the poems to insist on the residual unexposable, the silences, indefinabilities, the inviolable rest which can no more be clyped about than it can be denied. It is an increasing tendency but it is never wholly absent even in the early poetry. The teenage girls of 'Cloakroom' (*MFS*; *DF*, 151) have learned enough to know that desire is fuelled by the suggestion that there is more to come but they pay the penalty for their denial of self, in self-denial:

> Our eyes are blank
> of illusions
> but we automatically
> lengthen lashes, lacquer hair
> lipstick our lips for later
> and the too easily faked closeness
> of close-mouth kisses
> which always
> leave a lot to be desired.

The older speaker in 'The Last Hag' (*GS*; *DF*, 103) has learned a more hopeful way of retreating within herself to prepare for future plenitude:

> I want to winter a bit,
> honestly.
> Take pleasure as I move
> in empty rooms
> arrange dry grasses.
> Sweet to see my own stored pulses
> shelved.
> Bottling plenty – oh you'd not believe
> the goodies I've got
> salted away.
>
> Take each day
> one in front of the other.
> hayfoot strawfoot that's how.

> And in my own good time
> I'll let rip again.

At first it may seem hard to claim that the women of the deconstructed myths and fairy tales of *The Grimm Sisters* have much in the store cupboard other than trouble: Ariadne watching the black sail appearing on the horizon, Tam Lin's wife awaiting the less than magical transformations of the process of growing old, Rapunzstiltskin tearing herself in two. Yet in other poems in this collection Liz Lochhead suggests secret female reserves. The speaker in 'Bawd' sets out to be 'frankly fake' to 'flaunt herself', to be 'a bad lot', to give herself away; 'No one,' she claims 'will guess it's not my style'. The giving away of the fake self might seem merely to be a way of preventing involuntary giveaway, but she has 'hauled her heart in' off her sleeve and seems finally to be reserving a hidden strength rather than protecting a secret fear. And the transformations of 'Midsummer Night' (*GS*; *DF*, 89) confirm the potency of the indefinably strange:

> Remember the horses
> how silently they moved
> from dark woods.
> 'Would you call this a green glade?' you
> asking gravely with a glint,
> the lilac haze and three rooks on the long meadow,
> that russet shape that changed
> we could swear it, and stretched
> and lengthened to a fox and back to prick-eared
> hare again. Nothing tonight could decide
> what form to take.

> We are good and strange to one another and no mistake.

The goodness and rightness of strangeness is both rehearsed and asserted.

The lover in 'Midsummer Night' shares in the tranforming strangeness; the male bather in 'What the Pool said, On Midsummer's Day' (*DF*, 8) is less lucky. He is easily fooled by the misleading openness and gossipiness of the outer edges of the woman-pool:

> I've led you by my garrulous banks, babbling
> on and on till – drunk on air
> and sure it's only water talking –
> you come at last to my silence.

Here the pool's disarming directness is beginning to look more like a ploy for taking in the other than letting out the self. The man, now himself stripped and vulnerable, approaches the pool's icy depths and is afraid, and he should be:

> – Your reasonable fear,
> what's true in me admits it.
> (Though deeper, oh
> older than any reason).
> Yes, I could
> drown you, you
> could foul my depths, it's not
> unheard of. What's fish
> in me could make flesh of you,
> my wet weeds against your thigh, it
> could turn nasty,
> I could have you
> gulping fistfuls fighting yourself
> back from me.

Here the potency of ordinary language is brilliantly made to reveal the potency of the woman through time; almost every word is felt to carry a fearful weight of implication. 'What's true in me admits it' turns disarming frankness of admission into a claim that the pool and the act of penetrating its depths are tests of authenticity. The permutations of fish, flesh and foul (fowl) insinuate the indefinability of the woman-pool and the witty pun on 'weeds' insists on mystery through history. But this linguistic brilliancy is both flaunted and rejected in favour of simplicity which derives its force from the virtuosity that it discards:

> I get darker and darker, suck harder.
> On-the-brink man, you
> wish I'd flash and dazzle again.
> You'd make a fetish of zazzing dragonflies?
> You want I should rip myself up
> with the kingfisher's flightpath, be beautiful?
> I say no tricks. I say just trust,
> I'll soak through your skin and
> slake your thirst.
>
> I watch. You clench,
> clench and come into me.

The man is taken in once more and when he comes out, he will be out of the poem and he will not be the same. The poem's appropriation of male voyeurism is assertive but the effect goes beyond the trick of reversal to affirm trust in the unimaginable depths of the female subject.

In this poem language is more than giveaway; it is potent, pregnant with meanings and the poem's procedures suggest that only some of them are revealed. Thus revelation sanctions concealment and affirms that there is much, and much that is significant, to conceal.

This poem confirms that Lochhead's identification of language, poet and female subject importantly means that she is not as woman writer alienated from language, especially not from the people's language, the people's voice and from language in history. And it is after all as the People's Poet that she characterises Edwin Morgan to whose pressures on her work I shall return ('The People's Poet', *DF*, 17). Indicatively, too, she has always expressed herself suspicious of a separatist feminism which deprives the poet of past linguistic and experiential resources, which denies available potency:

> I'm interested in exploring issues without apportioning blame. I'm interested in female masochism, for instance. I suppose it's a feminist issue, but it's also a human issue. It's more ambivalent than I would feel it to be in proper feminist terms. Maybe quite wrongly, I tend to feel that feminism's about things I'm sure about, so there's nothing much to be said about them. Sure I'm interested in exploring people suffering from the lack of these things, but it's not a potent thing for me to write about constantly.[8]

I have described Lochhead as midwife to a natural function of language. But as we have seen 'it's only natural' is virtually synonymous with 'it's only painful', and if Lochhead in one of her poetic roles is midwife, in another she is herself the labouring subject, struggling to bring forth her own meaning, labouring with the painful consciousness that the birth may be abortive or monstrous, and that if it is it will tell tales about its mother – after all, 'Nobody's mother can't not never do nothing right' ('Everybody's Mother', *GS*; *DF*, 96). 'An Abortion' (*DF*, 9) describes the agony of a cow aborting a malformed calf, an agony that the poet watches from the window of the room where she herself labours 'at the barbed words' on her desk top. Lochhead says that she recognised after she had written it that the poem acts as a companion piece to the early 'Revelation' (*MFS*; *DF*, 124) in which she tells the story of an incident in her childhood when, sent to fetch milk and eggs from a farm, she is permitted a glimpse of the great black bull:

> I had always half-known he existed –
> this antidote and Anti-Christ his anarchy
> threatening the eggs, well rounded, self-contained –
> and the placidity of milk.

Although disturbing, the monstrous bull remains outside, threatening
femaleness without being part of it. Sixteen years later the cow's
abortion forces Lochhead to recognise what many of her other poems are
already demonstrating: there is nothing essentially placid about cows.

> I remember thinking 'Well, it's taken you sixteen years to come to
> some sort of full circle and realise that a cow is a very powerful
> creature.' By that time, of course, I was far more aware of gender
> issues. (Nicholson, 209)

The real suffering of the cow both parallels the writing process and
comments ironically upon it:

> Sunk again, her cow-tongue lolled
> then spiked the sky, she rolled
> great gape-mouth, neck distended
> in a Guernica of distress.
> That got through to me all right
> behind glass as I was
> a whole flat field away.
> It took an emblem-bellow
> to drag me from my labour
> at the barbed words on my desk top.
>
> (DF, 9)

As always Lochhead reveals her painter origins both in the ability to
look, which produces the appalling specificity of her picture of the cow,
and in the allusion that places the beast's agony in history. The words
that the poet is birthing will tear her but compared with the actual
suffering of the cow they are small things. Thus she conveys that respect
for her subject's story which is another validation of her right to tell it.
Here again the words suggest a power in excess of themselves.

> The thing is this. Left alone,
> that cow licking at those lollop limbs
> which had not formed properly
> with her long tongue,
> that strong tongue
> which is a match for thistles
> and salt-lick coarse as pumice stone
> tenderly over and over again at
> what has come out of her and she is responsible for
> as if she can not believe it will not
> come alive,
> not if she licks long enough.
>
> (DF, 10–11)

The cow's malformed calf tells a tale of failure and it is as a guilty thing that the cow is led away, but even failure becomes a kind of stamp of power and love.

Agonies of both magical penetration and birth structure the title poem of *Dreaming Frankenstein* (*DF*, 11) which tells in condensed form the story of *Blood and Ice*. It begins with the now familiar conjunctions of language, the female and creativity:

> She said she
> woke up with him in
> her head, in her bed.
> Her mother-tongue clung to her mouth's roof
> in terror, dumbing her, and he came with a name
> that was none of her making.

The monster is both self created and a created self. He comes as demon lover and is born as monstrous child:

> his buttons had bit into her and
> the rough serge of his suiting had chafed her sex,
> she knew — oh that was not how —
> but he'd entered her utterly.

> . . . Anyway
> he was inside her
> and getting him out again
> would be agony fit to quarter her,
> unstitching everything.

When the monster is born in Mary Shelley's fiction he will accuse his creator of refusing to take responsibility for what he has made him, he will hunt him down destroying Frankenstein's terrified attempts to conceal and deny his child. But the fiction itself, and Lochhead seems to me to be perceptive about Mary Shelley's sense of her own creativity as monstrous (Nicholson, 218), will tell tales, will clype about Mary Shelley, giving the lie to her surface desires for respectability and conventionality and proclaiming her guilt and her awful power.

'Mirror's Song', the closing poem of *Dreaming Frankenstein* (*DF*, 67), continues the figure of painful and destructive birth. The 'best black self' which lies coffined in ice behind the surface of the mirror is to be released by the gazing subject who is self-commanded to smash 'the looking-glass glass/ coffin' to release a Kali-like self whose whirling arms trash the offensive accoutrements of constructed femininity:

> the Valium and initialled hankies,

> the lovepulps and the Librium,
> the permanents and panstick and
> Coty and Tangee Indelible,
> Thalidomide and junk jewellery.

But in this poem the rejections go beyond those falsifications that women are induced to make of themselves, to tear up the 'herstories' in history:

> Smash me for your daughters and dead
> mothers, for the widowed
> spinsters of the first and every war
> let her
> rip up the appointment cards for the
> terrible clinics,
> the Greenham summonses, that date
> they've handed us. Let her rip.
> She'll crumple all the
> tracts and the adverts, shred
> all the wedding dresses, snap
> all the spike-heel icicles
> in the cave she will claw out of –
> a woman giving birth to herself.

'Don't/ let history frame you/ in a pretty lie' ('Construction For A Site: Library on An Old Croquet Lawn, St Andrews', *DF*, 21) or an ugly one either. The clearing away of these unacceptable constructed faces and public humiliations promises a story of new woman. But since she has had to endure the agonising struggle of self-conception and self-deliverance, she faces the danger of solipsism and severance from the past. I want to suggest that the poems of *Bagpipe Muzak*, Lochhead's most recent published collection, go some way towards tackling this problem, both by recapitulating the strategies of the preceding poems and by going on to provide a new sense of privacy and public meaning.

A first impression of the collection might be that it is a bit of a rag-bag. It begins with nine *Recitations*, follows with four presentations of *Characters*, three of them in prose, and concludes with ten *Poems*: this looks a little like a way of getting out what happens to be to hand. Two of the poems, however, provide a rationale for the collection and a justification for the remarkable integrity in difference of Lochhead's work. 'Papermaker' (*BM*, 71) describes the artist, Jacki Parry, making her own fine paper from miscellaneous materials all with their own hidden histories, 'Linen, worn cotton, tattered silk'. The joy in the making and the wholeness of the result are lovingly recorded:

You smile to yourself
satisfied to see a substance
obeying its own laws, cleaving to itself,
every fat fibre loving fibre
when you flip it, single, coherent
brand new on the blanket.
It is like a snowfall,
the first thinnest layer,
almost enough for just one snowball.

'Good Wood' (*BM*, 73) exuberantly records the varieties and uses of
wood, so many kinds, yet all versions of a single substance. The types of
Lochhead's pieces in *Bagpipe Muzak* seem to me to form a similar kind of
coherence in multiplicity.

The first four *Recitations* challenge female stereotypes in a fairly direct
way, employing the satiric function of tale-telling to expose social lies
and contradictions. And so the speaker in 'Almost Miss Scotland' (*BM*,
3) faces up to the dishonesty of the fictions of self that she is expected to
trot out:

Then this familiar-lukkin felly
I'd seen a loat oan the telly
Interviewed me aboot my hobbies –
I says: Macrame, origami,
Being nice tae my mammy –
(Basically I tellt him a loat o jobbies).
I was givin it that
Aboot my ambition to chat
To handicapped and starvin children from other nations
– How I was certain I'd find
Travel wid broaden my mind
As I fulfilled my Miss Scotland obligations.

And the 'jobbies' accuse more than the immediate audience of Miss
Scotland competitions of merely paying lip service to pieties that should
be moral imperatives – once the laughter has died away we find
ourselves rather uncomfortably included in the closing 'Away and get
stuffed'.

The second group of poems in *Recitations* point to Lochhead's always
present but growing interest in Scotland's story, in that public context
within which personal lives must finally find their meanings. She tells
Colin Nicholson of the increasing sense of nationality in her work:

I still have more of that Scottishness to explore, perhaps because
until recently I've felt that my country was woman. I feel that my
country is Scotland as well. At the moment I know that I don't
like this macho Scottish culture, but I also know that I want to
stay here and negotiate it. This place of darkness I acknowledge
mine; this small dark country. I can't whinge about it if I don't
talk back to it, if I don't have a go. (Nicholson, 223)

Well, she has a go. Without compunction ('I am one. I'm allowed') she
has the same kind of go at her country as she has had at her sisters. She
clypes about the dirty petticoats of the New Glasgow and the AIDS that
gives Edinburgh away as drugs capital as much as Festival City. In
'Con-densation' (*BM*, 16) she fleshes out the people's cliché of 1990 that
the only culture most Glaswegians saw was growing on their walls.
'Festival City: Yon Time Again' (*BM*, 20) punctures the flashy overkill
of yuppie Festival Edinburgh with its own contaminated needle.

Happily, as proved to be the case with female exposure, telling tales
on Scotland is a process which suggests a strength beyond the discarded
lies. The naming function of clyping, of telling it how it is, is explicitly
invoked in 'The Garden Festival, Glasgow 1988' (*BM*, 18) to validate
the claim that Glasgow has the potential for more significant
regeneration than the erzatz flowering and toy industry of the Garden
Festival:

> It'll cost a packet. It'll be a gey dear green place.
> The Garden Festival? I wish we had the courage
> To really call a spade a spade and Let Glasgow Flourish.

And 'Bagpipe Muzak, Glasgow 1990' (*BM*, 24), borrowing its
iconoclastic rhythms from Louis MacNeice's 'Bagpipe Music', whirls
through an orgy of demolition of the fake in the present and in the
history of Scottishness which parallels for the country the necessary
clearances of 'Mirror's Song'. It ends not with exhaustion and collapse
but with potency and threat: 'we'll tak' the United Kingdom and brekk
it like a bannock'.

The *Poems* with which *Bagpipe Muzak* concludes remind us that Liz
Lochhead dedicates the volume to her mother who died in the year of its
publication. For in these poems Lochhead seems to come to terms with
her own past, her own family and her own place and then finally to set
all these in the wider context of the political disruptions of Europe in
1990. Of course, concern with family and with place is not new in her
poetry. Poems about her grandparents feature in *Memo For Spring*, and
Islands charts the effect of difference of place on the individual
consciousness. A number of the poems of *The Grimm Sisters* and

Dreaming Frankenstein are located in Canada or America or the Middle East and the stories of these places are always made to matter, the relationships of here and there are always mutually illuminating:

> That was September, and
> now I am here and
> you are there
> but that is neither here nor there
> as far as what we feel
> or what, together,
> we will make happen.
>
> And that white-card
> cut-out of Liberty you sent her
> graces my sister's Glasgow mantel-
> piece, the week before her wedding.
> ('Sailing Past Liberty', *DF*, 31)

In 'In the Cutting Room' (*DF*, 34), the significance of the private life in the public place is explicitly signalled: 'Chaste on Broadway, we moved/ our privacy through the public streets'. What is new is, I think, a kind of poise which signals Lochhead's promising accommodation of her private self and her increasing public importance as a writer.

'After the War' (*BM*, 55) admires the loving restraint of her parents: her father's self-sacrifice after the war in renouncing his Capstan; her mother's, in making do with 'one mended featherstitch jumper'; and both of them 'loving one another/ biting pillows/ in the dark while I was sleeping'. 'View of Scotland/Love Poem' (*BM*, 56) merges childhood and present Hogmanays, thirty years apart, to celebrate past familial attentiveness and immediate adult harmony:

> And this is where we live.
> There is no time like the
> present for a kiss.

It would be nice to be able to claim that 'The Bride' (*BM*, 65) charts Lochhead's accommodation to her own marriage, but it wouldn't be true, for the poem although first-person, is not personal. Perhaps instead I might claim certain aspects of it as proleptic. Whatever, it high-heartedly shows that for a woman the achievement of equilibrium in a loving relationship may paradoxically depend on openness to the joy of the moment, in acceptance rather than forward planning. The Bride who speaks the poem tells us that on the morning of her wedding her mirror suddenly reveals to her that she is 'the absolute spit of Elsa

Lanchester'. Elsa Lanchester played the twin roles of the Bride
demanded of Frankenstein by the monster, and Mary Shelley in James
Whale's classic horror movie, *The Bride of Frankenstein* (1935). It is,
therefore, with a cargo of significance that Lochhead's Bride, now
getting on a bit, already living with her husband-to-be and fully
schooled in the pitfalls of matrimony, negotiates her comically
unconventional way to the 'altar of the registry office'. But, of course,
everything about a wedding crystallises to convention: Mum and Dad,
Bride and Groom and Guests squeeze into their appointed roles, and
even the attempt to refuse honeymoon is overborne by its imperatives:

> We unpack
> our paperbacks. We
> scorn such sentiment such institutionalizing as
> making love on this our wedding night
> and it's only
> after (sudden lust
> having picked us up by the scruff of the neck and
> chucked us into
> that familiar whirlpool) and
> practised and perfect
> we judder totally together
> into amazed and wide-eyed calm and
> I lie beside you
> utterly content that I know for sure
> that this is never
> ever going to
> work.

The poem ends with what we might call the new marriage superstition:
the relationship may be magically protected by not letting the fates
know that you expect it to last. And, as usual with Liz Lochhead,
language is working double time to take the couple out of the work-a-
day world, which for a writer might further suggest out of fiction and
into the real. Once again we have an art that claims dimensions beyond
itself.

'The People's Poet' (*DF*, 17) had recorded a reading by Edwin
Morgan at the age of fifty. The poem intersperses the performance of the
poet with speculations about the life of the city outside that he sings
about:

> But the winter city won't
> stay locked shut

> and that's what he sings out about.
> It's chocablock with life
> and lives we can make for.

The ability to make sense of the city and its people in history is again attributed to Edwin Morgan in '5th April 1990', the first of the 'Five Berlin Poems' that conclude *Bagpipe Muzak*. The poems are based on three separate visits to Berlin in 1987, '88 and 'after the wall was opened and one single city/ amazed/ and bursting at the seams in nineteen ninety' ('three visits'). The project of the poems is to make sense out of the apparently irreconcilable muddle of past and present, trivial and significant, and to make herself the kind of poet who can do so:

> And now I'm home
> with three painted Polish Easter eggs,
> Hungarian opera duets, Romanian symphonies,
> an uncopyrighted East German Mickey Mouse
> painted the wrong colours,
> funny tasting chocolate
> and the Rolling Stones 'in ctepeo'
> Made in Bulgaria *Made in the Shade*.
> And bits of the wall that are almost powder.
> I think who could make sense of it?
> Morgan could, yes Eddie could, he would.
> And that makes me want to try.
>   ('5th April 1990', *BM*, 77)

The modesty of this intention happily proves less inhibiting than it might have done, for the poems which follow work in ways which are not at all derivative. It is true that 'aquarium 2' perhaps unnecessarily underlines its political intentions, but the final poem in particular shows that Liz Lochhead has reached a kind of confidence that enables her to present Edwin Morgan and herself and their fellow writers as actors in a larger story, both private people and public poets. 'Almost-Christmas at the Writers' House' (*BM*, 83) is set during the 1990 visit. Edwin Morgan is about to photograph a Magritte-like scene from the balcony of the Writers' House in Berlin where the Glasgow writers are staying:

> Behind Morgan,
> Withers, Mulrine, McNaughtan, Lochhead,
> well-clad, scarved and booted
> stamp and laugh

(impatient for Gulaschsuppe and Berliner Weisse
at the restaurant by Wannsee S. Bahnhof)
then breathe, stilled
as his shutter falls, stopped
by this one moment's
crystalline unbroken vision
of the dreaming order in the
purring electric heart of the house of our hosts.

It is Liz Lochhead's poem, however, not Edwin Morgan's camera which
catches the meaning of the moment, which effects the link between the
pleasant ordinariness of human desires for food and wine and the
significance of this moment of perfect, yet strange, stasis in the
turbulent history of Berlin.

But it is not with this poem that I want to finish: my story begins to
have the appearance of falsification in its neat movement to the last
poem in the 1991 collection. I recollect Mary Shelley's remark in *Blood
and Ice* about Shelley's versified rationale for unfaithfulness – 'True love
in this differs from gold and clay/ That to divide is not to take away' – 'I
have learned to suspect any sentiment that rhymes that easily'.[9] Instead
I want to end with a woman who is not quite in the poetry at all: she is
the woman whose sharp heeltaps shatter the two minutes silence at the
Remembrance service that the poet as a child is listening to on the
radio, sitting on her father's knee:

My mother tutted, oh that it was terrible,
as over our air
those sharp heeltaps struck steel, rang clear
as a burst of gunfire or a laugh
through those wired-up silent streets around the Cenotaph.

'Why did she do it?' the poem asks. There can be no clear answer but
her shocking disruption of pieties, which the poem does not simply
dismiss, is felt, nevertheless, to be on the side of life:

Maybe it was looking at the khaki button eye
and the woundwire stem
of the redrag poppy
pinned in her proper lapel
that made the lady stick a bloody bunch of them
behind her ear
and clash those high heels across the square,
a dancer.

('Poppies', *GS*; *DF*, 102)

The woman's heels tell tales on her, broadcast her subversiveness to a hushed audience, but she retains her secret story. The dancing heels of that mysterious lady echo through Liz Lochhead's poetry.

NOTES

1 In *Night Geometry and the Garscadden Trains*. (Edinburgh: Polygon, 1990), 109–21.

2 In all quotations from poems originally published in the collections *Memo for Spring, Islands* and *The Grimm Sisters*, I give first the abbreviation for the original collection followed by the page reference in *Dreaming Frankenstein & Collected Poems*.

3 Jan Montefiore, *Feminism and Poetry: Language, Experience, Identity in Women's Writing*, (London: Pandora, 1987), 55.

4 Dinah Mulock Craik, 'Literary Ghouls', *Studies from Life*, New York, 1861, 13. This is one of a series of similar comments by women writers quoted by Elaine Showalter in her *A Literature of Their Own: British Women Novelists from Brontë to Lessing*, (London: Virago Press, 1982), 16. Mrs Craik elsewhere insists on silence as the central virtue of female friendship: 'Female Friendships', *A Woman's Thoughts about Women*, (London: Hurst & Blacket, 1858), 186.

5 Catherine Carswell, *Lying Awake; An Unfinished Autobiography and Other Posthumous Papers*; edited and with an introduction by John Carswell, (London: Secker & Warburg, 1950), 116.

6 My quotations from *Blood and Ice* are taken from the BBC Radio production, directed by Marilyn Imrie broadcast 11 June 1990.

7 *Sleeping with Monsters: Conversations with Scottish and Irish Women Poets*; research and interviews by Rebecca E. Wilson; edited by Gillean Somerville-Arjat and Rebecca E. Wilson (Edinburgh: Polygon, 1990), 10.

8 *Sleeping with Monsters*, 12.

9 Quoted from the BBC radio broadcast of *Blood and Ice*.

Three

The Voice of Revelation: Liz Lochhead and Monsters

S. J. Boyd

Dulle Griet by Brueghel . . .
I chose it for my History of Art essay, took pains
to enumerate the monsters . . .
             ('The Furies I: Harridan')

The enumeration of monsters, to judge by the reference here to a 'History of Art essay' which surely fixes the time as the latter part of schooldays, seems to have interested Lochhead from the beginning. Even here it is indicated that the process of studying the monstrous involves the poet's taking pains upon herself, that such taxonomy is a somewhat harrowing process, and this view is borne out by the first poem of Lochhead's first volume, 'Revelation' in *Memo for Spring* (*DF*, 124). This poem describes a rite-of-passage encounter with 'a monster' bull and it is, of course, the source of the title of this essay, being the first articulation of a voice that speaks through much of Lochhead's work in both verse and drama, a voice whose discourse is of the monstrous.

There is an amusing perversity in deploying 'Revelation' as a title at the *start* of a book and my own title here might well strike the reader as odd or inappropriate, suggesting perhaps a sublime or visionary poetic voice, hinting at loud blasts of the trumpet on behalf of the monstrous regiment of women. But stridency of tone and heaviness of matter are not qualities readily associated with Lochhead. Her poetic voice is generally familiar, by turns tender and wry; her poetic persona idealistic but down-to-earth too, 'silly like us', hard not to like.[1] Indeed, a nagging worry for the reader or critic might well be that the work is really rather lightweight. Lochhead's development as a writer tends to exacerbate this worry, since she has moved in the direction of performance art, her verse degenerating into rap, her voice delivering monologues that remind one painfully of *Naked Video*. Here, from *Same Difference*, is a sample:

> Her herrs always golden, her slippers are glass
> Though dumb she'll become some rich man's tits 'n' ass . . .
> She's had a bobbed nose job, she's lukked doon it since
> Hung oan to her cherry jist to merry a Prince
> Wi jumbo size ears and heid full o' mince
> That's why the Princess is a puke.

> *(TCNC, 95)*

That is not merely unworthy of the author of *Memo for Spring*, it is unworthy of a lavatory wall. This unfortunate movement down-market is no doubt largely the result of the baleful influence of the strange cult of poetry readings and festivals. It is, however, greatly to be regretted, since Lochhead has shown herself capable of creating poems of subtlety *and* substance. A study of her interest in the monstrous highlights particularly well the serious side of her poetic voice.

The word monster is derived from the Latin *monēre*, to warn, and the original *monstrum* was a divine portent or warning. It is also, however, connected with the notion of revelation, as it is etymologically close to *monstrāre*, to show. One definition of a monster is someone or something that deviates from the normal type, but the constant burden of Lochhead's writing on monsters is to warn that the monstrous inheres in the everyday, the familiar, to reveal the terror that lies just below the surface of the normal. Instances abound, from the early poem 'Revelation', where the Apocalyptic beast of a bull has the matey name 'Bob', to a recent poem 'Tupalik' (*BM*, 75), which contains the lines, 'It is domestic as dirty dishes,/ as ordinary as terror'. 'Tupalik', moreover, considers the similarity between the Eskimo art of the tupalik and the writing of a poem, and Lochhead, in interview, has indicated that for her the process of writing a poem can begin with a kind of bemonstering of language itself: 'A little bit of language goes funny. An ordinary phrase'll suddenly strike you in a new way. It'll turn itself inside out in some way.'[2] Hence the art of the 'new cliché'; giving ironic twists to familiar phrases, recycling linguistic bric-à-brac, and retelling and reinterpreting fairy-tales and myths.[3] 'The Ariadne Version' (*DF*, 96), for example, has the heroine 'applying more Ambre Solaire' as she sulks and plots over 'the family labyrinth'. That labyrinth of interconnected and tangled loves and tensions can have at its heart something monstrous, in the case of that unhappy Cretan family a fearsome bull such as frightened the childhood Lochhead in 'Revelation' and the monstrous product of illicit and unnatural love, the Minotaur. Such horrors (or, at any rate, comparable horrors) are not confined to old, forgotten, far-off things, as the poignant twisting of nursery rhymes in 'The Sins of the Fathers' (*TCNC*, 100) makes painfully clear:

> When I was one I ate a bun
> When I was two I buckled my shoe
> When I was three I hit my knee
> When I was four he shut the door
> When I was five, when I was five
> When I was five . . .

Memory tries to shut the door on language falters before the unspeakable, which is also, appallingly the domestic. At the heart of the family labyrinth a Freudian monster looms up. Indeed, it would be hard to find a better 'commentary' on this aspect of Lochhead's writing than Freud's superb essay 'The "Uncanny"', with its insight that 'the word "*heimlich*" exhibits [a meaning] which is identical with its opposite, "*unheimlich*". What is *heimlich* thus comes to be *unheimlich*.'[4] What is of the home turns out, oddly, to contain the weird, the monstrous. Lochhead's monsters belong to the Freudian class of the uncanny: 'the uncanny is that class of the frightening which leads back to what is known of old and long familiar.'[5]

An interest in the monstrous is, of course, what is known of old and long familiar in Scottish literature. Scotland, indeed, is particularly fertile ground for monsters, mythical, real, and in-between; from Nessie to Morag, from Ian Brady to Dennis Nilsen, from Macbeth (and his Lady) to Sawnie Bean, from Robert Wringhim to Mr Hyde. The combination of an interest in the bizarre with Dutch realism has been seen as a distinctive characteristic of Scottish literature.[6] Lochhead in 'Harridan' (*DF*, 74) places 'Mad Meg on my mantelpiece', sets the crazy and grotesque in the most *heimlich* context imaginable and frames herself and her work in a tradition that, like that of Flemish art, is strong on 'Realism' but with a 'surrealist' side to it as well. The most striking example of this in the present day is the work of Lochhead's friend Alasdair Gray, whose sketch of her as an icon of the early seventies adorns *Memo for Spring* (*DF*, 123). Gray's Jock McLeish, for example, a Dr Jekyll with a Mr Hyde kept in general on the leash of fantasy, describes his treatment of his lover Denny as 'Very ordinary and very terrible', a locution very close to that in Lochhead's 'Tupalik'.[7]

It would seem reasonable to ask whether there is anything particularly monstrous about Scotland and us Scots? One definition of a monster is a being which is compounded of elements from different types of creature, which is neither one thing nor another. Scotland's politico-cultural status can be seen as having this quality of monstrosity, being a strange mix of (or confusion between) nation and province: our national emblem, for MacDiarmid, is the 'monstrous thistle'.[8] For Lochhead, in 'Inter-City' (*DF*, 33), the train heading north-east towards Aberdeen is 'Hammered like a bolt/ diagonally through Scotland (my/ small dark country)', which images Scotland, especially given the title of the collection from which the poem comes, as a Frankenstein's monster, put together, no doubt, from all sorts of bits and pieces. This is undoubtedly the situation of the Scots as a people; ethnically, culturally, religiously, linguistically *split*, a 'routh/ O' contrairies that jostle'.[9] This is, to be sure, the case with many peoples and nations, but it is felt with particular intensity in Scotland because our loss of self-government tends to increase the need to establish a clear cultural identity. A sense of self-division within Scotland comes through strongly in Lochhead's 'Poem on a Day Trip' (*DF*, 139), in which Lochhead travels by train from her own native sod in the upper Clyde valley to genteel, cultured, anglicized Edinburgh. Lochhead's *persona* feels outclassed and rushes 'for Woolworth's anonymous aisles', where she can 'feel at home' in that 'You could be anywhere – even in Glasgow'. This might be an emblem of the plight of any Scots lad or lass o' pairts: journey to the capital of the Scots, make the necessary *gradua ad* the *Parnassum* of the Calton Hill, and you find you don't belong. Moreover, your own home territory is be-monstered:

> a hard land, a pitted
> and pockmarked, slag-scarred, scraped land.
> Coal. Colossus of pit bings . . .
> the black-gut and the quarried ash-red
> show in the gashes.

Who would want to go back to where hard men and poxy slags scrape a living, where the blood and guts of the life-struggle break through the 'veneer'?

In interview with Emily Todd, Lochhead makes clear her sense of the centrality of division in Scottish culture:

> I guess I would say that the big split in Scotland is between self and other self. In many ways I think that the big theme in Scottish literature is the split, from *Justified Sinner* to *Jekyll and Hyde*, and I think that's natural if you're Scottish when you are half English, really. There's a bit of you who's internalised all of that, so you're English, but you're Scots. So two different halves of you talk to

each other which is very similar to the states of the male and the feminine. (*Verse*, 90)

Lochhead here does a very fair impersonation of Lewis Grassic Gibbon's Chris Guthrie, *linguistically* split between a Scots and English self. It is this linguistic self-division which naturally looms largest in a writer's sense of the Scottish splits. The relatedness of this problem to issues of gender politics may be clarified somewhat by quoting Rebecca Wilson in her Introduction to a book of interviews with Scottish and Irish women poets:

> . . . many women writers are confronted with a creative tradition and a language that does not necessarily include room for their experience . . . To quote Adrienne Rich again, '*this is the oppressor's language / yet I need to talk to you*' . . . This struggle for creative expression is also relevant in relation to the concepts of nationality and cultural identity.[10]

The Scots writer may well feel that English is 'the oppressor's language' or that he/she is uneasily situated within it, but there remains the need to communicate. Other avenues are not promising. Retreat into dialect merely advertises self-division within Scotland and the use of synthetic Scots involves, of necessity, the creation of a *chimaera*, a monster. Edwin Muir, in the course of his devastating criticism of such tactics in *Scott and Scotland* (1936), describes MacDiarmid as trying 'to revive it [Scots] by impregnating it with all the contemporary influences of Europe one after another, and thus galvanize it into life by a series of violent shocks', which is very specifically to suggest the creation of a Frankenstein's monster.[11] Even MacDiarmid himself, whose achievements in Scots are miraculously impressive, characterises the very words themselves as 'Poor herds o'heich-skeich monsters, misbegotten', and that in the context of a poetic-linguistic call-to-arms, 'Gairmscoile'.[12] Lochhead herself has tried all tacks, from conventional English through varieties of Glaswegian to a thoroughly synthetic Scots that is as *ersatz* as the unfairly derided Harry Lauder. The latter two options tend to be chosen only for performance-based work, while what is essentially conventional English is deployed for lyrical material. This is a wise choice: the grotesque often goes down well in the theatre.

The field of gender politics (as distinct from issues of national identity or cultural imperialism) unsurprisingly throws up many images of monsters in Lochhead's work. In interview she too quotes from Adrienne Rich:

> I'm very interested in repression of various sorts, linguistic, sexual, whatever. I keep thinking of a line from a poem by Adrienne Rich: 'A thinking woman sleeps with monsters . . .' Yes, that's right.[13]

The interviewer, Gillean Somerville-Arjat, is able so readily to supply the line because, despite its considerable potential for schoolboy-humorous interpretation, it provides the title of the book in which this interview is contained, *Sleeping with Monsters: Conversations with Scottish and Irish Women Poets*. There is more than a hint here that men are the monsters, and perhaps even that Scots and Irish men have regimented their women in an especially monstrous way. In 'Obituary', a nostalgic poem from *Memo for Spring* (DF, 132), Lochhead recalls, 'We two in W.2 / walking / down Byres Road'. They might have passed me in Tennant's having a pint, for I lived in those days in 'the Taggart country', but Ms Lochhead could not have joined me because women were barred. Perhaps that was a little monstrous. On a slightly higher cultural level, our most famous poem 'Tam O' Shanter' divides the female, from a homeward-bound drunk man's point of view, into the dreaded moralising nag at home and the wicked, tempting go-go dancer. That *is* somewhat monstrous, and it's a form of splitting that Lochhead specifically complains of, albeit here in a jocular enough way:

> I'm not Jezebel
> And I'm not Delilah
> I'm not Mary Magdalen
> Or the Virgin Mary either.
>   ('What-I'm-Not Song', *TCNC*, 55)

In the age of feminism in which Lochhead is living and writing, an age which can acknowledge as a champion of truth and freedom a woman who writes that 'Men love death. Men especially love murder',[14] it would be surprising if man did not sometimes appear, as in that disturbing sudden intrusion of the masculine pronoun 'he' in the fourth line of 'The Sins of the Fathers', as a threat, as the other, the alien, the oppressor, a monster. But perhaps such a presentation of the male is also in part the product of more local cultural determinants.

Man, or the male, makes a spectacularly threatening entry into Lochhead's poetic world in the early poem 'Revelation'. The poem describes the *persona's* memory of an encounter with a monster male 'when a child at the farm for eggs and milk' (a phrase which gives a subtle feel of linguistic immaturity, as does the later 'a roar to be really scared of'). It is a tale of the transition from innocence to experience, and it is interesting to note that, as Rebecca Wilson suggests, encounters with monsters are often associated with such transitional states:

> Monsters symbolize a fusion of contradictions. Human and animal
> bodies . . . are joined in a single shape. In many cultures such

creatures . . . are associated with a *rite de passage*, the centre point
of a transition from one state of being to another.[15].

Though the bull in 'Revelation' does not literally join human and
animal bodies (or body-parts) it is specifically called a 'monster' and it
may be said metaphorically to join together the human and animal in a
disturbing way, a way that suggests to the little girl protagonist the
dangerous animal violence latent in the male. The girl is 'shown the
black bull' (*monstrāre*) and that revelation of darkness is a warning
(*monēre*) of the unpleasantness of the human farmyard. In interview
Lochhead has indicated her early fondness for the poetry of Heaney and
Hughes (*Verse*, 87), both poets whose work contains examples of similar
youthful encounters with the darker side of nature. Indeed, perhaps the
most obvious intertext of Lochhead's poem is Hughes's 'The Bull Moses'
from *Lupercal*,[16] its emphasis on 'blackness', 'darkness', 'reek' suggesting an influence on 'Revelation'. The child in Hughes's poem leans over
the half-door and gazes into the byre's 'Blaze of darkness', like the
protagonist of Lochhead's poem, but the difference of gender seems to
have an important effect. For Hughes this moment of revelation is 'a
sudden shut-eyed look/ Backward into the head', a recognition of
something that is in himself, as a male (it would be hard to think of a
more *patriarchal* name than Moses). For Lochhead's protagonist, though
the encounter does involve some recognition of her own animality, the
bull remains an embodiment of threat from without, *to her* as a female.

This meeting, which is characterized as apocalyptic (the title; the
bull is 'Anti-Christ'), is also presented as a simple product of the
common day: the monstrous, once again, is just below the surface of the
normal. The poem opens:

> I remember once being shown the black bull
> when a child at the farm for eggs and milk.
> They called him Bob — as though perhaps
> you could reduce a monster
> with the charm of a friendly name.

The second half of this opening section neatly presents as naive
speculation what is a well-known fact: the propitiation of dark powers
by friendly names is a common phenomenon and an extremely well-
known Scottish poem, Burns's 'Address to the Deil', plays wittily with
the idea. Perhaps the child is right to be sceptical about the efficacy of
such tactics however. There have been human monsters with similarly
innocuous names (Ian, Dennis, Peter), who perhaps frequented pubs
called *The Black Bull*, surely the commonest of all pub names. The
threat comes not from the exotic, from some equatorial heart of

darkness, but from a farm which is evidently just up the road, where a child can be sent for eggs and milk.

The child is held by the hand at the 'threshold' of the bull's byre, like a novice at some ancient *Mithræum* about to be initiated into the mysteries, about to cross the threshold from one state of being to another. She peers inside: 'At first, only black/ and the hot reek of him'. The awareness is of darkness and of the hot breath/ smell of the *male*. The images that follow, to the end of the first verse-paragraph, suggest awe-inspiring sexual potency, a power and threat which the girl does not quite understand (and which, in keeping with this, is never fully articulated in the poem) and which she attempts to flee. In the second verse-paragraph it is noted that life goes on despite such monstrous presences: the hens pick about 'oblivious' to the presence of the bull, now described with an over-emphatic use of capitals as 'that Black Mass'. The *persona* admits:

> I had always half-known he existed –
> this antidote and Anti-Christ his anarchy
> threatening the eggs, well rounded, self-contained –
> and the placidity of milk.

This eruption from the earth-darkness is not inappropriately identified as Anti-Christ since his appearance threatens to smash the fragile world of innocence to pieces, an apocalyptic happening from the child's point-of-view. Moreover, he might be a Cretan Bull, a Mithras, a pagan god of Dionysiac anarchy, the kind of figure the prudish early Christians anathematised as the horned-beast figure of the Devil. He might even be a Celtic deity, such as Heaney catches a glimpse of in 'The Forge' in *Door into the Dark*.[17] Perhaps the child's half-knowledge is a racial memory. However that may be, the dark male's threat is towards emblems of femaleness, the eggs and milk.

The final verse paragraph needs to be quoted in full:

> I ran, my pigtails thumping on my back in fear,
> past the big boys in the farm lane
> who pulled the wings from butterflies and
> blew up frogs with straws.
> Past thorned hedge and harried nest,
> scared of the eggs shattering –
> only my small and shaking hand on the jug's rim
> in case the milk should spill.

The child runs, but fails to escape masculine threat: the 'big boys' in the lane combine in two monosyllables two signal qualities of the bull, largeness and maleness. And boys will be boys! These wanton boys, in a fashion that calls to mind Ian McEwan's nearly contemporary short story 'Butterflies',[18] further illustrate male violence towards innocent nature. The girl, trying to prevent the milk from spilling and the eggs breaking, presents a poignant emblem of the female desperately trying to keep the household together, keeping things tidy and putting food on the table, in the face of male irresponsibility and violence that threaten to spill everything at once, to harry the nest: it's an emblem the force of which would not be lost on many a Scots woman. What causes panic is also, more simply, a nascent awareness of the power of *desire*, a power which can lead to the literal shattering of a female's eggs and the flow of her milk in motherhood. These images also suggest perhaps the culmination of male desire, a view perhaps supported by the French expressions *'casser son œuf'* (to ejaculate) and *'laitance'* (ejaculation). Such things are understandably a source of fear, especially in a girl on the threshold of adolescence. It perhaps bears saying, however, that desire is not necessarily to be regarded as a dark and dreadful thing. It is a driving force of nature: we are all, of necessity, human farmyard animals, as Will Guthrie explains to his young sister Chris, who asks him about their mother's pregnancy: *'What has father to do with it?* And Will stared back at her, shame-faced, *Don't you know? What's a bull to do with a calf, you fool?'*[19] The girl, too, is involved in the world of animality and desire: she has 'pigtails', suggesting perhaps the role of passive victim (as in 'a stuck pig') and certainly indicative of her femininity (especially since the word 'pig' is cognate with words that mean girl). Her hand shakes 'on the jug's rim', suggesting a reflex of clutching the breast in fear, but also hinting at desire and the erotic. The child glimpses male desire as a threat but also catches sight of desire for the male within herself. Mary Shelley, in *Blood and Ice*, will articulate what the child here cannot: 'When man and woman lie down together they are at once each other's strange wild savage beasts and each other's sacrificial victims' (*PW*, 114). A mere glimpse of this is sufficient to end innocence, but the child's panic is by no means the one proper response. Not for nothing did our pagan forebears honour such dark gods. The very milk that the child fears to spill (and *threatens* to spill by her panic) is a wholesome everyday product that could not exist without the dark sexual world of bull and coo. She is herself, of course, (like all of us) a product of such messy origins.

This sense of male threat and female fear in the realm of sexuality is not uncommon in Lochhead's work. In 'Song of Solomon' (*DF*, 86) the male lover is 'as happy as a hog rooting for truffles' but the female hopes 'he would not smell her fear'. 'Beauty & The' (*DF*, 79) opens:

> Beast
> he was hot
> he grew horns
> he had you
> screaming mammy daddy screaming blue
> murder.

The new twist to the old story here is to re-interpret the fairy-tale as symbolizing the unfortunate position of the female, having to kiss the 'old crocodile', pressured into sleeping with the monster: 'So you (anything for a quiet/ life) embrace the beast, endure'. Horror and glum acceptance are not the only responses recorded to beastly *machismo* however. In 'Rapunzstiltskin' (*DF*, 78), a poem from the same sequence ('Three Twists') as 'Beauty & The', the distressed maiden's reaction to her Prince is described thus: 'Well, it was corny but/ he did look sort of gorgeous/ axe and all'. Complicity is also a possible reaction. In interview Lochhead declares: 'I don't think anybody could have seen *Dracula* and called it feminist. I'm interested in female masochism, for instance'.[20] Interest in a subject does not clearly define one's attitude towards it, but the juxtaposition with the first sentence suggests a sympathetic interest. That said, feminism is a broad church and it is possible to find feminist writers who are openly enthusiastic about the dark delights of lesbian sado-masochism. Lochhead might sit oddly in such extremist company ('True Confessions' [*TCNC*, 3] speaks of 'The night she was *almost* tempted by lesbian advances' [italics mine]), but the common thread is perhaps a determination to attack the *repression* of female sexuality and all attempts (even feministic ones) to turn little girls into sugar and spice and all things nice. As Mary Shelley says towards the close of *Blood and Ice*: 'What are little girls made of? Slime and snails and . . . What are monsters made of?' (*PW*, 112). In the sequence 'Dreaming Frankenstein' (*DF*, 11–15) it is the *female* imagination, the *female* fantasist, that creates the sexually aggressive monster who 'entered her utterly', 'the rough serge of his suiting' chafing her sex, his buttons biting into her. She is the monster's 'maker'.

Speaking of Mary Shelley, Lochhead is quite clear about the evil influence of repression:

> So I was interested in people's darker natures, what makes somebody who has all the ingredients of a rational life turn to darkness. It's suppression. The more you to try to suppress the dark bits of yourself, the more they well up.[21]

and again:

Why would Mary Shelley write about monsters? I was haunted by
that phrase from Goya: 'The sleep of reason produces monsters'. If
you try to force things to be too rational the dark and untidy bits
will well up and manifest themselves in quite concrete ways.[22]
The Laingian spirit of the seventies is evidently still alive. What is
remarkable here is that Lochhead wholly ignores what one might call
the primary sense of Goya's ambiguous epigraph, the idea that when
one puts reason to sleep and lets imagination, fantasy, the dark side, run
riot, one inevitably unleashes monsters. The play, however, is arguably
wiser than the playwright.

In *Blood and Ice* Byron takes the same line on repression when
questioned by Mary regarding his affair with his half-sister: '*I love my
sister Augusta*. Too much to subject that love to the warpings of
platonics. Frustrated love perverts, produces monsters' (*PW*, 100). Both
he and Shelley in the play are free-spirits, libertines who would kick
over the traces of conventional sexual morality.

> SHELLEY: Ladies, Wollstonecraft said: 'Make brothers and equals
> of your husbands and lovers'. Shelley says: 'Make
> husbands and lovers of your brothers and equals' — if
> you so desire. Let love know no limit!
>
> BYRON: Bravo, Bravo, the Snake! Well, Shelley, you do have a
> trickier tongue than the serpent in Eden.
>
> CLAIRE: Monsters.
>
> (*PW*, 93)

Liberation here is producing monsters. Byron at one point (*PW*, 94)
commends contraception to women so that they can 'liberate
[themselves] . . . from the enforced labour of the childbed', but also so
that men 'need no longer be the slaves of our unsatisfied lusts'. It is, to
employ an oxymoron, pure Sade, one of the 'Libertines for Liberty' of
the French Revolution that Byron here refers to, and might almost have
been lifted from the grotesque theorisings of his Dolmancé. Liberation
of women from repression, a worthy enough cause in itself, can be
exploited by men to further their own dark ends and female complicity
in this can be very dangerous indeed. Claire Clairmont, shocked by the
monstrous thoughts of the young Romantic poets, is earlier prepared to
play along. She explains to Mary her wearing a '*thin red velvet ribbon
round her throat*': 'The brave beldams of the French Revolution affected
it. It is called '*à la victime*' . . . Oh, only a fashion, Mary, but I'm sure
the gentlemen will love it' (*PW*, 88). In the sexual revolution, as
evidently here in the French Revolution, women are always in danger of

ending up '*à la victime*' (and one might add that Claire seems to be guilty of contributory negligence in this respect). It is hard to regard revolutions with such outcomes as glorious. 'Let love know no limit!' But throwing out sexual morality wholesale is no answer. In an early scene Mary apologises to the maid Justine for Shelley's sudden appearance in the nude:

> MARY: . . . But he is a good, good man, he is against all viciousness, and cruelty, and tyranny and owner-ship. What is nakedness compared to . . .
>
> *Pause. Elise is withholding.*
>
> ELISE (*shrugging*): It's only nature, Madame.
>
> (*PW*, 85)

It's a fine ambiguity. Is not nature itself (as Sade, for one, frequently asserts) full of viciousness and cruelty and tyranny and ownership? Doubtless the rules have been established in the wrong places (as witness the inability of Jonathan and Mina in Lochhead's *Dracula* to accept that the other can desire anyone else [*MQD*, 146]), but abandoning (rational) rules altogether unleashes monsters and re-drawing the lines is a devilishly difficult matter. Lochhead takes pains to enumerate the difficulties of solving the David Lodge question that must haunt our post-pill paradise like a serpent in Eden: *how far can you go?*

Blood and Ice ends with a true confession by its heroine:

> I am the monster, poor misunderstood creature feared and hated by all mankind. And then I thought: it is worse, worse than that, I am the female monster, gross, gashed, ten times more hideous than my male counterpart, denied life, tied to the monster bed for ever.
>
> (*PW*, 115)

It's an odd mixture of Schopenhauer and feministic protest at the wrongs of woman. It shows a clear awareness of the other side of the gender politics of monstrosity: that *man*kind may be inclined to fear and hate the female as the alien, the other, 'gross, gashed', cleft not crested. Lochhead's writing shows a strong commitment to the revelation of what's monstrous about the monstrous regiment (to misuse that phrase in the usual way) of women, though the *unheimlich* turns out, for the most part, to be reassuringly *heimlich*.

Lochhead is indubitably a feminist, but she rather plays down the importance of this in her work: 'I think feminism's basically very, very simple. It's about equal pay, equal opportunities, abortion on demand, free childcare. So what could you write about such things'[23] *Sancta simplicitas*! There are those of us who think that there is something (other than the merely lexical) monstrous about abortion. Lochhead's *forthrightness* about feminine matters in general is a feminist aspect of her work that might have seemed to earlier generations a monstrous quality in a woman. Her literary *persona* is not that of an extreme or highly theoretical feminist, but rather someone with a large fund of (Scottish working-class?) common-sense and humour, the kind of person who might produce the beautifully Prufrockian couplet in 'Spinster' (*DF*, 75): 'My life's in shards./ I will keep fit in leotards', someone more at home with leotards than Lyotard, someone who knows more about 'self-help coffee mornings/ with your speculum and mirror' (*TCNC*, 44) than about *Spéculum de l'autre femme*. The wry humour, however, does not exclude seriousness: the speculum and mirror are emblems of self-exploration and self-recognition, of a woman's coming to terms with herself. The poem (or 'rap') from which those emblems are taken, 'Feminine Advice' (*TCNC*, 42), for all its jokey, sceptical tone, shows awareness of the seriousness of such matters:

> But I'm aware and now I know
> that men are overrated.
> I've cast my simpers, found myself,
> I'm Spare-Rib liberated.
> I fly above False Consciousness
> I love me more, I love him less
> I use Real Words for parts of me
> Which formerly I hated.

Finding oneself, learning to love oneself; these are elements in a *redemptive* process. Those monstrous words have to be redeemed too, so that the very parts of the body may no longer be hated.[24]

Without ever being obscene, Lochhead is forthright about such 'speculative' matters. 'Song of Solomon' from *The Grimm Sisters* (*DF*, 86) offers an amusing inversion of the figurative tactics of one of the most celebrated and influential of love poems, the Canticle of Canticles. 'Solomon' in that book heaps extravagant praises upon the beloved and her body: it can appear as a kind of cosmetic process:

> Thy lips, O my spouse, drop as the honeycomb:
> honey and milk are under thy tongue . . .
> Thy navel is like a round goblet, which wanteth
> not liquor . . .[25]

In Lochhead's version the male lover is appreciative of the olfactory qualities of his partner: 'You/ smell nice he said/ what is it?/ Honey?' His partner, however, is uneasily aware of the male imperative underlying the second line quoted (women *ought* to smell nice) and of the fact that his pleasure is in part the product of what is literally a cosmetic effect, produced by such things as 'chemical/ attar of roses at her armpit'. She is afraid of the *reality* of her own body, which becomes *thereby* an ugly reality:

> never think of the whiff of
> sourmilk from her navel
> the curds of cheese between the toes
> the dried blood smell of many small wounds
> the stink of fish at her crotch. [26]

Cosmetics betoken the alienation of the woman from herself and our alienation (along lines of gender) from one another. The last line quoted is rather shocking, but that shock is a measure of our alienation from ourselves.

A number of the aspects of the monstrous that have been considered come together in a splendidly rich little poem, 'Inter-City' from *Dreaming Frankenstein* (*DF*, 33), which opens with an image of Scotland as a Frankenstein's monster:

> Hammered like a bolt
> diagonally through Scotland (my
> small dark country) this
> train's a
> swaying caveful of half-
> seas over oil-men (fuck
> this fuck that fuck
> everything) bound for Aberdeen and
> North Sea Crude.

Here there be (male) monsters, atavistic brutes whose language seems to consist entirely of sexual threat or boasting of sexual conquests (this latter deftly suggested by the odd lineation). These barbarians have invaded and conquered the female space ('cave') of the carriage in a way that might be seen as matching the violent penetration by the train (conceived of as a whole, a masculine symbol) of Scotland, associated by means of a pun on one of those 'Real Words' with the speaker's sex. The poem, however, is no mere diatribe against those objectionable louts who let their empty lager-cans 'roll like ballbearings/ underfoot' and outrage decent people with their loud obscenities. The poem's *persona* understandably tries to look away from this gross scene, but she is 'not even pretending to read' her 'artsyfartsy magazine', perhaps because she is responding sexually to the well-lubricated *machismo* of these oil-men.

This monstrous admission is communicated obliquely, chiefly through imagery. The train sways with the ferrovialic rhythm that is proper to it but also in imitation of another, more natural rhythm, the to-fro of 'this fuck that fuck'. 'North Sea Crude' may sum up their vulgarity and bad manners but this phrase too has its erotic edge, 'crude' being etymologically close to 'cruel' and deriving from the Indo-European root KRU, 'to be hard'. As the *persona* turns away to look out of the window she finds she can see 'bits of my own blurred/ back-to-front face'. Another side of the self is seen, though the image is not quite focused. The image appears in a frame filled with the 'black absolutely' of the night world outside. It's a portrait of a dark self, though the *persona* sees 'fizzing starbursts' of streetlights, firework imagery that might remind one of that used by Joyce to symbolize Gerty MacDowell's orgasm in the 'Nausicaa' episode of *Ulysses*,[27] and 'windows', feminine spaces again, that are 'lit-up': her mind is 'elsewhere'. The magazine, which she calls 'artsyfartsy' as if her mind-set had shifted to something resembling that of the crude roustabouts, is

> wide open
> at a photograph called Portrait of Absence.

Thus, beguilingly, the poem ends. The penultimate line strongly hints at female arousal and there is a rather obvious and crude interpretation of the nature of what is *absent* here that one might venture! This female desire is, in a sense, absent from the poem, since it is never explicitly articulated. Such monstrous complicity with gross *machismo* is a subject likely to be absent from any 'artsyfarsy magazine'. It is, however, a presence in the art and portraiture of *Dreaming Frankenstein*, a book of monstrous imaginings and fantasies.

Though I have characterised Lochhead as a non-extreme feminist, her valorising of hitherto despised or monstrous roles for women shows traces of the influence of a very radical feminist indeed. Mary Daly, in her *Gyn/Ecology* (1978) celebrates woman as Hag, Spinster and Fury. In *The Grimm Sisters* (1981) one finds sections entitled 'Hags and Maidens' and 'The Furies', the latter being divided into 'Harridan', 'Spinster' and 'Bawd' (*DF*, 94, 74). Daly writes:

> Haggard writing is by and for haggard women, those who are intractable, willful, wanton, unchaste . . . As Furies, women in the tradition of the Great Hags reject the curse of compromise.[28]

While there is something grotesquely unfair about electing Liz Lochhead to the ranks of the Great Hags, one must remember that for Daly this is a term of praise and does not have its usual connotations. 'The Furies' certainly looks like 'haggard writing'. In 'Harridan' the *persona* 'more than sympathise[s]' with the 'maddened slut', the 'Virago' of Brueghel's *Dulle Griet*: she *empathises*, taking on the role of hell-raising Fury herself:

> Oh I am wild-eyed, unkempt, hellbent, a harridan.
> My sharp tongue will shrivel any man.

For Lochhead, Mad Meg is not simply a quaint figure from Flemish legend, someone who belongs merely to 'History of Art', but an emblem of woman driven to extremes by the 'mass of misery' of male-imposed domesticity: she carries a 'kitchen knife', the commonest weapon in cases of female on male domestic murder. Again, in 'Bawd', the *persona* parades qualities of wilfulness, wantonness and unchastity:

> I'll be a torment, haunt men's dreams
> I'll wear my stockings black with seams.

This perhaps echoes Daly's etymological interpretation of 'hag' as nightmare (for men), but in Lochhead's version (as in the quotation from 'Harridan' above) there is also a Jane Russell-esque erotic charge to the image. Lochhead may assert in 'What-I'm-Not-Song' that she's not 'Thinking Man's Crumpet' (*TCNC*, 55), but her verse can be seductive all the same, a tendency which culminates in the dazzling eroticism of 'What the Pool Said, On Midsummer's Day' (*DF*, 8), the *persona* a kind of Celtic river-goddess celebrating a pagan feast day in style:

> The woman was easy.
> Like to like, I called her, she came.
> In no time I had her
> out of herself, slipping on my water-stockings,
> leaning into, being cupped and clasped
> in my green glass bra.

An 'easy' woman is wanton, unchaste. In the mirror-like pool, like Eve in Paradise, she sees and is drawn to her like, *amans amare* ('Like to like'). The near-brutality of the third line is superbly counterbalanced by the suggestions of quasi-mystical experience in the union of the woman and the *persona*, 'in no time', 'out of herself'. Even as the woman steps (presumably naked) into the pool, she is imaged as being clothed by the *persona* in fetishistic underwear (which is, nonetheless, the *persona's* very self). *Et in Arcadia ego*!

The poem which perhaps most forcefully deploys the idiolect of Mary Daly is 'Mirror's Song' (*DF*, 67), the *finale* of *Dreaming Frankenstein*. Here the public face cosmetically applied before the mirror is to be destroyed by the smashing of that 'glass/coffin', thereby unleashing the 'best black self' of womanhood: 'Smash me she'll whirl out like Kali'. The image of monstrous Kali, destructive yet with the promise of new life, is reminiscent of Daly's notion of the 'spinster':

> A woman whose occupation is to spin participates in the whirling movement of creation. She who has chosen her self, who defines her Self, by choice . . . who is Self-identified, is a Spinster, a whirling dervish, spinning in a new time/space.[29]

'Mirror's Song' calls for the 'trash[-ing]' and 'junk[-ing]' of cosmetics, anodynes and other symbols of male control and female subservience thereto; 'whalebone and lycra', 'underwires', 'lovepulps and the Librium'. It's a furious clear-out of which Daly would approve:

> Furies rush forth and collect the shreds of the deadly deceivers' costumes. We throw the threads and shreds into a heap. We toss onto the pile the combustible samples displayed by the Obsessors, such as magazines and bras. We set the pile afire with the flames of our combined fury.[30]

'Mirror's Song' builds towards its final image of the establishment of a true female identity:

> . . . Let her rip.
> She'll crumple all the
> tracts and the adverts, shred
> all the wedding dresses, snap
> all the spike-heel icicles
> in the cave she will claw out of –
> a woman giving birth to herself.

It is a final image of monstrosity, conveying powerfully the birth-pangs of a new self, but it is also suggestive, as is every moment of birth, of new hope for the world, a Revelation.[31]

NOTES

1 The phrase 'silly like us' is from Auden's 'In Memory of W. B. Yeats' (l. 32).

2 *Sleeping with Monsters: Conversations with Scottish and Irish Women Poets*; edited by Gillean Somerville-Arjat and Rebecca E. Wilson (Edinburgh: Polygon, 1990), 9.

3 One might suggest that during the past decade the city of Glasgow itself has been acting out of the fairy-tale 'The Emperor's New Clothes'.

4 Sigmund Freud, 'The "Uncanny"' (1919), in *The Complete Psychological Works of Sigmund Freud*; translated from the German under the general editorship of James Strachey in collaboration with Anna Freud, assisted by Alex Strachey and Alan Tyson, vol. 17, 224.

5 Ibid., 220.
6 The *locus classicus* is Gregory Smith's *Scottish Literature: Character and Influence* (London: Macmillan, 1919).
7 Alasdair Gray, *1982 Janine* (Harmondsworth: Penguin, 1985), 30.
8 Hugh MacDiarmid, *A Drunk Man Looks at the Thistle*, annotated edition; edited by Kenneth Buthlay (Edinburgh: Scottish Academic Press, 1987), 50 (l. 2064).
9 Ibid., 88 (ll. 1111–12).
10 *Sleeping with Monsters*, xii.
11 Edwin Muir, *Scott and Scotland*, with an introduction by Allan Massie (Edinburgh: Polygon, 1982), p. 9.
12 Hugh MacDiarmid, *Complete Poems 1920–1976*; edited by Michael Grieve and W. R. Aitken (London: Martin Brian and O'Keeffe, 1978), vol. 1, 73 ('Gairmscoile', l. 41).
13 *Sleeping with Monsters*, 14.
14 Andrea Dworkin, 'Why So-Called Radical Men Love and Need Pornography' in *Take Back the Night: Women on Pornography*; edited by Laura Lederer (New York: William Morrow and Company, 1980), 148.
15 *Sleeping with Monsters*, xi.
16 Ted Hughes, *Selected Poems 1957–1967* (London: Faber and Faber, 1972), 41.
17 Seamus Heaney, *Door into the Dark*, second edition (London: Faber and Faber, 1972), 19.
18 In his *First Love, Last Rites* (London: Jonathan Cape, 1975).
19 Lewis Grassic Gibbon, *Sunset Song*, Heritage of Literature Series (Harlow, Essex: Longman, 1971), 38.
20 *Sleeping with Monsters*, 12.
21 Ibid., 13–14.
22 Ibid., 13.
23 Ibid., 12.
24 This is the kind of redemptive process engaged in by D. H. Lawrence, a prime example of a would-be liberator of womankind who nonetheless wished them to end up '*à la victime*'.
25 Song of Solomon 4.11; 7.2 (King James Version).
26 A passage from Freud's 'The "Uncanny"' has some relevance here:
    It often happens that neurotic men declare that they feel there is something uncanny about the female genital organs. This *unheimlich* place, however, is the entrance to the former *Heim* [home] of all human beings . . . In this case, too, then, the *unheimlich* is what was once *heimisch*, familiar; the prefix '*un*' is the token of repression. (Ibid., 245)
27 James Joyce, *Ulysses*, Corrected Text; edited by Hans Walter Gabler with Wolfhard Steppe and Claus Melchior (London: Bodley Head, 1986), 300.
28 Mary Daly, *Gyn/Ecology: The Metaethics of Radical Feminism* (London: The Women's Press, 1979), 16.

29 Ibid., 3–4.
30 Ibid., 422.
31 I would like to thank Dr Mary Orr of the Department of French at St
     Andrews for some helpful discussions about Liz Lochhead and related
     matters while I was working on this article.

Four

The Two-faced Language of Lochhead's Poetry

Robert Crawford

Pun is one of the main engines supplying Lochhead's verbal energy, especially in the early poetry. Her first collection, even if it now seems to her 'written by somebody else' (Nicholson, 204), was accomplished and brimming with promise, particularly since its author was only twenty-five; but sometimes the puns in *Memo for Spring* are uneasy, 'Your egg collection/ Shatters me' (*DF*, 147) or 'corny old autumn' (*DF*, 149). Puns are trying hard in 'the sea's/ cold summersault' (*DF*, 142) and 'forge my ironies from a steel town' (*DF*, 128); they are less ostentatious but more assured in 'Inventory' (*DF*, 135) which opens with the line 'you left me' before cataloguing a list of abandoned objects, last of which is 'a/ you shaped/ depression in my pillow'. *Memo for Spring*, through its puns, indicates and initiates a number of Lochhead's preoccupations. The themes of mirrors and of the circumscribing of a woman's life are present in 'Morning After' with its:

> Me, the Mirror
> reflecting only on your closed profile.
> You, the Observer
> encompassing larger, Other issues.
> (*DF*, 134)

In this acute small poem, the speaker (whom we assume to be female from the gender roles in this and the surrounding poems, though no sex is here assigned) has for herself the demotic tabloid, though she is also aware of the higher-brow broadsheet, and is conscious of the value (and gender) judgements implied in flicking 'too quickly/ too casually' through the 'colour section'. The 'Mirror' here is not just the *Daily Mirror*, it is also the daily mirror of the woman obliged to present herself to male observers. It is for those male observers that the speaker of 'Obituary' is punningly making her purchases:

> Christmas found me
> with other fond and foolish girls
> at the menswear counters
> shopping for the ties that bind.
> March found me
> guilty of too much hope.
> > seems silly now really.
> > (*DF*, 134)

Here again we are aware of the speaker's fascination with 'the ties that bind', but also of her awareness that shopping for these may be 'fond and foolish' or 'silly'. That last adjective might conjure up the ghost of the dismissive phrase 'silly girl', yet we can hardly fail to be aware that this poem is not simply a conventional lament for lost love. It is also a poem about growing older and wiser, and that maturing involves a perception that the gender roles assigned to 'fond and foolish girls' who go 'shopping for the ties that bind' are to be resisted or wriggled out of, or at least warily watched. The verbal mobility of puns is part of this wriggling process of liberating escape in a book whose 'I' is always aware of and attracted to 'Something I'm Not' (*DF*, 138). The self in these poems seeks to be as unstable as a pun, and so to win free of the social and gender clichés in which it might too easily be fixed. It is once more pun which articulates and carries out the determination to escape from being caught when in 'Phoenix' (*DF*, 131) the speaker sees that the slipperiness of words can be turned to her own advantage:

> When crowsfeet get a grip on me
> I'll call them laughter lines
> I'll think of burnt-out romances
> as being my old flames.

This phoenixing looks towards the later, more complex 'woman giving birth to herself' (*DF*, 68), while it may also draw on the self-resurrecting power of Sylvia Plath's 'Lady Lazarus' as Lochhead punningly subverts and appropriates the phoenix emblem which D. H. Lawrence tried to make his own.

Though we live in the century of Joyce, I suspect many readers still feel that images and metaphors are more genuinely 'poetic' than puns. Puns were essential to the popular stand-up humour of the sixties and seventies – they were vital, for instance, to Ronnie Barker – and they are the stuff of (often bad) jokes. Puns, which depend fundamentally on a homophonic (soundalike) rather than homographic (lookalike) quality, lend themselves to oral delivery and it is fitting that they are so prominent in the early work of a writer who attends so carefully to the performance of her work. When George Mackay Brown (quoted on the blurb to *BM*) praises Lochhead as 'a truly modern poet in that she writes – I almost wrote, *speaks* – in the very tone and accent and rhythms of the 1980s', he is drawing attention to the orality that is so important to Lochhead's work, and that comes to the fore in her fidelity to speech, her love of spoken 'wrong', rather than the 'correct' written forms, and her delight in puns that may at times work better aloud than they do on the page.

Lochhead comes from a culture which delights in the oral and the way it can interfere with the literary. Her senior Glaswegian contemporary, Adam McNaughtan (see *BM*, 83), who 'prefers to publish in sound rather than in print' feels obliged to apologise for the 'somewhat laboured pun of the title' of his 'Oor Hamlet' when it appears in print in *The Best of Scottish Poetry* gloriously subverting Shakespearean tragedy with demotic Glaswegian in a breakneck verse-summary of the play ('Then he cried "The rest is silence!" That was Hamlet hud his chips./ They firet a volley ower him that shook the topmaist rafter/ An' Fortinbras, knee-deep in Danes, lived happy ever after.')[1] McNaughtan, who studied at Whitehill School and Glasgow University before becoming a teacher in 1962, has produced songs and take-offs which are familiar in West of Scotland oral culture, and some of which, such as the gloriously punning 'The Jeely Piece Song' (1967), blend the consciously urban and Glaswegian with older music-hall and ballad traditions. As a young poet, Lochhead would have been familiar with McNaughtan's work, just as she knew the work of her early mentor Stephen Mulrine, most celebrated for his use of Glasgow working-class speech in 'The Coming of the Wee Malkies' (1967), another energetically urban poem whose refrain is all the more effective in oral delivery.[2]

Though she did not immediately put demotic rhythms to full use in her poetry, Liz Lochhead grew up in a climate where younger poets and singers were making confident use of Glasgow speech, sights and sounds. Ian Hamilton Finlay's 1961 'Glasgow Beasts, an a Burd, an Inseks, an, aw, a Fush' was followed by the poems of Tom Leonard, Lochhead's friend and contemporary, who was able to produce some of the finest Scots poetry since MacDiarmid by turning away from the dictionary towards the oral and urban. Leonard, like Lochhead, was encouraged in this by the recent American poetry and poetics which were championed in Scotland by Edwin Morgan. Charles Olson's 1950 manifesto 'Projective Verse' encouraged a free verse that paid attention to 'Laws and possibilities of the breath' while the work of Creeley and Williams gave rise to a relaxed, improvisatory verse whose short lines were at times close to the hesitations and rhythms of clipped speech.[3] American poetics and a Glaswegian love of 'patter' in McNaughtan, Mulrine and others (which may be related to the strength of the pantomime tradition in Scotland (Stanley Baxter, Rikki Fulton)) combined in the sixties and seventies to encourage in Lochhead a reliance on the orality of poetry.

As a woman writer, Lochhead was emerging into what was perceived in Scotland around 1970, as very much a male domain. Here again, orality offered certain strengths. If one looks at Scottish anthologies of the period, the preponderance of male writers is striking. In the anthology *Contemporary Scottish Verse 1959–1969* edited by Norman MacCaig and Alexander Scott only two out of the two hundred and forty or so poems in the book are by women. Charles King's 1971 school text *Twelve Modern Scottish Poets* contains only male poets. Well under ten percent of the poems in the 1966 second edition of Maurice Lindsay's Faber anthology *Modern Scottish Poetry* are by women.[4] These anthologies are typical in their representation of the sexes. Today, some of the exclusions, such as that of Muriel Spark, may be striking, but the anthologists are not likely to have been consciously misogynistic; their choices reasonably accurately reflect Scottish culture at the time. If it is still hard to argue that the major voices of mid-century Scottish poetry were female, it is now obvious that male anthologists did little to help the position of women writers. The mid century was scarcely an encouraging time for Scottish women poets.

Part of the problem was the legacy of the still living Hugh MacDiarmid. Lochhead has spoken of 'implicit, incredible sexism' in *A Drunk Man Looks at the Thistle*, and she recalls that for her as a young poet MacDiarmid was 'the big black devil' against whose work younger poets, both male and female, reacted.

> Most of the young writers certainly in Glasgow that I knew at that time, we all agreed very much with MacDiarmid about the oppressive power of English English, but instead of being attracted towards the things that he had done I think at that time there was an enormous attraction towards American poetry. You know it was all William Carlos Williams, Creeley and the breath, the voice – things that are actually there in MacDiarmid as well. But perhaps it was too close, you know, perhaps it was the devil that we knew in so many ways, or the devil that we thought we knew. There was a feeling – once again, it's not MacDiarmid's fault at all – but there was a feeling that he was a kind of prison and, you know, such a giant oppressive figure – that the thing to do about it was to ignore it and do something quite different.[5]

MacDiarmid had become in many ways reactionary, dismissing the work of Ian Hamilton Finlay and scorning the US Beat poetry admired by Morgan. Lochhead was attracted to these younger male poets whose work relished the acoustics of Glasgow, and she felt a certain jealousy of Jean Milton, another young Scottish woman poet who had begun to publish American-influenced breathy verse impressions of Glasgow.[6]

Lochhead's early puns are only one indication of her fidelity to the oral. Her later poetry revels in the spoken word in other ways that may be related to modes favoured by women artists, often artists regarded as unserious, and uncanonical. The female monologue tradition developed by the American Ruth Draper and the English Joyce Grenfell offered Lochhead one model of a female performance art that was at once popular and acute, drawing its strength from fidelity to the quirks and particularities of the voice. Though this monologue tradition was far from exclusively female, and though it may now seem old-fashioned, it was a tradition in which women had clearly excelled. Lochhead has worried that some of her own monologues 'seemed . . . steam-radio-Stanley-Holloway-meets-Flanders-and-Swann-meets-Joyce-Grenfell-old-fashioned. (I *liked* the radio when I was wee)' (*TC*, 2).

More recently she has spoken of how 'The subversive laughter of the music hall appeals to me a great deal . . . At some point I'd like to do something about the male impersonators of another era, like Vesta Tilley and her 'Burlington Bertie' routine' (Nicholson, 221). Through the music-hall-derived media of revue and cabaret, Lochhead has moved the female monologue away from the rather polite, but precisely crafted pieces of Grenfell towards a more adventurous, taboo-breaking feminist humour. What she has kept is Grenfell's fidelity to the spoken voice, a fidelity encouraged by contemporary trends in Glasgow writing, and probably by the Scottish tradition as a whole. Lochhead remembers that 'the Border Ballads . . . were among the only poems I had liked at secondary school' (Nicholson, 211) and Catherine Kerrigan has argued that the ballad tradition, so crucial to the development of Scottish culture, 'is one of the most readily identifiable areas of literary performance by women'.[7] Such an argument is consonant not only with Lochhead's use of ballad materials – whether Scott's 'The Young Tamlane' in 'Tam Lin's Lady' or 'The Twa Corbies' in *Mary Queen of Scots* and elsewhere – but also with the feminist argument propounded by Jan Montefiore that women poets have been fascinated by myth and fairytale, fairytale attracting 'those poets whose idiom is closest to ordinary speech'. Quoting Walter Benjamin's 1936 essay 'The Storyteller' to the effect that 'Experience which passes from mouth to mouth is the source from which all storytellers have drawn', Montefiore goes on to point out that Lochhead's poem 'The Storyteller' (*DF*, 70) 'reads like a feminist gloss on [Benjamin's] essay'.[8] Certainly by the time of *The Grimm Sisters* we can see the oral and the feminist properties of Lochhead's work working together to produce verse which (though she does not discuss Lochhead) seems to follow exactly the paradigm outlined by Liz Yorke in her book *Impertinent Voices: Subversive Strategies in Contemporary Women's Poetry*:

> *Anywhere that experience, memory, fantasy or dream can be retrieved, whether in words or images, it may be revalued, and re-presented. This effort of retrieval may permit different textures, colours, aspects, lights and shadings to be heard, seen and felt: such feminist transvaluation is a continual re-processing.*[9]

In *The Grimm Sisters* Lochhead celebrates a world of female speech which may 'subvert from within' (Nicholson, 216), a spoken 'herstory' that runs counter to male history, male myth, and male fantasy in a way that is again orthodoxly feminist in quite complex ways. We might usefully apply to Lochhead's poetry what Liz Yorke writes about the feminist 'history' advocated by Catherine Clément and Hélène Cixous:

> The history written by women will not be a 'true' history but will be reconstituted, re-membered out of the exclusions and negations of patriarchy, and will be written by those who play out their lives 'between symbolic systems, in the interstices, offside'. Thus, the history produced by women, in Clément's and Cixous' terms,
>
> > is a history, taken from what is lost within us of oral tradition, of legends and myths – a history arranged the way tale-telling women tell it. And from the standpoint of conveying the mythic models that powerfully structure the Imaginary (masculine and feminine, complex and varied), this history will be true. On the level of fantasy, it will be fantastically true. It is still acting on us. In telling it, in developing it, even in plotting it, I seek to undo it, to overturn it, to reveal it, to *expose* it.
>
> Far from the universalising and ahistorical versions of myth produced within a religious or Jungian perspective, this mythology of reminiscence emerges from a specific cultural and historical context, and articulates an individual, culture-bound mode of relating to the symbolic system.[10]

In *The Grimm Sisters* and elsewhere Lochhead's celebration of and use of orality can be seen as disrupting the fixed, orthodox forms of the written-down. The oral world is fluid and dialogic; it is also particular rather than universalizing. Where Tom Leonard, Stephen Mulrine, James Kelman and others maintain a fidelity to the particularities of

West of Scotland speech as a means of disrupting so-called 'standard English,' the dominant language of the Anglocentric, male-ordered canon, Lochhead's use of the oral functions not only as a Scottish – even Glasgwegian – disruption of Anglocentricity; it also functions as a spoken female subversion and disruption of the masculinist written world. Opposing those Scottish anthologies whose textuality was fixed as almost exclusively male, Lochhead sets up the woman's shifting *voice*. That is why it is so important to be aware of a delight in the oral even in the poems of her first book with their careful attention to the minutiae of speech, signalled here in the italics and break-up of the last word:

> what *is* the difference between a
> republican & a
> dem - o - crat?
>   (*DF*, 144)

Here, on the page, we sense mischievous orality disrupting Standard English ('democrat' isn't usually pronounced 'dem-o-crat'). The slangy, the colloquial is available on call – 'Oh it was a scream' (*DF*, 125); '(oh I forgot)' (*DF*, 139); 'Sure' (*DF*, 141); 'a dead ringer' (*DF*, 146); 'they really are a riot' (*DF*, 149). Yet at the same time a much more literary register is present in such phrases as 'gold embroidered gorgeousness' (*DF*, 139), or 'unironic lips' (*DF*, 129) – a phrase lifted from Edwin Morgan's poem 'King Billy'. The presence of another established male poet is felt in 'Revelation' (*DF*, 124) which is more 'literary' in tone and so appeared 'closer to what a poem should feel like' (Nicholson, 208). 'Revelation' seems to draw on the animal poems of Ted Hughes. Yet (though it did not appear so to the young Lochhead) it is also a poem about the female's need to negotiate with and slip past the admired yet also fearsomely monstrous male in order to preserve her own particular gift. If Lochhead's first book establishes patterns which will be developed in her later work – such as monsters, mirrors, and midsummer – it also establishes the ongoing dialogue in her work between male and female, a dialogue related to and conducted alongside the tensions between the oral and the literary.

These latter tensions are subtly present in the rather different collection *Islands*, which looks in its subject matter towards the familiar Scottish literary territory of MacCaig and Crichton Smith, while its opening words 'Another Life' might call to mind the Morgan who had recently (in 1968) published *The Second Life*. The literary description is sharp – 'Sheep come apart in handfuls' (*DF*, 107) – but we are also aware that the journey to the Hebrides is a journey to an oral culture in which what women say, however self-dismissively, is important:

And when the butter wouldn't churn
there was a saying if you took a pan –
having first shut fast the windows and the door –
and gave some of that slow milk
a right good scald over the fire
the witch that was the one that cursed it
had to come.
It worked.
That auld bitch knocked my father said
and afterwards the village knew her.
Over our drink it seems
Dolidh will tell us – if she's pressed –
of the witches of Tolsta.

And och it's all nonsense . . .

(*DF*, 108–9)

The 'other world' of the Hebrides is to an important degree an oral and
female one; not the feminized Celticism of Arnold, but a more authentic
and gritty femininity is what the poems articulate in their presentation
of the young women of the place who:

giggle
or go blank
or bat back smart answers
to the young dogs (sealegs,
cuffed wellingtons) moving easily
among nets and hooks and weights.

(*DF* 111)

In these poems, alert to the actual contemporary islands with 'the
Pakistani draper's shop', a modern female Hebridean point of view is
articulated, perhaps for the first time in Scottish writing. Though
Lochhead does not conceal her outsider's status, she sees the importance
of paying attention to what the women do as having its own lyrical pull,
complementary but also different to that of the much more frequently
celebrated male fisherfolk of the islands.

At Woolworth's beauty counter
one smears across the back of her hand
the colour of her next kiss.
The other nets in her wiremesh basket
Sea Witch.
Harvest Gold.

(*DF*, 111)

Here, with a loving irony, the shopper fishing for cosmetics in Woolworth's is made to continue the tradition of such Gaelic songs as 'Golden Harvest', which she has ostensibly 'not much time/ for'. Lochhead's use of an actual shop name, like her mention throughout her poetry, of actual product names – 'Clark's sandals' (*DF*, 65); 'Bush radios' (*DF*, 117); 'Meadow's Minimarket' (*DF*, 117); 'Mothercare' (*BM*, 67) – is at one with her love of orality, of what people actually say. Literature/Poetry has a habit of purifying away the details of actual shopping, in which it is important to say, exactly, which product you want. Larkin, for instance, writes not about a named shop but about 'The Large Cool Store'. He never specifies what sort of 'Electric mixers, toasters, washers, driers' his 'cut-price crowd' want to buy in 'Here'. He is keeping himself poetically aloof from actual shopping. But Lochhead is different. She is not interested in literary generalisation. She is interested in what people really buy, and her particular interests presents her shoppers with a dignity which Larkin's aloofness withholds. Where Larkin plays safe, not mentioning ephemeral brand-names, Lochhead enters into the ephemeral and actual, to be closer not to the word of Literature, but to what women really *say*.

It is this urge, this fidelity, which leads her to 'The Storyteller Poems' of *The Grimm Sisters*. In a poem such as 'Laundrette' (*DF*, 116), she had been learning how to derive energy from treading the borderline between speech and writing. Here a command of pun and of idiomatic phrasing had conspired with a more literary allusiveness.

> The dark shoves one man in,
> lugging a bundle like a wandering Jew. Linen
> washed in public here.
> We let out of the bag who we are.

In *The Grimm Sisters* there is still a sharp use of oral popular material, signalled in the way Lochhead is able to unite her love of pun with her use of idiomatic and proverbial material. So in 'Last Supper' she puns on 'the cooked goose' (*DF*, 93) and in the butchery 'Everybody's Mother' she puns on 'a bloody shame' (*DF*, 95), while in 'The Other Woman' we have a cut-up run of folk insults as the direct speech of the protagonist's 'spies' and the voice of the protagonist run fluidly together:

> I send out spies, they say relax
> she's a hag she's just a kid
> she's not a patch she's nothing to she's
> no oil painting.
>
>   (*DF*, 92)

Here the oral switchback gives life to the shape-changing identity of
'The Other Woman' who is simultaneously 'hag' and 'kid'. Yet while
there are clear instances in *The Grimm Sisters* of language which is at the
oral end of the spectrum, it is at least as common to find the celebration
of the storytelling world being conducted through the medium of a
much more literary register. So we may be reminded again of Plath's
'Lady Lazarus' when we hear in 'The Mother' (*DF*, 72) that 'she's always
dying early,/ so often it begins to look deliberate,' or we may think of
Plath's bee poems as well as of popular idiom when 'My Rival's House'
concludes 'Lady of the house./ Queen bee' (*DF*, 77). We are closer to the
world of feminist textuality than to the world of speech when we are
told 'Everybody's mother/ mythologised herself' (*DF*, 95) and we sense
the conscious literary construction that (despite the hint of the oral in
'we could swear it') lies behind;

> that russet shape that changed
> we could swear it, and stretched
> and lengthened to a fox and back to prick-eared
> hare again. Nothing tonight could decide
> what form to take.
>
>   (*DF*, 90)

A similarly literary feel is present in earlier lines of the same poem,
'Midsummer Night', when the oral — 'Get us' — meets the allusive:

> Get us, half enchanted and undecided
> whether or not to give in to it,
> wandering the wide woods on such a night like
> the wrong pair of ill-met demi-
> lovers we most likely are
> in far too high a pollen count for
> anybody's comfort.
>
>   (*DF*, 89)

Reading those lines we are aware that Lochhead's sharp sense of
language refuses to deliver what we expect. We don't get Kenneth
Grahame's Wild Wood; we get 'wide woods' instead. In place of
universalising we are presented with a modern world in which lovers
bother about the pollen count. At the same time we are aware of the
'half enchanted' world of *A Midsummer Night's Dream*, the fairytale play
of shapechanging in which the worlds of the demotic and the erotically
supernatural cross over and intermingle. It is surely this Shakespearean
world, in part at least, which lies behind Lochhead's delight in
midsummer, which recurs in her poetry from 'On Midsummer

Common' (*DF*, 126) to 'What the Pool Said, On Midsummer's Day' (*DF*, 8). In these midsummer poems shifting erotic allure is focused and refocused. The ludic shiftiness of pun is taken on by the metamorphising human form. Shape changing is what *The Grimm Sisters* is all about. Those poems offer us not Shakespeare's sister but the sisters of the Brothers Grimm, and the narratives of the men's folktales are changed to take on a feminist slant and bite.

To do this not only do narrative lines have to be shifted from their familiar forms; language must also be rescued from cliché, the verbal analogy to the hackneyed, fixed ideology of masculine domination. So in 'Rapunzstiltskin', 'our maiden' comes to reject the 'strung-together cliché' of her would-be rescuer (*DF*, 78). The woman's liberation in these poems must be generated by the woman herself. The poems offer us shifting, shape-changing female identities. At one moment we hear 'I was scholarly' (*DF*, 74); at another 'I'll paint my face up, paint the town,/ have carmine nails, oh/ be fatal dame' (*DF*, 76). That 'oh' is again the marker of orality, while the phrase 'fatal dame' is closer to the folk performances of panto than to the conventional literary phrase 'femme fatale' or even to Keats's 'La Belle Dame sans Merci' (which Lochhead in any case Glasgwegianly subverts in her 1991 short story 'La Belle Dame sans "Thingwy"').[11]

As befits a collection remade from an anthology of stories based on spoken sources, *The Grimm Sisters* operates best along the smudged boundary between oral and written. This is the case, however, not just with this one collection of Lochhead's verse, but with her poetry as a whole. She is conscious, even anxious about what she perceives as a split in her work:

> . . . that interest in performance, which seemed slightly to split away from an interest in writing . . . It feels to me that I write two quite different things, although I don't think other people see these as two . . . I feel as though they are written by two different people . . . you know how there is the black book and the white book [laughs]: there's *True Confessions* and there's *Dreaming Frankenstein*. (*Verse*, 86)

Yet what I am trying to suggest in this chapter is that the 'split' in Lochhead's work is not nearly as simple as this, any more than Burns's work is simply split between spoken and written, Scots and English. Rather, the poems in *Dreaming Frankenstein* are constantly animated by their situation in a 'debatable land' between speech and writing, so that they partake of energies that come from both. Lochhead likes to define her work in terms of splits or binary oppositions – female/male, Scottish/English, Scot/Celt, working-class/middle-class, performance/

text. Certainly these pairs of opposites are useful in the discussion of her writing. However, when one thinks of them not in isolation but as operating simultaneously in Lochhead's work, one begins to see that (as was the case with Burns) a complex amalgam of divisions in her personality as a writer may be a strength rather than a defining limitation. Given that she sees herself as so multiply divided (*Verse*, 90), it is no surprise that Lochhead is interested in shifting selves and plural identities – puns of the self. Developing a technique tried out in *Blood and Ice*, 'human puns' abound in *Mary Queen of Scots Got Her Head Chopped Off* where 'the Queen' means Mary one minute, Elizabeth another; Elizabeth is also Bessie, is also Leezie, while Mary is Marian is Mairn. Lochhead has taken the theatrical convention of 'doubling' and has adapted it to the animation of three dimensional puns as identity shifts and slides in front of the audience. Mary both is and is not the same as Mairn. Child and adult, queen and commoner, victor and victim are all kaleidoscopically interchanged in front of the audience: same difference.

What seems fixed in Lochhead's work is usually open to becoming fluid. Just as a pun takes an apparently clear message and enriches it by introducing another possibility, so the 'doubling' multiplies the meaning of the character Mary, and so the Grimm folktale takes on a powerful alternative gloss. Using the terminology of Mikhail Bakhtin, what seems 'monologic' (having one fixed, uninterruptable meaning) in Lochhead's work turns out to be 'dialogic' (susceptible of interruption, contradiction, and reinterpreting intervention).[12] This is all the more evident given the orality of Lochhead's work, since what is spoken invites (or at least gives the illusion of permitting) interruption and contradiction much more readily than what is written and so fixed. Lochhead's excitement at American poetry from Plath to the Beats and Olson was sparked by the element that 'made poetry about breathing, about talking' (*Verse*, 91). Lochhead's fidelity to the sounds, idioms, and situations of West of Scotland speech means also that her language is explicitly 'heteroglossic' in Bakhtin's terms; that is, it is explicitly composed of a variety of different languages and registers – demotic and literary, or (in the case of a few poems and several plays) Scots and English. In *Tartuffe* for instance, Lochhead delights in what she describes as:

> a totally invented and, I hope, theatrical Scots, full of anachro-
> nisms, demotic speech from various eras and areas; it's proverbial,
> slangy, couthy, clichéd, catch-phrasey, and vulgar; it's based on
> Byron, Burns, Stanley Holloway, Ogden Nash and George
> Formby, as well as the sharp tongue of my granny; it's deliberately

varied in register – most of the characters except Dorine are at least bilingual and consequently more or less 'two faced'. (*T*, 'Introduction')

The 'two-facedness' of Lochhead's language was clear in the many puns of her early poetry; by the time of *Tartuffe* and *Mary Queen of Scots Got Her Head Chopped Off*, that 'two facedness' has become a full-blown split between two languages. Yet, like the oral and literary languages of the poetry, the two languages cross over and intermell. Puns are conventionally double-sided; actually, they're more like a Möbius strip. Similarly the Scots and English in those plays, like the oral and literary language of the poems tend to infect one another, so that it takes a careful and conscious effort even to start to try and separate them. Much of Lochhead's writing is at its best in the border territory where self and other (as Bakhtin likes to have it) partake of each other, the zone of crossover, fluidity, shape-changing, pun.

Nowhere is this clearer than in one of Lochhead's finest poems, 'What the Pool Said, On Midsummer's Day' (*DF*, 8), which introduces us at once to the world of orality with its 'garrulous banks, babbling/ on and on'. Accompanying this orality is the slippery love of pun present in 'it's only water talking': from one angle this means literally that the poem's voice is that of a pool; from another angle, though, the poem puns on the popular idiom 'it's only the drink talking'. Orality maintains a strong presence in this spoken poem, yet it is mixed up with word-craft that comes from a clear literary artifice heard in 'gonging' and 'the kingfisher's flightpath' for instance. The poem operates not only in the crossover zone between the spoken and the written; it also hints, more than hints, at other kinds of intercourse and metamorphosis, 'What's fish/ in me could make flesh of you.' A sense of metamorphic fluidity is heightened by the realisation that this is one element trying to lure another in, to convert another. In one sense the poem is a love poem, but like most of Lochhead's love poems, such as 'The Bride' (*BM*, 65), it also acknowledges the sex war and is concerned to avoid stereotypical sentimentality – 'I could have you [the enjambment heightens the sexual meaning]/ gulping fistfuls fighting yourself/ back from me.' The poem takes place also in an ambiguous area between surface and depth. Its last stanzas refuse surface beauty (the sort of fetishistic female beauty of flash and dazzle which men want of women), offering instead a potentially fearful but stronger depth. Eventually, the 'you' is submerged in the pool, an action syntactically enacted by the last stanza which opens with 'I', closes with 'me', and contains 'you'. Throughout the poem the personal pronouns have interchanged constantly. This is a poem about the sexual act, but it is also more widely a poem that deals

with the unstable enhancing play between self and other – one of the
subjects of A *Midsummer Night's Dream*. 'What the Pool Said, On
Midsummer's Day' is one of Lochhead's poems which draws strength
from an interchange between speech and writing, using that fluid
interchange to reinforce the metamorphic intercourse at its heart. It is a
'live' poem, one of Lochhead's best, not because we can say it is spoken
in her own voice, but because it communicates a sense of an actual,
restless speaking voice which seems to be engaged in dialogue, in
argumentative seduction, with the 'you' of the poem. The enjambments
heighten this sense of dialogue, so that the line 'Yes, I could' presents
for the moment an assertive statement (with the word 'could'
functioning as a principal verb) before we read on and the next line
makes us realise that 'could' in the larger context is to be read as an
auxiliary verb. In these lines Lochhead's sense of pun is again at work,
operating through enjambment and the fine possibilities of syntax:

> Yes, I could
> drown you, you
> could foul my depths . . .

The repetition of 'you' functions initially as if it was a spoken emphasis
on the particular (you, yes you) rather than simply the opening of the
next sense unit ('you/ could foul my depths'). These subtleties in
enjambment are yet another indication of the sharpness of Lochhead's
ear, and of her fidelity to the rhythms of an actual voice. It is just that
fidelity which is so apparent in her rap pieces such as 'Favourite Shade'
(*TCNC*, 123). Here again there is a sense of dialogue in the monologue;
there is not just the voice we hear, there is also the implied voice which
is being argued against and talked about. Lochhead's playful articulation and punster's whirl produces the close-to-tonguetwisting line:

> You've got bugger all bar black, Barbra

in which 'Barbra' is both the West of Scotland pronunciation of the
name Barbara and a play on the word 'bar', just used, and 'bra' (which
calls to mind black bras). As suits a rap, Lochhead generates here a
mischievous alliterative music which gives the speaker's voice a
distinctive signature. Lochhead inhabits what seems an actual,
idiomatic voice ('eh no?') working at full tilt and earthed in popular
idioms:

> Black!
> As well oot the world as oot the fashion.

Lochhead also inhabits the world of actual, not literary shopping, the world of 'Polyester everything Easy-kerr' and 'Miss Selfridge'. As in 'Heartbreak Hotel' with its 'Teasmade', tradenames are part of the poem's attachment to the actual. Though 'Heartbreak Hotel' is in the 'white book' rather than the black one, it has an equally unmistakable delight in the sung and spoken, heard in its enjoyment and gentle mockery of:

> Syrup from the radio's
> synthetically soothing late night show
> oh remember, remember
>
> (*DF*, 44)

and heard also in its appropriation of storytelling, fairy-tale talk:

> Mirror, mirror on the wall
> does he love me enough,
> does he love me at all?

Those rhythms are kept in the poem's consciously modern, but also acoustically 'folk' conclusion':

> Oh it'll take more than this aerosol
> to fix it all, to fix it all.

Once more the point is not that this is an autobiographical poem (it may or may not be), but that Lochhead has developed in it a voice that is absolutely credible, that is individually situated yet also acoustically akin to that of her community. She is articulating not only a female identity but also a particular Scottish female identity.[13]

The convincing particularity of Lochhead's best work comes primarily through orality, through the sharp quality of the sound; but it is also present in clinching images, see nowhere better than in the poem 'The Offering' (*DF*, 60), where remembered sensations are communicated with salutary precision and alertness:

> Sunday,
> the late smell of bacon
> then the hard small feeling
> of the offering in the mitten.
> Remember how the hat-elastic cut.
> Oh the boredom,
> and how a lick of spittle got purple dye or pink
> from the hymn-book you worried.

This attention to the other senses does not mean there is a dimunition in

Lochhead's acute hearing. When we hear of 'the one about Nic-/odemus' we realise not only that the story is presented as if it were a joke being told ('Heard the one about *x*?') but also that 'Nicodemus' has been syllabically unpicked (like 'dem-o-crat') so that the name comes to resemble a Scottish-style name like 'Tam o' Shanter'. Converting Nicodemus's name into a rather irreverent noise, the speaker tries to drown out the original message, just as the people who 'turned their televisions up' try to drown out the sound of the Brethren. The poem ends strongly with a note of stubborn, ungiving resistance, with 'the offering/still hard and knotted in your hand'.

It is hard to imagine that last line as part of a colloquial conversation. Instead, it is the more consciously measured conclusion to a poem. This is not to suggest that in recreating or re-presenting orality on the page Lochhead does not have to use craftsmanship to project an accurate impression of orality; but that is a rather different skill from the one involved in the conclusion of 'The Offering'. If Lochhead herself has tended to separate her performance pieces ('the black book') from her 'poems' ('the white book'), it is good to see both together in one book *Bagpipe Muzak*, though the division between 'Recitations', 'Characters' and 'Poems' persists. While such divisions can be useful, I have been trying to suggest in this chapter that Lochhead's work draws its characteristic strength from operating in the border zones between such categories, the areas where the one category 'infects' the others. So, for instance, there is a Stevie Smith quality to the 'recitation' 'Advice to Old Lovers', though we may think of Stevie Smith as a 'poet' rather than a writer of 'performances' (actually her use of rhythm, rhyme, and vocabulary has much in common with that of Lochhead). Or, to choose a different example, there is a quality of over-the-top energy that recalls the Dunbar of the flytings in 'So, he lifts the spoon up to his mouth, in it goes, burns the roof of his mouth, scalds his tongue, sears his epiglottis, he leaps to his feet reaching for the waterjug which I have made quite sure is empty and by this time he's dancing and I just go "Now, do be careful, sir, it's rather *hot*" and I flounce off to swap gay banter with the camp barman' (*BM*, 32). The controlled explosions of energy here are impressive, though less impressive is the awkward deference to the literary master, Edwin Morgan, in the touristic 'Five Berlin Poems' (*BM*, 79), where an act of homage becomes too apologetically deferential. Because Lochhead's poetry occupies the shifting ground between speech and writing, it may risk failure more often than other poetries, particularly when it moves beyond the culture and speech patterns in which it is rooted. At its punster's best it is both sharp and evasive, accurately shaped and shape-changing, its re-presented orality and its literary construction working together as one.

NOTES

1 Adam McNaughtan, 'Oor Hamlet' in Robin Bell, ed., *The Best of Scottish Poetry* (Edinburgh: Chambers, 1989), 21.

2 'The Jeely Piece Song', 'The Coming of the Wee Malkies' and Glasgow poems by Ian Hamilton Finlay and Jean Milton, along with work by Lochhead's friends Tom Leonard and Tom McGrath are reprinted in Hamish Whyte, ed., *Noise and Smoky Breath: An Illustrated Anthology of Glasgow Poems 1900–1983* (Glasgow: Third Eye Centre and Glasgow District Libraries Publications Board, 1983).

3 Charles Olson, 'Projective Verse', reprinted in James Scully, ed., *Modern Poets on Modern Poetry* (London: Fontana, 1966), 271.

4 Norman MacCaig and Alexander Scott, eds., *Contemporary Scottish Verse 1959–1969* (London: Calder & Boyars, 1970); Charles King, ed., *Twelve Modern Scottish Poets* (London: University of London Press, 1971); Maurice Lindsay, ed., *Modern Scottish Poetry: An Anthology of the Scottish Renaissance*, second edition (London: Faber and Faber, 1966).

5 Liz Lochhead in a 1992 radio programme, later published in lightly edited form in Robert Crawford et al., 'Hugh MacDiarmid: A Disgrace to the Community', *PN Review* 89 (January–February 1993) 21–2.

6 Lochhead mentions Jean Milton on p. 84 of the *Verse* interview, though her name appears there as 'Millington'.

7 Catherine Kerrigan, ed., *An Anthology of Scottish Women Poets* (Edinburgh University Press, 1991), 2.

8 Jan Montefiore, *Feminism and Poetry: Language, Experience, Identity in Women's Writing* (London: Pandora, 1987), 39–41.

9 Liz Yorke, *Impertinent Voices: Subversive Strategies in Contemporary Women's Poetry* (London: Routledge, 1991), 23.

10 Ibid., 81. Yorke is quoting from Catherine Clément and Hélène Cixous, 'The Guilty One' in *The Newly Born Woman*; translated by Betsy Wing, introduction by Sandra Gilbert (Manchester University Press, 1986), 6–7. It is worth noting here that Lochhead's reading in feminist thought seems confined to British and North American feminism. Though it might be appropriate to the interpretation of her work, there is no evidence that she has read, e.g., Luce Irigaray, *Speculum of the Other Woman*; translated by Gillian C. Gill (Ithaca, New York: Cornell University Press, 1985).

11 Liz Lochhead, 'La Belle Dame sans "Thingwy"', short story broadcast on BBC Radio 4, 24 September 1991 (producer: Bruce Young of BBC Radio Scotland).

12 For a short introduction to Bakhtin's work in the context of Scottish literature see Robert Crawford, *Identifying Poets: Self and Territory*

in Twentieth-Century Poetry (Edinburgh University Press, 1993),
Introduction. The last chapter of that book sets Lochhead's use of
Scots in a contemporary context.

13 On this see Marilyn Reizbaum, 'Canonical Double Cross: Scottish
and Irish Women's Writing' in Karen R. Lawrence, ed., *Decolonizing
Tradition: New Views of Twentieth-Century 'British' Literary Canons*
(Urbana, Illinois: University of Illinois Press, 1991), 165–90. I am
grateful to Ms Lorraina Pinnell for drawing my attention to this,
which is a useful background piece, though not always accurate (e.g.,
Agnes Owens appears as 'Agnes West').

Five

Hearing Voices: Monologues and Revues

Jackie Clune

I

'Wouldn't it be good to get a structure and maybe costume, a few props anyway and learn the poems off by heart, not read them, nose buried in a book, dropping them out your looseleaf onto the floor, scrabbling around picking them up again in the wrong order.' (Marcella Evaristi, *TCNC*, preface)

In 1978, Liz Lochhead teamed up with Marcella Evaristi, ostensibly to perform some of their poetry. It was to herald something of a watershed in Lochhead's career as it was the first time she had ventured into the arena of performance. Previously she had been involved in more traditional poetry readings which had become a popular feature of the Beat Generation poets but had used only the bare minimum of theatricality, namely, vocalisation. Her collaboration produced *Sugar and Spite*, an evening of poetry, monologues and songs which was performed in Glasgow during 1978, and it was this which began an interest in the many different levels of performance which now form her profile. The nature of her performances and – subsequently – the style of her writing are the subject of this chapter. The move from the early earnestness of poetry readings to the broad theatrical sweep of the most recent revues offers some interesting insights into the very essence of theatre and performance. Lochhead and what we might call her 'performity' allow us to examine what constitutes a theatrical act. Her use of poems, sketches, songs, voices and monologues expresses a culturally diverse and truly 'popular' aesthetic, rooted in a fascination with the female psyche.

The use of monologues and characters (or voices) in revues is a long established tradition in British theatre. From the comic turns of Vesta Tilley, Jenny Hill and Marie Lloyd in the Edwardian Music Hall, through the use of character comedy in the work of Joyce Grenfell, to the television monoliths such as the wonderfully kitsch character Kitty invented by Victoria Wood, it is evident that monologue has an illustrious history in the canon of female performers. It is perhaps significant that women, so often silenced in life, have used a form which can be characterised quite simply as an *uninterupted* series of statements. The power of the genre is rooted in the strength of performance needed to carry it off as much as in the empowerment of gaining solitary access to the stage, a domain which has traditionally been under the jurisdiction of men. Indeed it could be argued that this form of performance is particularly suited to women as writers and performers, since the solitary nature of many women's lives lends itself to solo speeches. Who can forget the 'Wall' as the only audience to the eponymous Shirley Valentine's musings? The writing and acting of solitary figures who are often ensnared by their environment is understandable given the social and economic isolation of many women in contemporary society.

The distancing that women experience as a result of the patriarchal structure of society can result in a keen awareness of the idiosyncracies of others. Women, forced so often to observe rather than participate, can become ruthless commentators on contemporary mores, both in their writing and what they bring to performing comic characters: character acting is a female forte. It is argued that while women can't or won't tell jokes, they excel at portraying a wide variety of ridiculous and eccentric women. Edith Evans' Lady Bracknell, Margaret Rutherford's Miss Prism, Hylda Baker's "She knows, ya know!"' and Joyce Grenfell's 'George, don't do that!' have all become current currency.[1] This form of comedy is distinct from other types of humour in that the characters tend to be short-lived and have largely appeared in revues rather than as a whole evening's entertainment in themselves; 'the monologuist dips in and out of character and often appears on stage, initially and intermittently, as herself, there is a greater distance between actor and character, a greater opportunity for satire.'[2]

Alan Sinfield makes an interesting distinction between two broad types of dramatic monologue and the purposes these types can be said to serve. The audience receives the monologues as coded communication, the encoding being primarily enshrined in the attitiude of the writer towards her subject. The first category Sinfield identifies is the Sympathetic Monologue. In this code, the writer uses the 'sympathetic draw of the first person'[3] in order to invite the empathy of the audience towards the (often oppressed) character, who is shown to be under the strain of her/his oppression. The audience may be prompted to take issue with the the character's acceptance of his or her lot in life and will certainly feel the sense of indignation implicit in the writing and performance of the piece. Above all the character will be treated with a great deal of compassion by both the playwright and the majority of the audience, who will receive the code and respond with appropriate sympathy. The second category is the Satirical Monologue. Inscribed in this code is the implicit contract between the audience, the performer and the playwright that everything uttered on stage is to be heard in inverted commas, as it were. We must take nothing for granted and must look between the utterences for what is *not* said. Monologue of this kind provides the opportunity for a more complete story to be told, because if an audience perceives that a character is making key omissions in her version of events, the character 'will appear to be justifying themselves',[4] will be judged and found wanting. Above all, the audience is to be made to react *against* the speaker. In this way the playwright can intimate or directly communicate a version of the truth about a certain situation or character. These two approaches to categorising dramatic monologue seem particularly helpful in criticism of Lochhead's use of the genre. The pageant of women she parades before us seems at first to fall into the latter category, although it could perhaps be argued that the process of the demoticisation of these voices has an humanising effect, at least on Lochhead's perception of the characters and the people from which they are drawn. The voices and characters in both *True Confessions & New Clichés* and *Bagpipe Muzak* often sit on the boundary between a satirical depiction of and a sympathetic attraction to the idiosyncracies of modern Scottish women. Ultimately, we are left with an ambiguous relationship towards the characters. This ambiguous relationship is a dichotomy women often face within themselves. We are at once critical of and compassionate towards ourselves as constructs of an often misogynist society. Siobhan Redmond, an actress who worked extensively with Lochhead during the early period of her revue work, bears witness to this horrified identification on the part of women in the audiences:

> . . . one thing I remember laughing about a lot was that invariably people who even *sounded* like the women in those monologues, who even spoke in the same kind of voices we'd chosen for our characters, would come up and say 'I know someone just like that!', and you'd think 'Well, yes it's *you*, isn't it!'[5]

The character monologues in *True Confessions* and *Bagpipe Muzak* were not written as self-contained performance pieces, however. They slot into a wider range of material and as such are perhaps best considered within the context of the revue form. Songs, poems, raps and voices as

well as sketches interspersed with the monologues create quite a
different performance context, which in turn directly colours the way in
which we receive the characters. The order in which the material was
performed is in accordance with the traditions of Old Variety (the
various different 'turns' such as contortionists, stand-up comics, cross-
dressing monologuists, paper tearers which characterised the Edwardian
Music Hall) and New Variety (the contemporary version of the Music
Hall, as can be witnessed at any of the comedy/cabaret nights at
London's recently restored Hackney Empire Theatre) which encourages
differently-pitched acts; serious or more obviously targeted satirical
pieces are contrasted with lighter, more palatable items. Poems follow
monologues, songs change the atmosphere again and the raps use a
modern youth-culture performance style borrowed from such urban
commentators as MC Hammer in America or Betty Boo in Britain to
popularise the poetry/lyrics. The effect of this is to create a varied
evening of entertainment which is not precious in the same way as a
performance of a play is. The audience/performer divide is much less
rigid, making direct contact possible, and the consequences of missing
five minutes of the action through going to the bar are less drastic: a
constant span of attention such as one needs to follow a plot is not
needed. Revue draws on popular traditions which are (potentially)
politically transgressive because the communication between the
peformers and the audience is less rigidly coded. Bourgeois theatre,
with its predilection for the unravelling of complicated plots and/or
intellectually aerobic subject matter, can be described as a closed form,
a form which denies access to those unfamiliar with what we might call
'high' culture. Lochhead's use of the revue form is significant given her
subject matter. The use of revue to explore sexual politics from an
intensely personal point of view allows her to address potentially
explosive and politically difficult subjects without risking alienating her
audience. It is a form which befits her gentle brand of satire and which
also allows her to include poems, thus transgressing the boundary
between 'high' culture's traditional poetry readings and 'low' culture's
variety entertainments.

    This cross-pollenation can be seen in the material included in *True
Confessions & New Clichés*. The issue-based material covered in this
selection includes divorce (paralleled neatly with the imminent
demolition of a street in a run-down area of Glasgow), Page Three girls
as political decoys, the objectification of women in fine art, age
stereotyping, the Arts and the conservative establishment, Incomers
and blood-sucking tourism, party politics and adultery. Similarly in
Bagpipe Muzak we find monologues and voices concerned with misogyny

and the Bible, the oppression endorsed by 'beauty' contests, the annual invasion of Edinburgh by pretentious artistes as well as the 1990 invasion of Glasgow as European City of Culture. Serious issues presented in a constantly shifting pattern of mood thus rendering the 'preaching' accusation, so often levelled at feminist theatre, redundant.

II

Of the many characters included in *True Confessions* and *Bagpipe Muzak*, Verena towers above the unlikely urban chroniclers as the most inadvertently articulate. She started life as a character in *True Confessions* before earning her two-hander with Derek in *Quelques Fleurs*. Bored and ill-tempered due to her isolation whilst her husband works shifts on the Oil-Rigs, Verena knocks around her suburban house with its new shagpile carpet and its Beverage-Master Cappuccino maker, trying to disguise her unhappiness with a general air of superiority. She signals the embodiment of the dissatisfied overly-material consumer culture of the Eighties. The monologues expose her as a materially obsessed woman with a neat turn of phrase. We laugh at the quiet viciousness she delivers about everyone she encounters. We are charmed by her neat observational humour, even though she does not seem to discriminate between her targets. She is a seeming nihilist with little tolerance for anybody. Above all, she is not very *nice*; in itself a liberation from the caring, nurturing depictions of womanhood so often mooted as the norm. It is perhaps the outrageousness of exploring such a negative representative of the female gender which makes the character stand out from the other women in *True Confessions & New Clichés*. It has long been the case in feminist theatre that we must, in reclaiming images of women for the stage, present *positive* images of women which would redress the balance of virgins, whores or mothers so often projected by male playwrights as the only three ways to be a woman. My own experiences with Red Rag Women's Theatre Company have often confirmed that there has been a received notion of politically correct representations of women amongst our audiences and any character who defies this should not be placed in the public arena on stage in case our male 'enemies' should use these characters as further proof of our lack of worth as human beings. Verena stands in opposition to that rather suffocating and prescriptive agenda; she refuses to be nice to or about anyone, not even other women. On the one hand she explodes the myths about the nurturing (good) woman with one-liners like, 'Is a kid compatible with an off-white fitted carpet, that's the question . . .', whilst on the other she is no easy sister in the feminist struggle with her (bad) slimmasoups, her Carmen Heated Rollers and her suspicion of Moira McVitie's women's book group. In the transition from *True Confessions* to *Quelques Fleurs*, Verena emerges as a complex representation of the psyche of a modern Scottish woman.

Siobhan Redmond was the first actress to play Verena. She provided the 'bazically' which Verena uses to string her sentences together, and it was her success in the role which led Lochhead to write more Verena monologues. Redmond became part of the Merryhell Theatre Company and appeared in productions of Lochhead's revue work (*Tickly Mince* in 1982 and *The Pie of Damocles* in 1983). Redmond, according to Lochhead herself, played a large part in the success of the early revues.

Redmond first appeared in *True Confessions* in 1981–2 at the Tron Theatre, Glasgow, where the show was heralded as 'a warm, witty feminist revue shot through with Glasgow's backgrounds, speech rhythms and dry humour. . . . The fun, the absurdity and deep underlying pain of being a truly modern woman who keeps trying, against her better judgement, to form happy relationships with men.'[6] The move towards the new 'Young, Wacky, Zany' type of comedy in the early eighties was the beginning of much of the revue work we are now familiar with on television (*Not the Nine O'Clock News*, *Three of a Kind*, *Al Fresco*, et al.) and this was the cultural context for *True Confessions*. Popular audiences, made of non-traditional-middle-class theatre goers, began to patronise theatres hungry for the new products that were being made fashionable via television light entertainment programmes. The format of these TV and stage revue shows closely followed a pre-existing variety format, but the content was often of a politically challenging nature. Satire, pastiche and direct political comment on very contemporary issues became a hallmark of the genre, which sometimes led to the companies producing the work being accused of 'preaching to the converted'. The performer/audience relationship demanded a shared set of opinions and assumptions about the world in order for the humour to work. For women performers, interested in addressing feminist issues, the space to create their own political agendas in an entertaining way, the genre proved to be highly useful and many feminist revue companies were formed during this period: Scarlet Harlets, Spare Tyre, Sensible Footwear, The Millies, Fascinating Aida, early French and Saunders, early Wood and Walters, and so on.

It was, then, within this atmosphere that *True Confessions* was first performed. I spoke to Redmond about her involvement in the creation of Verena, and there now follows an edited transcript of this interview.

JC   If you think back to when you played Verena in *True Confessions*, how did you form the character? Liz credits you with the 'basically' Verena uses to link everything together with.

SR   That was a very annoying habit that a flatmate of mine had at the time. It wasn't even 'basically' it was 'bazically' in a way that nobody ever says it! Like people who say 'Rad-e-aytor' or 'Him-arl-eeyas' instead of 'radiator' or 'Himalayas'. I said it once in a rehearsal and so more of it had to be put in!

JC   Did you improvise first and then would Liz script it?

SR   No, no there was always a script. Particularly noticeable with the later shows was the fact that all the writers would be in the rehearsal room.

I found Verena very difficult at first. I think because of her natural authority. I didn't know if I had a big enough soul to play her. I don't mean that you have to be generous towards her or be sympathetic in any way . . . She's just a colossal-sized character. I didn't know if I was quite capable of it. Then I decided I'd just have a go at it anyway and I mean she does take you over! But the Verena in *Quelques Fleurs* is quite different. You see different bits of her.

JC   It's quite poignant isn't it? Liz calls her the 'deadly' or 'dreadful' Verena . . .

SR   I'm sure that's because she gets into your system! I'm sure it's not because she says anything that's so terrible. Verena just says things that you're thinking but wouldn't actually say. People used to laugh a lot because of that I'm sure, because they recognised they had some of the same attitudes! Not that there's anything wrong with those attitudes, but they're not the sort of things one usually voices.

JC   It sounds as if Liz's writing offers great opportunities for actors in terms of being able to create really strong characterisations.

SR   Yes. One of the reasons I find Liz's work so pleasing to do, so *physically* pleasing to do, is that her dialogue is very toothsome. It's a real pleasure to *say*. It's great when you have a huge long 'chocolate eclair' of a phrase – in terms of the senses it's very gratifying to perform.

JC   Did you find that women identified with Verena in a empathetic way – or is she a character that everyone likes to laugh *at*?

SR No I think everyone knows there is a part of them in Verena.
    We've all had a quick look round the 'Fuck Me' pumps in the
    House of Fraser. And everybody knows someone like Moira
    McVitie with her book club. You don't *always* want to be reading
    things like *I Stand Here Ironing*. And everyone's fallen out with
    their mother, sibling rivalry, etc. which is very extensively covered
    in *Quelques Fleurs*. Also, Verena is witty in her own right. You
    don't just laugh at Verena with your hand over your mouth
    thinking, 'Thank God I'm not like that.' She commands your
    respect.

    I think Liz is very gentle. She always manages to make you see
    not just two sides to a situation but also the good things about the
    argument. Her writing has got teeth but she's not at all
    unforgiving, it's not vicious. I think that's why so many people
    identify with what she writes and how she writes. It's very moving
    and sometimes it's quite shocking but you don't feel distanced by
    what she writes – I never have – and I don't think people felt
    alienated by those characters. The number of people who came up
    to us afterwards is testament to what I've been saying. But it's
    certainly not twee or cosy. It sits in a very comfortable spot.

JC Some of the characters and the songs remind me quite a lot of
    Victoria Wood's work on television.

SR Do you know why that is?

JC I think it's that same sense of looking at odd characters and
    showing them in a gently mocking yet compassionate way. Some of
    her characters are quite pitiful but we laugh at them

SR But they all have their dignity, or redeeming characteristics. They
    all have something that you owe them some respect for.

JC I wonder why she has not been snapped up to write for television. Is
    it perhaps the fact that she may be seen as too particularly Scottish
    to appeal to the TV programmers' idea of the 'mainstream'
    audience?

SR She has been told by one person that her language is too *theatrical*
    for television. Some people think that the exuberance of her
    language would register an unreality on television, but TV isn't real
    life either! I wondered if maybe the reason you thought of Victoria
    Wood was because there are so few women who are successfully
    funny.

I have to say that the reaction from men on the whole was that they were immensely flattered. They thought it was marvellous that Liz had noted with such detail how they were.

JC   Do you think it was therefore a failure? That they were flattered by it?

SR   No, I think it's what you call *selective hearing!* I think they liked the fact that she had a good point and she made it in a way that made them laugh. Her work is very humane, and a lot of women writers have similar criticisms made against their work; they take the very small and delicately piece it together and the whole world is here on this piece of tapestry. But Liz doesn't just work in little stitches, she paints in bold colours on a very big canvas. That's one of the things I really like about her work – it's big.

III

. . . between plays and poems odd new characters do begin monologuing away and asking to be written down. Old ones pipe up again on other subjects. Mrs Abernethy grows more awful and Verena is no nearer to what she still can't seem to own up to as her heart's desire. (*TCNC*, 111)

Verena found new life in *Quelques Fleurs*, whilst her companions in *True Confessions* and *Bagpipe Muzak* were busy forging their own identities as commentators on the Scottish woman's psyche. Lochhead uses laughter to pinpoint important social issues through character. We see Sharon, a young schoolgirl in love with her teacher, impressed by the beanbags and the books in his house, and we are made to ponder on the nature of class and identity. We meet Vicki, the waitress in the Glasgow theme restaurant 'The Hungry 'Thirties' and we consider the hijacking of Glasgow during its time with the onerous title of European City of Culture, 1990. Her cynicism about the 'Depression Broth' menu points to the appealing way in which many Glaswegians remained suspicious of the glamorising of their cultural identity; 'Sectarianism is coming back into fashion as a sort of Fun Thing' (*BM*, 29). We find Mrs Abernethy, the Minister's wife, with her tight-lipped endurance of the forth-coming Hogmanay celebrations, a word she is none-too familiar with, and we examine the role of the Presbyterian puritanism which allows women to make victims of themselves. We encounter Norma Nimmo with her Kelvinside preoccupations with wealth and gossip, and we recognise the voice of a lonely provincial woman, hinted at in her throwaway last line, 'Anyway I'm going out with her for a wee G & T on Gordie's squash night' (*BM*, 35).

These characters are broad types drawn with precision. My interest on meeting Lochhead herself lay in the treatment of the characters and their situations given that monologue is a powerful form of voice. I was also concerned with the use of comedy; was the humour derisive, or merely laughter of recogntion? Perhaps the answers lay in the *performance* of these pieces. Do we need the physical presence of the performer plus their attitude towards the character in order to assess properly what to make of the voices we are hearing? The difference between acting and performing also struck me as an important issue when considering Lochhead's revue work. Were we, as an audience, to be *transported* into the world of each character and swept along by their voice, or were we to be *transformed* in some way by remaining outside of their experience and therefore more critical of it? There follows a transcribed interview with Liz Lochhead which took place on 18 November 1992.

JC   The first thing I wanted to ask you about was the whole notion of *otherness* and performance. In your monologues you literally give voice to your dual oppression as a Scot and a woman, and that, I feel, in performance is a powerful statement in itself. Was this your intention when you reluctantly began to perform?

LL   No! [Laugh] I think that's the kind of thing people say about your work afterwards, then you go 'Oh, that's right, that's what I did!' You just get the idea for a character. All these other things come out unconsciously, or they come out in the writing process. In the writing rather than the performing. The performing's just a sideline really, just for fun.

JC   And do you find it fun? Do you find it enjoyable? You've been performing in *Quelques Fleurs* haven't you?

LL   But that was like *acting*. Well, it wasn't *really* like Acting, but I did have to wear different costumes and do things like sellotape up a parcel while talking to people, or put on eyeshadow. It was funny, different from just standing there doing stand-up. Normally my body doesn't do anything, it's just my voice.

JC   Yes – you made that distinction when you started reading your poetry – it's not Acting, you don't do it as an actor . . . What's the difference?

LL   Usually in a poetry reading I'm just reading out poems. Revue is half-way between that and acting. You begin to slightly perform the characters, or you're working with someone as wonderful as Siobhan [Redmond] and you learn a lot from them. It would be terrible not to make some attempt to perform when you're on with somebody like her. At the same time when I was working with her she was really doing something quite different. She really *became* the people. Although she was very good at pulling back and becoming part of the whole thing.

Reading poems is quite different because the poem's got a voice but that's not a *character*. Very few poems are dramatic monologues and those that are tend to be dramatic monologues of *psychic states* rather than dialogue, what someone would *say*.

JC   That's interesting, the point where you say it's somewhere between just reading it out and acting it at a level of performance.

LL   There are different levels. There are different things you can do. You can just read poems. For some reason if you don't have the book in front of you it becomes a bit more essential to 'up' the performance slightly. Of course you're always performing anyway, and you ought to be aware of that. It's very hard to do poems without the book in front of you.

JC   Have you seen other performing poets like John Hegley or Benjamin Zephaniah? What do you feel about their work in performance rather than on paper?

LL   John Hegley's much better on stage rather than on paper!

JC   You need his physical presence to let you know that what he's saying is ironic a lot of the time?

LL   The best of his I really enjoy. He's more of a stand-up comedian. Benjamin Zephaniah is more like a performance poet. He goes half-way to rock music or singing. Certain things I do are more like that, certain raps. You're not becoming somebody different from you. It's hard to do a poem like 'Revelation', which is a childhood memory. It's very hard to do it to an audience without a book because then you feel you are having a personal memory and why are you telling them?

JC   So the book is a guard between you and the audience?

LL   Yes, but you still look at them. You probably don't even look down at the book, but that's just for real poems. I discovered the first of this in 1978 when I did *Sugar and Spite* with Marcella Evaristi. It was just going to be a poetry reading we were going to do, but she said, let's do a poetry reading where we actually get some nice smart costumes and actually learn them. Do them like the Russians do – learn them and declaim them! And it's impossible to do things like that, I didn't feel at all comfortable; so I began writing new things. That was the first of any kind of revue. The first prose bit was Sharon, the school girl. When I performed those, at first I couldn't remember it very well, I had to read it and pretend I was doing an essay but that didn't work! I only had two poems I felt comfortable doing without a book – 'The Spinster' and 'Bawd' which are sort of dramatic monologues. A lot of other poems work alright done like that because it's like a song without music, like 'The Other Woman' or 'The Hickey' – quite confessional little romantic things . . .

JC   So when you're performing and you're reading from a book, the book acts as a signifier that you're not *acting* it. Who are we watching then?

LL   I would only read things from a book which didn't have a character speaking them – they were either third-person poems or poems where the 'I' speaker was not a person. Something like 'What the Pool Said', which is a sort of dramatic monologue with the pool speaking, I'd prefer to have the book because otherwise you've got to look into the distance. It's no too bad if it's dark but you don't want to catch someone's eye because you're not telling them something as *yourself*. The other sort, where you have a character, it's daft to have the book. Mrs Abernethy, Sharon, Vicki – you can't *read* them. There are three different levels of performance. There's poetry reading, which I'll be doing tomorrow night, and I'll be reading from the book. In that I'll also do some characters and I know those. Then certain really daft 'performance' poems. You wouldn't want the book for those.

JC   Is it the difference between *showing* them and *being* them?

LL   That's what it is with revue, yes. That's what the difference is with doing Verena and Derek in a little realistic setting. Then you've got to *be* them. The revue style is really demonstration.

JC   And what's the difference in terms of an audience? Is there more distance when you are showing?

LL   Probably, but I don't know if they perceive that. It's just how comfortable I feel about it. For instance, tomorrow night I'll probably do two or three characters and put them together. I'll try and do it so that I don't have to say anything to introduce it, so that they know that these are characters who speak quite differently from each other. They'll know it's not *me*, I think. I might say something like 'Here's two or three ladies. I hope you don't find them too familiar.' I might get quite into them, but I won't be dressed as them and I won't be doing anything more than standing up or sitting down. It doesn't take that complete commitment that it takes to go that stage further.

JC   Catherine Kerrigan, in her introduction to *An Anthology of Scottish Women Poets*, bears witness to 'The chorus of voices, different in class and education, but which offers a broad and complex picture of the psyche of women'.[7] The Scottish ballad and oral traditions: in a sense your work could be seen as part of this tradition.

LL   I hope so. I try to present different people. With a dramatic monologue where it's an actual character, not a poem that pretends to be a dramatic monologue (there are tiny wee gradations), I try to credibly have what that person would actually say out loud. Hopefully you show the gaps behind the words. With Verena it would be her lies and evasions. Whereas if it's a poem which is slightly more stylised you might put in the subtext of what somebody's saying and not write the surface. But with the monologues you've got to have a reason, a dramatic present tense reason why the person is saying it now.

JC   So do you see yourself in that tradition?

LL   Yes, but it's equally akin to Stanley Holloway and Joyce Grenfell as it is to the ballad cacophony. Ballads are not exactly dramatic in the classic sense of the word. They're often melodramatic in their subject matter, but they were for doing out loud. They are storytelling. Drama and storytelling are not the same, but it's the storytelling aspect of drama that I like. And if you present characters, then you are telling a story. The first Verena that I wrote for Siobhan to do, it's probably just character but there is a fragmentary story there, the tip of an iceberg.

JC   Alan Sinfield's book *Dramatic Monologue* defines monologues as 'truncated plays' using 'the sympathetic draw of the first person'. It's as if the character is saying 'Look at it this way' for the duration of the monologue. It's therefore quite powerful for women, I think. Women are often interrupted or silenced in life but you are literally giving them a voice and a stream of consciousness.

LL   My dramatic monologues don't tend to be all that sympathetic. They use the power of the 'I' voice to say to the audience 'This is only this person's point of view. You don't have to believe this.' It's the *unreliability* of the narrator that I'm interested in. I probably take for granted the fact that it's powerful. A dramatic monologue like *Shirley Valentine* where there isn't a gap between what the person is telling the audience and what the audience is meant to perceive, I find that unsatisfactory dramatically. Attractive enough as the character might be there's no conflict and I think the conflict has to be between what the person thinks they are saying and what the audience actually hears. Often one is writing about unconscious people. The author is conscious of some of the things they are trying to write about but with the people you are showing, you are interested in their dramatic strategies for *not* listening to themselves, or the hidden agenda in what they're saying. You could write a monologue where there was no gap and it would be interesting for a short while if the person was talking about an experience which was quite new to you but with *Shirley Valentine* I just thought 'I know all this.' I'm quite a Willie Russell fan actually. I like *Educating Rita* very much but that is a *play*, there is conflict between two people who are drawn very sympathetically. With *Shirley Valentine*, I didn't believe that this person had this powerful voice, this powerful overview of herself. It was quite an interesting story, maybe, to those who had maybe not thought about these things before, and it was dead popular. But that was a disappointing example of dramatic monologue. There was no drama.

JC   Do you have more distance from your characters? The voices aren't you, they're not autobiographical. Are you aware of a wider judgement you are making whilst you are writing them? With Verena or Norma Nimmo, Sharon or Vicki?

LL   Oh yes, I think they start off quite satirical, although I gradually become more sympathetic towards them as I'm writing them. I'm not saying that I don't do all those things myself – I'm sure I get a lot of those strategies from watching myself.

JC   Your use of comedy interests me. You mentioned satire which is a political form, and I find the monologues quite political in the feminist slogan 'The Personal is Political' sense.

LL   They might very well be. I remember being scared at first that I might get drummed out of the Feminist Brownies! The characters are very intimate – the things in *True Confessions*. I didn't think at the time 'Oh now I'll do this very intimate voice'. Most of the charm of writing them was for Siobhan who was so wonderful at doing them and she had a wonderful voice. It was sort of saying 'Come closer, listen to what people are really like'. And men loved it. It wasn't really very nasty about men. I wasn't saying that men weren't the problem but I took that for granted. I'm interested in what people do to themselves as well as what other people do to them.

JC   Did you think that that might make you unpopular with the 'Feminist Brownies' because they would want to see the problems as being totally outside of women's control?

LL   Maybe. I'm not saying that there aren't reasons why we have these strategies but these reasons aren't within the scope of a person who is trapped within them, which is what the characters are.

JC   You can't show women with consciousness?

LL   No – because it's boring! [laughs] I am a feminist and that's no problem to me at all but I don't think my writing is feminist writing with any kind of agenda. Naturally I write more intimately about women and, yes, there is something political about that but that's not the reason why I do it. I can see that because it's not done often, especially in Scotland, that that becomes a political act. That's not why I decide to do it. There were two scary things about *Quelques Fleurs*. The first was writing a monologue from the man's point of view because it demands such intimacy. On the one hand a satirical put down of the character but also to command a sympathy for the wee things that they would do. It was getting it right. Stuart (Hepburn) helped me, he helped to get the voice better . . . My friend Ian Heggie was always saying to me 'You've got to write men monologues', you know, not monologues where women are saying '*Men*!!' but monologues for men to say. I wondered could I make them rich enough? Because I don't know enough about the wee strategies men use to avoid facing themselves. The things that Derek had to do had to be an ironic counterpoint to Verena.

JC   Do you think your humour is quite gentle? It is quite satirical at points. I wondered what your aim is in using comedy? With Merryhell Theatre Company were you trying to confront the audience or affirm them?

LL   I don't set out to be gentle or satirical or to change anybody's mind about anything. All I try to do is make someone alive, that's interesting enough to me.

JC   Sinfield talks about two distinctly different kinds of monologue;
     sympathetic or satirical. Obviously yours fit into the latter
     category, on the continuum from Chaucer's *Wife of Bath*, if you
     like.

LL   [laughs] Yes, although I don't think they are exclusive. I always
     like writing characters for whom my sympathy at the beginning is
     quite limited and then I find through the writing of them that my
     sympathy is fairly unlimited really. Some people find Verena
     unkind as a piece of writing. They think it's very very snobbish,
     that she was an easy target which she is, I suppose. She's got no
     wit, she's humourless really. My comedy is based on the people
     doing it not getting it! With *Miss World*, well that's not a real
     person anyway, it's a sort of mental version of a consciousness-
     raising process or something. She's not a real 'Miss World' – I felt
     quite comfortable to perform that out loud, I didn't feel that I had
     to really be like that. The jokes that she does make, she knows she's
     making them. She's different.

JC   In an interview in *Verse* (*Verse*, 86), you talk about the black book
     and the white book, the first being poems for publication and the
     second for performance. What's the difference when you are writing
     them? You say that you select the more 'performable' ones; what is
     the criteria for the more performable ones?

LL   Things that come across in a single reading. They may be ballad-
     like or song-like. It depends on what kind of performance it is.
     These categories are comforting to me but they may be less rigid in
     practice. It's a question of a certain kind of tone. *Bagpipe Muzak* is a
     good example of the way I would split up the categories. They are
     all out loud things, not necessarily my best work. They are all
     based on verse and they are there for their basic entertainment value
     that the rhymes contain. Then there are the characters which are all
     in prose although occasionally there might be a character written in
     verse like 'The Redneck', which is sort of a poem but why is she a
     poem rather than a character? I suppose because she is quite short
     and because she's not so much a specific character as a stereotype, or
     an archetype if you wanted to be kind! Also because there's
     something more mysterious about it in the end.

JC   So your performance work is more about communicating directly in
     an uncluttered, 'unliterary' way?

LL It's all performance.

JC I'm interested in the serious internal world of the poet for publication and the perhaps louder more humorous jester-like persona for performance. Is that a divide you see within yourself?

LL Yes, although I think they blur together a lot. Some poems are about the performance of a mood, even if it's a private performance of that mood for the page. I don't mind publishing the characters but I wouldn't want anyone to think they were poems. I'm unclear sometimes which category things should go into. There's the audaciousness of saying private things out loud – using performance techniques to say private things. I'm thinking of something like *Stooge Song* which is a performer speaking but is really a private, internal monologue. So they blur.

JC Are the audiences different depending on whether it's a revue or a poetry reading? Is there a poetry reading audience and a revue audience?

LL Oh yes. If you do a reading with someone like Roger McGough you'll get people in who wouldn't normally go to a poetry reading. If you're doing a revue you'll also get people who wouldn't usually go to a poetry reading but you can do a few poems and they get that, just like songs.

JC What about reaching a wider audience? What have been your experiences of television?

LL We've just done a TV version of *Nippy Sweeties*,[8] a revue with a lot of the things in *Bagpipe Muzak*. We did it for Scottish Television. They like the writing and wanted to film it. But we weren't allowed to wear our own costumes and they never came to see the stage show before they filmed it. There was lots of timed turning of heads and the camera would be one beat behind us. It was a bit like *Acorn Antiques* on Victoria Wood's show—using TV techniques badly – it makes you laugh. They set us in this large maroon and brown disco in the middle of an acre of dancefloor with the audience around the edges but they couldn't hear what we were saying. They were extras really, with drinks. Then they came to see it live and they said it was much better than on the telly and I said 'Yes I know!' So no, I wouldn't really like to write for telly. It gobbles up loads of material too. What I do is blurred – it's not so palatable. It's never going to be that *popular*. I really like being a poet and a dramatist. And performing occasionally just for fun!

NOTES

1 Morwenna Banks and Amanda Swift, *The Jokes on Us* (London: Pandora, 1987), 88.

2 Ibid., 102.

3 Alan Sinfield, *Dramatic Monologue* (Critical Idiom series, 36, Methuen, 1986), 6.

4 Ibid., 14.

5 Interview with Siobhan Redmond, 12 November 1992.

6 Joyce McMillan reviewing *True Confessions* in the Glasgow *Sunday Standard*, 17 January 1982.

7 Catherine Kerrigan, *An Anthology of Scottish Women Poets* (Edinburgh University Press, 1991), 2.

8 Liz Lochhead founded a double act with Elaine C. Smith in 1986, performer on the highly successful *Naked Video* television comedy series.

Six

Lochhead's Language: Styles, Status, Gender and Identity

Lynda Mugglestone

Language, as Lochhead is well aware, is neither monolithic nor neutral. Selections from its linguistic repertoire offer images of identity which embrace the social, cultural and the national; it is language which, in David Crystal's words, provides 'the most natural badge, or symbol, of public and private identity'.[1] Its variations structured, as modern sociolinguistic research has revealed, in line with speaker variables, such as age, status, and gender, as well as influenced by situational and stylistic constraints, the heterogeneous nature of language in use hence acts as a means by which individuals may be located, or indeed may locate themselves, in a multi-dimensional social space. Whether dealing with the hegemonies of English over Scots, or indeed male over female, or delineating the urban experience of life in a 'scheme', or the dynamics of power, status and solidarity in sixteenth-century Scotland, such preoccupations form recurrent topics in Lochhead's own work.

Voice and its role in 'forging an identity' appear, for example, as a pervasive construct within Lochhead's comments on the art of writing; 'poetry is very much about getting exactly the voice and tone', she stressed in 1991 (*Verse*, 87), and it is this 'sense of voice' which determines relative estimates of success or failure from her own point of view: 'I'm interested in voice, whether it's in drama, whether it's in poetry, or whether it's in fiction. I'm not particularly interested in poetry in which I can't hear the voice' (*Verse*, 89). The fact of being Scottish adds of course an extra dimension to this sensitisation to the spoken word, the linguistic repertoire in Scotland incorporating not only Gaelic, but also the use of Scots and English in varying measures along a bi-polar continuum. Correlations between style, status and language in Lowland Scotland range, for example, from the use of a more prestigious Standard English, in varieties which embrace both Scottish and non-Scottish, to, at the other end of the spectrum, 'fully local non-standard varieties, in which the choice of Scottish elements (and Scottish phonology and phonetics) is maximal'.[2] Voice as a result can embody a sense of national identity distinct from that of England, or, in its alignments towards the norms of Standard English, it can conversely betray aspirations for social and cultural identity which are targeted at the assumed social superiorities of 'educated' English usage.

The complexity of the modern linguistic situation in Scotland is embedded in its history as nation state, one initially independent with its own laws, government, court and monarch, and one later integrated, at least formally, as a part of Britain. The Union of the Crowns in 1603 led to the removal of James VI and his court to London; the Act of Union of 1707 led to the laws and administration of Scotland being determined there too. This loss of political autonomy was, in a number of ways, not unrelated to the loss of linguistic autonomy as well; Scots, functioning through the sixteenth century as an emergent standard in its own right, lost status through the relocation of king and crown, as English gradually took over the role of administration, law, education and religion. In addition, no Bible was translated into Scots, and in the religious upheavals of the Reformation, the fact that English assumed the mantle of religious authority was far from insignificant. By the eighteenth century, Boswell, like many others, took lessons in elocution to help eradicate the stigma of his native tongue, and Beattie published a list of Scotticisms so that their use might be avoided by those who sought to indicate propriety rather than provincialism in their speech. Scots came to be seen as a dialect, English as the 'standard' and imposed norm, and, just as the upper classes in the eighteenth century sought to assimilate to the norms of London speech, so in the twentieth century do the middle classes incline in the same direction. Usage of Scots is now, as Leith notes, 'found most consistently among the working classes',[3] though language loyalty will, in addition, regularly lead to the use of some Scots forms in the speech of those higher in the social scale as well.

Language use in Scotland is therefore highly complex in the schema of differentiation it offers, and it is presumably this circumstance which leads Lochhead to assert the supreme value of Scots as a 'language for multiplicity of register' (*Verse*, 93) and for the foregrounding of social, gendered and geographical divisions, the modulations of voice and register which inevitably accompany every exchange. It is certainly an aspect which Lochhead herself explores and exploits, to a considerable extent in her own work, drawing upon the emblematic aspects of language as a symbol of national identity in *Mary Queen of Scots Got Her Head Chopped Off* or upon the resources of graphological deviation to suggest a working class and Glasgow identity in a number of poems in *Bagpipe Muzak*. What is described by Fishman as 'contrastive self-identification' in language choice, for example,[4] is made to encode more fundamental differences related to questions of nation and nationalism; Mary and Elizabeth, in *Mary Queen of Scots*, are visually opposed in Lochhead's stage directions ('MARY *and* ELIZABETH *raised up at either corner*' (*MQD*, 12)) and verbally opposed in their use of, and attitudes to, language; as Mary visibly succeeds in assimilation to the norms of Scottish speech, manifest in the contrast between utterances such as 'How could ma belle-mere think o't?' (*MQD*, 13) or 'it's cauld enough to gie me *chair de poule*' (*MQD*, 16) and others such as 'Henry Darnley, you ha'e nae richt to ma throne eftir ma death' later on (*MQD*, 40), so does Elizabeth maintain a rigid physical and linguistic distance, plain in the stereotyped usages which Lochhead allots her ('Methinks they do try to play me and my Scotch cousin off against each other', 'We do not think we could marry a subject' (*MQD*, 14)), and in English assumptions about the nature of Scots, expounded by her maid:

ELIZABETH   What are her other amusements?

MARIAN   She writes poems apparently . . .

ELIZABETH   Poems? In English?

MARIAN   In French. And in 'Scots'. [*scornful laugh*]
(*MQD*, 17–18).

The dismissive inverted commas framing ''Scots'' indicate already the sense of superordinate status which English was increasingly to assume; from the point of view of Elizabeth and her court, Scots is not a language. For Mary, her Scottish kingdom, and indeed for Lochhead herself, however, it is, serving as an emblem of nationhood and national aspiration; 'Mary did not learn to speak English, She came to the Scots', as Lochhead comments on the play (*Verse*, 94).

Attitudes to languages, and language varieties, as Downes reminds us in the context of modern sociolinguistics, commonly 'reflect social and political processes at work',[5] a fact which Lochhead rarely forgets in this play; dealing as it does with 'two queens in one island, both o' the wan language – mair or less' (*MQD*, 15), the emphasis is decisively placed upon the 'mair or less'. Sharing antecedents in the related dialects of the Anglo-Saxon invaders of the fifth century, by the sixteenth Mary and Elizabeth neither literally nor metaphorically 'speak the same language', a fact which irrevocably impedes true communication between these two nation states and their two queens.

'Speaking the same language' can in fact be seen to evolve into a significant principle of discourse in Lochhead's work, used to good effect in more recent poems such as 'The Garden Festival, Glasgow 1988', with its juxtaposition of the glib (and English) registers of advertising, with the localised and Glaswegian narrative voice:

> Yet now 'One hundred acres of riverside
> Right in the heart of Glasgow at Princes Dock
> Close to the airport and a few minutes' walk
> From the city centre with its many fine hotels' —
> (Aye, pu' the other wan that's got bells).
>
> (*BM*, 18)

The idiomatic interruption disrupts the flow of rhetoric, as well as the persuasions it enacts upon the reader; more than that, it disrupts equally the sanitised image of Glasgow which such advertising-speak is intended to suggest. Again issues of language and identity converge; whilst the discourse of advertising in its declamatory sentences ('It's new! It's healthy! It's educational!/ Attracts tourists! Reclaims the Wasteland! It's recreational!' (*BM*, 18)) intimates a repackaged and commercially viable identity for the city, the colloquial directness of the narrative voice offers instead a ready injection of realism, stressing the reality of Glasgow as a city 'Wi' muck on its hauns and a durty face' and punning on contemporary speech-based forms of broad Glaswegian to subvert the re-creation of Glasgow as a once-industrial theme park:

> Well, jolly japes
> Like cutting hedges inty fancy shapes
> And trying to make some kinna eighth wonder
> Oot o' plantin' oot the coat o' arms in floribunda
> Are making Scotland just a theme park,
> A dream park,
> A Disneyland where work disnae exist.
>
> (*BM*, 19)

Scots, as used here, and indeed in the reminder of the other work written in Scots by Lochhead, is of course far from that synthetic and idealised Scots used by MacDiarmid and followers, drawing not on the dictionary and the linguistic legacies of the past, but on the colloquial, urban, and demotic legacies of the present. Her work abounds in the forms conventionally stigmatised as shibboleths and 'vulgarisms'; 'to lose the heid', 'up to high doh', 'tumshies' rather than 'neeps', the use of 'awfy' as intensifer, or the localised enunciations such as *squerr* [skwɛr] for *square, shoat* for *shot*. Often presented in contrast to the 'guid' Scots of Burns and the conventional literary language, it is this, described by David Murison, for example, as 'a debased industrial variety which . . . can hardly be described as Scots',[6] which is regularly adopted as both poetic and dramatic vehicle by Lochhead.

Denied aesthetic value in popular attitudes to the language, and castigated for its 'laziness' and 'ignorance',[7] such demotic Glaswegian, together with its embedded social meanings, is revealed as a flexible, racy and resonant medium of expression in works such as *Tartuffe* or in poems such as 'Almost Miss Scotland'. The latter with its distinctive rhymes and rhythms based on the patterns of spoken urban Scots (*whistles* : *missiles, origami*: *mammy*) will be discussed in more detail later in connection with Lochhead's working out of the inter-relationships of language and gender; Lochhead's translation of Molière's *Tartuffe*, however, offers considerable scope for an examination of the use of these varieties of Scots as prime social and stylistic discourse. Of course, such patterns of language use are not, and are not intended to be, entirely mimetic; *Tartuffe* employs what Lochhead has termed 'theatrical Scots' (*T*, Introduction), though elsewhere she does not dispute its links to 'actual Scots' too in large sections of the text (*Verse*, 94). Its qualities, in terms of language, are those of the 'proverbial, slangy, couthy, clichéd, catch-phrasey, and vulgar' (*T*, Introduction); it is direct, vigorous, idiomatic, and colloquial, and, as Lochhead stresses, it is, in addition, 'deliberately varied in register' (*T*, Introduction).

It is in these gradations of usage along continua of social and stylistic meaning in which a major focus of interest in the text can be seen to reside, as characters shift their language habits in line with the identities they wish to convey. Themes of hypocrisy can, as Lochhead clearly recognises, be brought out in the manipulation of verbal masks as well as in other, non-linguistic, ways; images of language convergence and divergence can suggest meanings beyond the mere import of what is overtly being said. Interactions between Dorine, the servant, and Marianne, Orgon's daughter, for example, can be used to exemplify these hidden agendas of language use, as Marianne, ordered by her father to marry Tartuffe, adopts the registers of fake tragedy queen rather than facing up to the reality of her love for Valère. Scene Three opens with Dorine and Marianne on stage, immediately after Orgon's edict:

DORINE   Huz the cat got your tongue, or whit?
              Leavin' me tae say your bit!
              The hale thing's ridic-ulous, nae sense t'it
              But naw, ye nivir said a word against it.

MARIANNE   Ma faither's the Big Boss, let's drop it —

DORINE   Say onythin', dae onythin', but *stop* it.

(*T*, 20)

Dorine's directness forms a hallmark of her character; unabashed by her supposed 'betters' she sees the substance which lies below the projected surface of those she encounters. Her language, unlike that of the majority of the other characters in the play, forms a stable discourse; as Lochhead comments, 'most of the characters except Dorine are at least bilingual and consequently more or less "two faced"' (*T*, Introduction). Marianne's discourse, in contrast, thus displays marked instability: using a level of Scots enunciation in this section akin to that used by Dorine herself, her construction of herself as a martyred heroine, on the lines of those familiar from the tragedies of Corneille and Racine, leads her to adopt an increasingly artificial (and anglicised) mode of speech. Even in the utterance given above, her grasp of linguistic labels and identities is shaky; Orgon, specified in French as '*un père absolu*', and transformed here, with vivid colloquialism, into 'the Big Boss', has already been revealed as nothing of the kind, having consistently been portrayed as the kind of traditional dupe who can be fooled by anyone, as indeed he is by Tartuffe. Marianne's construction of him as a man with absolute power and control is hence highly comic, as is indicated by Dorine's immediately disbelieving 'C'moan!' (*T*, 20). A few lines later, however, Marianne is adopting the stock response of the heroine whose love has been thwarted by a power beyond her control, in a register and role which are again undermined by Dorine's own rejoinder:

MARIANNE   I'll kill myself before I'm forced to marry such a man.

DORINE   Oh very good! Ah must be daft to no see
            The easy wey oot o' a' this hertbrek is tae dee!
            Is yon no awfy sensible, the very dab!
            My! Self peety fair gies ye the gift o' the gab.

(*T*, 21)

As in *Mary Queen of Scots*, conflicting patterns of language serve to signify the wider issues of distance and solidarity, the rapid upward convergence of Marianne's language being made to suggest her distance not only from Dorine (who remains rooted in her proper role, and speech) but also from reality:

> Abandon me to this Living Hell, you
> Abandon me to Death. I'll die, I tell you.
>
> (*T*, 22)

In contrast, Dorine's language sets forth the pragmatic rather than the histrionic, the down-to-earth rather than the elevated, as she specifies the delights of Tartuffe as husband 'wi' his rid, plooky grunzie' (*T*, 21), a description far surpassing in its concrete immediacy the French of the original: *'l'oreille rouge et le teint bien fleuri'*. Such patterns of linguistic difference continue into the next scene, Dorine's attempt to make Marianne (and Valère) see sense ('Yiz'll be the daith o' me/ Don't be stupit! C'mere the baith o' ye' (*T*, 26)) with its complex of markers redolent of a richly urban vernacular, is intentionally counterpointed by Marianne's 'Dorine, what do you want with us?', the language devoid of native idioms, as Marianne intentionally pulls linguistic rank as mistress over maid.

Such nuances of status are, as already indicated, firmly embedded in the details of language use; Orgon, as *nouveau riche* uses a language still rooted in his social, and working-class origins ('Ye ken nothin' aboot nothin' so will you shut/ That mooth o' yours, brither, afore Ah get upset?' (*T*, 10). Elmire, his wife, confirms her upward social mobility by linguistic habits which, whilst not denying Scots elements entirely, reduce their frequency in keeping with her assumed status:

> Whit! I emm don't think we need to move so fast —
> Too soon spent kisses never last!
> I promise all the happiness of which dream's
> Around the corner, if you don't push it to extremes.
>
> (*T*, 48)

Using on occasion those fronted vowels deemed resonant of social pretension ('Right enough, but about this other Metter' (*T*, 33)), she suggests a measure of linguistic propriety entirely in keeping with those heightened sensibilities to the linguistic markers of prestige systematically evidenced for women within modern sociolinguistic studies on speech variation. She is, however, as Lochhead notes, 'not too Bearsden voiced' (*T*, Introduction), a comment drawing upon contemporary linguistic stereotypes of the different areas of Glasgow and their respective socio-symbolic affiliations. Bearsden, connotative of the upper-middle-class enclave of the managerial and professional classes, conveys both social and linguistic identity, as indeed does that more pervasive stereotype of the Kelvinside speaker, a target elsewhere of Lochhead's linguistic satire as in, for example, the monologue 'Meeting Norma Nimmo' in *Bagpipe Muzak*.[8]

The dramatic world created within *Tartuffe* thus sets forth, via language and its significant variations; a social and stylistic matrix in which characters are differentiated by their varying commands of the standard and vernacular forms at their disposal. Tartuffe himself fits ambiguously into this framework, his linguistic duplicity foregrounded in the incompatibilities of his favoured registers of the ascetic and the sensualist, as well as in his strategic modulations of language between an urban and intensely Glaswegian demotic, and his other and more formal rhythms of discourse. A versatile performer, Tartuffe is made to style-shift with ease, as he moves between Biblical English ('How doth the city sit solitary that was full of people! How is she become a widow she that was great among the nations and princess among the provinces' (*T*, 30)), a broad Glaswegian which in its graphological modifications (though not perhaps in its idiomatic vigour) is made to parallel that of Dorine ('Ach, *chist* a minute there, Ah'll thank yi/ Afore ye speak tae me tae tak' this hanky/ In the name o' a' that's holy and religious' (*T*, 31)) and the diminished colloquialisms (and heightened religious rhetoric) he uses in, for example, the opening of his conversation with Elmire in Act Three, Scene iii:

> May merciful heaven grant to thee and thine
> Health, wealth and grace baith temporal and divine.
> I, God's humblest servant ask, and ask in all sincerity,
> May He crown all your days wi' bountiful prosperity.
>
> > (*T*, 32)

With particular aptness, 'sincerity' is made to rhyme with 'prosperity', the one thing about which Tartuffe is of course sincere.

The excesses of his religious facade readily lend themselves to linguistic parody, as Dorine illustrates by means of Lochhead's strategic reallocation of speeches in Act Three, Scene ii; Tartuffe here makes his first entrance in the play, blazoning the devotional exertions in which he has (supposedly) been occupied:

> Laurent! Awa' an' lock up ma King James Bible.
> An' bring me linament – Ah'm awfy liable
> Tae rheumaticks wi' bein' so lang oan the caul' flair, kneelin'.
>
> > (*T*, 30)

Concluding with the further injunction to 'pit ma bookmerk in whaur Ah wis readin', as well as a regurgitated section of the Bible for further effect, Tartuffe's verbal mask is immediately adopted to good comic effect by Dorine. Using the figure of hyperbole, aptly described by Puttenham in the sixteenth century as 'the loud liar or over-reacher',

Dorine transcends even Tartuffe's religious pyrotechnics to expose the dichotomy between assumed voice and true identity:

> 'Laurent! Knot ma scourge again, mak' shair it hurt.
> An' hem an extra awfy jaggy bit on ma hairshirt.'
> Whit a big ham! He must think Ah'm green.
>
> (*T*, 31)

As this makes clear, the trappings of religious language are, in the hands of the hypocrite, merely a vehicle for outward display. The disharmonies which can exist between outward signification and underlying meaning are, of course, further exposed in the attempted seduction scene with Elmire in Act Three, in which the discourse turns on the religious and secular polysemies present within Tartuffe's addresses to Elmire, where 'loving-kindness' has quite another meaning from that intended by Tyndale, and 'Blissful Ecstasy' suggests satisfactions which are less of heaven than of earth.

Though less subtle in a number of ways than Molière's original in this section, Lochhead's use of Scots in the play as a whole offers a vigour and directness which, on the other hand, the French can lack. As H. Gaston Hall has noted, 'Molière's vocabulary leans heavily towards words with an ethical rather than visual background';[9] it is here that the vividly colloquial Scots can have its advantages, perhaps most notably in the 'intact Scots' of Dorine. Representations of her speech imbued with graphemic devices which suggest the broader enunciations of Glasgow Scots ('poat' for *pot*, 'stoap' for *stop*), she deploys a range of idioms which present her ideas with graphic clarity, and without those linguistic subterfuges adopted by, as we have seen, a number of other characters in the play. Orgon's foolish infatuation, described by the French Dorine in the terms of the way '*il est devenu comme un homme hébété*', is, for example, transposed by the Scots Dorine into the resoundingly dismissive 'his heid's full o' mince' (*T*, 7), drawing on those idiomatic contemporanities of modern Glaswegian in which, as Munro notes, the word 'mince' has assumed a linguistic versatility in meaning quite unwarranted by its etymology.[10] Semantic nuances possible within Glasgow Scots are employed to good effect in the same context; whereas the French describes Tartuffe's entry into Orgon's household using more neutral verbs ('*un gueux, quand il vint, n'avait pas des souliers*'), Dorine gives the more emphatic, and exclamatory 'To breenge in here, a raggity bare-fit tink,/ Wi' the bareface to tell us whit to think' (*T*, 4) in which *breenge* is not merely a localised form of *bring* but carries with it the sense of impetuous, ill-considered, action which is precisely the hallmark of Orgon in the play.

The labels Dorine applies to Tartuffe himself similarly offer a telling illustration of the versatility of urban Scots in Lochhead's hands, giving a strength and directness to Dorine's discourse unsurpassed in the original. Molière's '*Il passe pour un saint dans votre fantaisie:/ Tout son fait, croyez-moi, n'est rien qu'hypocrisie*' receives a much more pointed, and idiomatic, opposition in Lochhead's *Tartuffe*: 'You think wan thing, Ah think anither/ You cry him a saint, Ah cry him a blether' (*T*, 4), where *blether* (from ON *blaðra*) carries the entirely appropriate sense of 'a person who talks foolishly or too much'. More than that, he is accorded the evocative label of *gaberlunzie* on p. 17 and that of *puggy-ape* five pages later, dismissed as a *cuddy* on p. 8 and a *sumph* (an idiot, or slow-witted oaf) on p. 29, and condemned as a *galoot* on p. 30. It is perhaps the Officer in the final scene who provides, however, the most apposite term for Tartuffe:

> Mr. Prince is proof against the con-man's art
> Not wan to fall for any cock and bull,
> Nor tae let nae silvertongued pattermerchant pull the wool.
>
> (*T*, 61–2)

The 'patter' standing as the local label for the urban demotic of Glasgow itself, and explicitly referred to elsewhere by Lochhead as in 'Bagpipe Muzak, Glasgow 1990' (*BM*, 24), 'patter-merchant', another term of local currency, conveys precisely that sense of the glib, intentionally persuasive talker which can be seen to fit Tartuffe exactly.

Lochhead's manipulation of the resources of Scots, whether lexically, idiomatically, or stylistically in *Tartuffe* clearly substantiates her vision of herself, articulated with reference to *Memo For Spring*, as 'forging out a Scottish and female and working-class and contemporary identity as a writer' (*Verse*, 89). The notion of 'femaleness', specified here along with issues of class and nation, is clearly important to Lochhead as a writer; as she stresses, 'the female voice has to exist' (*Verse*, 92), and its existence in her own works is asserted in a number of ways, not least in Lochhead's use of language, and her considered awareness of, among other things, the gendered nature of language and representation.

The politics of representation are, of course, involved in Lochhead's work in a number of ways, influencing, as we have seen, conceptions of Scotland's identity, whether in the diachronic terms of *Mary Queen of Scots Got Her Head Chopped Off* or in the commercialisation and repackaging of the modern Glasgow, including its language, in 'Bagpipe Muzak, Glasgow 1990':

> . . . marketing men will spill out spiel
> About how us Glesga folk are really *real*

(Where once they used to fear and pity
These days they glamorize and patronize our city —
Accentwise once they could hear bugger all
That was not low, glottal or gutteral
Now we've 'kudos' incident'ly
And the Patter's street-smart, strictly state-of-the-art,
And our oaths are user-friendly).

(*BM*, 24)

Just as English is seen to exert its hegemonies over Scotland, so too does male often seem to influence female, issues which are explicitly linked by Lochhead in the contrast of 'dominant cultures and undominant cultures' in which 'the Scots is in some way in the position of being the feminine with regard to Britain' (*Verse*, 90). Voice is salient to both, and in her articulation of areas of female experience, and her examination of gender stereotypes within and about language use, Lochhead foregrounds some of the dichotomies, the prejudices and preconceptions which can attend women and their representation in language.

Language is, of course, of prime importance in encoding the values and assumptions of a particular culture, evidencing notions of bias and inequality, of hierarchy and social stereotypes, in the divisions of semantic space which result. In terms of gender, the consequences of this are marked; linguistic representations, as Cameron points out, 'give a clue to the place of women in our culture', one in which 'sexist assumptions are embodied by linguistic choices'.[11] Lochhead's poem 'The Alternative History of the World Part One', with the imagined feminist discourse with which it (hypothetically) credits Eve, offers a striking exposition of these ideas. Giving, as the title suggests, an 'alternative' reading of the myth of creation, it examines the androcentricity (both social and linguistic) resulting from the fact of 'The Lord Our God being a Male God', as well as from an Adam in whose hands the power of naming, according to Biblical authority, was assumed to lie. The world into which Eve comes is thus already ordered on patriarchal lines, with still-familiar gender roles already mapped out. Eve's role as 'helpmeet' in the Biblical version is disambiguated, and dysphemized, into that of 'slave', with all its attendant consequences:

And soon she was worn to a frazzle
Waiting on His Nibs
Ironing his figleaves
Barbecueing his ribs
While home came the hunter
With the Bacon for the table

> She was stuck raising Cain
> And breastfeeding Abel.
>
> *(BM, 13)*

As the narrative voice comments: 'Some Garden of Eden!'

From the point of view of language, and the gendered nature of representation within it, the main import of the poem rests in the Whorfian conceit that if only Eve had articulated at that point the sheer unacceptability of the role in which she was placed, and the labels which came to attach themselves to it, subsequent history (of both language and feminism) could have been radically changed:

> She could've saved us all a whole lot of trouble if only she'd told him right at the start:
>
> > I'm not your Little Woman
> > I'm not your Better Half
> > I'm not your nudge, your snigger
> > Or your belly laugh.
> >
> > *(BM, 13)*

The list goes on, as Lochhead itemises the terms by which images of women's identity polarise into madonna and whore, Virgin Mary and Mary Magdalen, all of which are, however, prefaced here by an emphatic and anaphoric denial. Rejecting archetypes and stereotypes alike, Lochhead anatomises the imbalances in semantic space in which women are constructed as items for male consumption ('Thinking Man's Crumpet', 'Tart-With-a-Golden-Heart'), and demeaned and diminished by the lexis applied to them in popular culture: 'I'm not your Living Doll/ I'm not Poetry in Motion' *(BM, 14)*, avers the assertive voice with which Eve is endowed, vigorously negating such collocations which depict female identity in terms of toys and playthings. Words, as Casey Miller and Kate Swift have stressed, act as 'semantic symbols of deeply rooted cultural assumptions'[12] and in these contexts they can be seen to embody the premises of patriarchy and androcentrism, and the ideologies of power which exclude the female, or define it in terms of male possession, as the Other and as the different.

'Almost Miss Scotland' similarly confronts notions of female image and identity, not this time through a vision of a recreated feminist Eve embracing a role as linguistic activist, but instead through the feminist awakening of an aspiring beauty queen competing for the title of Miss Scotland. Written in a broad urban vernacular, and immediately parodic ('The night I/ Almost became Miss Scotland/ I caused a big

stramash/ When I sashayed on in my harristweed heathermix onepiece/
And my 'Miss Garthamlock' sash' (*BM*, 3)), issues of language again
prove significant, as in the skewed alignments of language and gender
revealed by Lochhead's subversive defamiliarizations of language use:

> How would *thae guys* like to be a prize –
> A cake everybody wanted a slice of –
> Have every leering schoolgirl consider them a pearl
> Everybody kennt the price of?
> How would *they* like their mums to say that their bums
> Had always attracted the Ladies Glances,
> And nothing wrang wi it, they's gone alang wi it
> And encouraged them to take their chances?
> And they were Good Boys, their Mum's Pride & Joys,
> Saving it all for their Future Wives?
> And despite their fame they still steyed at hame
> And lived real clean-living lives?
>
> (*BM*, 5)

Disrupting those linguistic conventions which present women as sex
objects as well as items for male consumption, Lochhead inverts
characteristic applications of language, constructing men as 'cake', as
'Good Boys', as virginal creatures 'saving it all for their Future Wives'.
The evident incompatibilities which result, perhaps most notable in the
collocation of 'leering schoolgirls', concisely reveals the existence of
those inequities and double standards which pervade both language and
society. In a culture which judges women by their outward appearance,
imposes divergent standards of sexual morality and contributes a
plethora of other inequalities, in which the beauty contest stands as a
prime example of both sexism and exploitation, the only solution, once
feminism dawns, is to make a hasty exit, as indeed the narrator does,
though rejecting possibilities for other feminist conversions on the way:

> Now I'd love to report that I was the sort
> To speak out and convert the other lassies
> Pick bones wi aw the chaperones
> And singlehandedly convert the masses
> Till in a bacchanalian Revenge of the Barbie Dolls
> Crying 'All for One and One for All!'
> We advanced on the stage, full of bloodlust and rage –
> But, I cannot tell a lie, the truth is that I
> Just stuck on my headsquerr and snuck away oot o therr
>
> (*BM*, 5)

'Almost Miss Scotland' ends with the recognition that 'Every individual hus tae realize/ Her hale fortune isnae in men's eyes' and with a refutation of the importance of body image which a number of Lochhead's other narrators could do with, from Lucy in 'Lucy's Diary' ('This gross flesh I will confine/ in the whalebone of my very own/ hunger' (BM, 62)) to the references to dieting which permeate poems such as 'The Bride', 'The Redneck', or monologues such as 'Quelques Fleurs' in Bagpipe Muzak. Domains of usage again peculiarly female, and triggered by the pressures exerted upon women by modern cultural constructions of gender and femininity, such images recur in Lochhead's work. Other notions of femininity, in linguistic as well as cultural manifestations, receive emphasis elsewhere: Marianne's silence in the face of Orgon's dictates in Tartuffe, for example, being explained in terms of the silence that belongs to 'proper' women, especially when it concerns speaking about the men they desire: 'Is it no kinna unfeminine to flaunt/ Before the whole wide world how much I want/ Valère? Should a lassie disobey her faither?' (T, 21), a precept ironically endorsed by Dorine in her own reply:

> Of course she shouldny, no when she'd raither
> Have yit another auld man to belang tae!
> (T, 21)

Elmire too is made to play with conventional stereotypes about women's linguistic behaviour in her endeavours to expose Tartuffe as hypocrite:

> Dear Tartuffe, you don't know women, you're so innocent!
> A refusal like that! You surely never thought I meant
> It? We women struggle so with modesty when we transgress
> But you know that we say 'no' when we mean 'yes'!
> (T 47)

She is in reality, of course, entirely in command, controlling a discourse in which Tartuffe is revealed as consummate religious hypocrite, prepared to twist divine law to sanction profane love ('Heaven forbids certain things, oh aye, bit we'd better/ Mind we're enjoined tae follow the spirit o' the law and no the letter/ under certain circumstances these . . . gratifications that I mention/ Micht be richt – accordin' tae Purity o' Intention' (T, 48)).

It is Dorine, however, who emerges as perhaps the strongest female voice in Lochhead's work, her language pithy, spirited, and direct; it is she who confronts Orgon with his own stupidity, pointing out the folly, as Marianne should have done, of his ludicrous proposals that she should marry Tartuffe: 'What would yon bigot want wi' oor wee lassie' (*T*, 17). Consistently assertive, outspoken, refusing to be subdued or to conform to feminine models of propriety in language,[13] her speech is marked by a supreme colloquial verve. As seems entirely just, in Lochhead's *Tartuffe*, though not in Molière's, it is Dorine who gets the last word:

We'll be happy ever eftir. And the band will play.

NOTES

1 D. Crystal, *The Cambridge Encyclopaedia of Language* (Cambridge University Press, 1987), 17.
2 A. J. Aitken, 'Scots and English in Scotland' in P. Trudgill, ed., *Language in the British Isles* (Cambridge University Press, 1984), 527.
3 D. Leith, *A Social History of English* (London: Routledge & Kegan Paul, 1983), 163.
4 J. Fishman, *Language and Nationalism* (Massachusetts: Rowley, 1976), 52.
5 W. Downes, *Language and Society* (London: Fontana, 1984), 36.
6 D. Murison, 'The Future of Scots' in D. Glen ed., *Whither Scotland?* (London: Gollancz, 1971), 178.
7 See R. K. S. Macauley and G. D. Trevelyan, *Language, Social Class, and Education. A Glasgow Study* (Edinburgh University Press, 1977) for a detailed sociolinguistic examination of language use and language attitudes in modern Glasgow.
8 'I have not clepped eyes on you since the Sixth Year Leavers's Social. I mind of you diving round in bleck tights and a big fisherman's jumper shoogling up esperins in Coca-Cola' (*BM*, 34). As Aitken comments, such varieties are 'widely disapproved as supposedly indicating pretentiousness of affectation . . . the result of inaccurate, 'overshooting' or 'over-compensating' attempts to adjust the native realisations of sounds to the more prestigious RP pronunciation.' ('Scottish Speech: A Historical View with Special Reference to the Standard English of Scotland' *Languages of Scotland* A. J. Aitken and T. MacArthur, eds., (Edinburgh: W. & R. Chambers, 1979), 113.)
9 H. Gaston Hall, *Molière: Tartuffe* (London: Edwin Arnold, 1960), 61.
10 M. Munro, *The Patter. A Guide to Current Glasgow Usage* (Glasgow: Glasgow District Libraries, 1985), 46: 'this prosaic word for humble fare has blossomed into one of the most versatile words in the dialect', taking on the meaning of 'nonsense, rubbish', as in Dorine's application of it, and, in other uses, suggesting extremes of denseness, indicating the marked absence of animation, and even being used to express the experience of taking the wind out of someone else's sails, as in 'That's sickened his mince for him.'
11 D. Cameron, *The Feminist Critique of Language* (London: Routledge & Kegan Paul, 1990), 12, 16.

12 C. Miller and K. Swift, *Words and Women: New Language in New Times* (New York: Anchor/ Double day, 1976), xii.

13 See, for example, the exchange between Dorine and Orgon on p. 18.

ORGON   . . . A clever lass can aye mak' a man tae fit her template.

DORINE   'She canny mak' a silk purse oo a soo's erse!

ORGON   The language!

DORINE   An eejit is an eejit, nothin' worse!

Plates

PLATE 1: Liz Lochhead's poster poem of 'My Rival's House', 1976.
Photograph: Douglas Maclean.

PLATE 2: Liz Lochhead and Siobhan Redmond performing a rap in *True Confessions*, 1981.

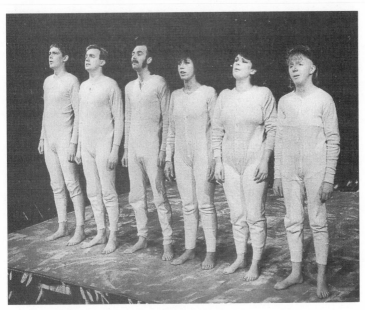

PLATE 3: *Same Difference*, directed by Hugh Hodgart, Wildcat Theatre Company, 1984. Photograph: Sean Hudson.

PLATE 4: Elaine C. Smith as Josie in *Same Difference*, directed by Hugh Hodgart, Wildcat Theatre Company, 1984. Photograph: Sean Hudson.

PLATE 5: Isabella Jarrett as Mary and Michael Mackenzie as the Creature in *Blood and Ice*, directed by John Carnegie, Winged Horse Touring Company, 1986. Photograph: Douglas Robertson.

PLATE 6: Bev Willis and Amanda Pointer as Dracula and Lucy, in *Dracula*, directed by Ian Forrest, Dukes Theatre, 1988. Photograph: Arthur Thompson.

PLATE 7: Anne Lacey and Alison Pebbles as Mary and her maid, in *Mary Queen of Scots Got Her Head Chopped Off*, directed by Gerald Mulgrew, Communicado Theatre Company, 1987. Photograph: Ginny Atkinson.

PLATE 8: Alison Peebles as Elizabeth in *Mary Queen of Scots Got Her Head Chopped Off*, directed by Gerald Mulgrew, Communicado Theatre Company, 1987. Photograph: Ginny Atkinson.

PLATE 9: The company in *Jock Tamson's Bairns*, directed by Gerald Mulgrew, Communicado Theatre Company, 1990. Photograph: Sean Hudson.

PLATE 10: Liz Lochhead as Verena, in *Quelques Fleurs*, directed by Joyce Deans, 1991. Photograph: Frank Higgins.

PLATE 11: Jimmy Chisholm in the title role of *Tartuffe*, directed by Hamish Glen, Dundee Repertory Company, 1992. Photograph: Sean Hudson.

Seven

Re-enter Houghmagandie: Language as Performance in Liz Lochhead's *Tartuffe*

Randall Stevenson

Tartuffe was one of the most successful productions of the eighties, impressing critics and packing the Royal Lyceum Theatre in Edinburgh nightly in January 1986 – a time immediately after the Christmas period when audiences are more often very sparse. Liz Lochhead's translation has gone on to become a popular, influential part of the Scottish repertoire: its initial success, however, was based partly on strengths already established for the Scottish stage, and it is worth examining these first before considering the particular achievements of the play itself.

Since the war, and especially since the sixties, drama has become an exciting, rapidly developing part of Scottish literature, largely through discovering, or rediscovering, three principal areas of interest and potential – the transcription for dramatic purposes of the vitality and particularity of Scots speech; the use of Scottish history as a source of often-colourful subjects and themes; and the staging of a politicised, socially-aware vision of the impoverished reality of Scottish urban or working-class life. Lochhead's work has not been much involved with the last of these areas, but it has in various ways both profited from and added to the resources of the first two. *Mary Queen of Scots Got Her Head Chopped Off* (1987), for example, shows Lochhead participating in a second phase, a kind of new generation of dramatic treatments of Scottish history – one which moves beyond the initial steps taken by earlier writers such as Robert Kemp. In treating the reign of Malcolm and Margaret in *The Saxon Saint* (1949); the struggle of Robert the Bruce in *The King of Scots* (1951); or the time of Mary's reign in *Master John Knox* (1960), Kemp provides little more than historical accounts of his periods and their people – expository dramatic pageants, tenuous in conflict or characterisation. Much the same narrative straightforwardness and slightness of dramatic analysis is apparent in other historical dramas of this time, such as Sidney Goodsir Smith's *The Wallace* (1960), or R. S. Silver's *The Bruce* (1951). But a new vigour and variety in Scottish historical drama begins to appear in the seventies. Performed at the Royal Lyceum in 1977, Ian Brown's *Mary*, for example, is less interested in the actual events of Mary Queen of Scots's life than in the problems she defined and has continued to pose for the Scottish imagination in general. Her complex, multi-faceted influence on later generations Brown dramatises through a multiplicity of styles, tones and historical points of view. Produced at the Lyceum ten years later, after a successful run on the Fringe, *Mary Queen of Scots Got Her Head Chopped Off* followed similar tactics, dramatising in a range of flexible, inventive and often unusual forms not only Mary's life itself, but also ways it has been conceived by later generations; ways actual events and personalities are transformed towards myth, and the effects this has on a nation's sense of itself.

Though *Mary Queen of Scots Got Her Head Chopped Off* shows Lochhead sharing in new styles and subtleties in treating Scottish history, her principal achievement for the theatre – as might be expected of an author initially valued mainly as a poet – has been in terms of language: in diversifying and consolidating, in *Tartuffe* particularly, the use of Scots speech and idioms on the stage. The origins of this revival of Scots as a dramatic language can also be retraced to the influence of an earlier generation of post-war playwrights – to the work of Alexander Reid and Alexander Scott as well as Robert Kemp. Reid insisted in the fifties that the Scottish theatre could progress only by returning to the 'meaning and sincerity' offered by Scots speech,[1] a principal resource of his own drama at the time. Significantly, Robert Kemp's theatre writing was much more effective when he worked as a translator and adaptor, with Scots language as a centre of his interest, rather than in his historical plays, usually written in a bland English influenced by contemporary English verse dramatists such as T. S. Eliot and Christopher Fry. It was Kemp's shortened, modernised version of Sir David Lindsay's *Ane Satyre of the Thrie Estaitis* which Tyrone Guthrie used for his Edinburgh Festival production in 1948, one of great influence in the post-war reawakening of Scotland to the native strengths of its stage. Another such event – potentially at least – was the launch in 1981 of Scottish Theatre Company, probably as close an approximation to a National Theatre, during its brief success in the eighties, as Scotland will see in the twentieth century. Kemp's work in Scots played its part here, too: Scottish Theatre Company's first production in March 1981 was *Let Wives Tak Tent*, Kemp's excellent Scots translation of Molière's *L'Ecole des Femmes*.

Given the company's emphatic, widely-publicised commitment at the time to Scotland and Scottish material, its opening choice of a French play might seem surprising – at least until some further thought is given to the matter of translation and the interrelations of languages. As most commentators and theorists in this area are quick to point out, the ease or completeness with which one language can be made the susbtitute for another relates to the extent of congruence between the cultures each language represents. The literal meaning of most statements in one language can be rendered, more or less, in any other, but the extent to which such translated material is really 'audible' – genuinely significant and apprehensible within another imagination – is highly specific culturally. What matters to one culture may be largely irrelevant to another, however exactly it can be understood superficially. In this way, the success of translations into Scots both derives from and indicates what the Scottish imagination finds most illuminating and closest to itself in other cultures. Ibsen, for example, has recently worked well in translations by Tom Gallacher and several others. Something of Ibsen's vision of remote, gloomy communities – victims of a dreadful climate and stringent, often hypocritical morality – bears obvious relation to Scotland: appropriately enough, Scottish Theatre Company ended that first season, begun with Molière, with a translation of Ibsen's *Ghosts*.

Some of the relevance of Ibsen's concerns for Scotland is shared by Molière, at least where severe but specious morality and piety are concerned. In Lochhead's *Tartuffe*, Cléante appropriately suggests that Tartuffe is typical of 'False Heroes and Holy Willies' and the kind of 'kiddology' that they practise (I, v). Figures of monstrous, hypocritical self-righteousness have long interested Scottish literature, for example in Robert Burns's 'Holy Willie's Prayer'. Though an extreme figure, Tartuffe is probably more familiar in life, as well as literature, to Scottish theatre-goers than to many another audience around modern Europe. Pernelle, too – the grandmother of the play and Tartuffe's principal supporter in Orgon's household – is a figure easily placed in the context of an older Scottish generation's continuing allegiance to unforgiving moral laws and willing subjection to the grey hand of the church: no wonder Lochhead records in her Introduction 'the sharp tongue of her granny' as one of the inspirations for her *Tartuffe*.[2] A Scottish context even offers Lochhead the chance to *extend* Molière's original resistance to religious hypocrisy. At a crucial moment in her version, when Orgon looks as though he really might be persuaded by his daughter's Mariane's genuine love and distress, she unfortunately hits on the plea 'Let me turn Catholic! In God's honour, He/ Bids me live my days out in a nunnery' (IV, iii) – a suggestion which immediately destroys all traces of Orgon's fragile patience. In seventeenth-century France, Molière had less chance of extending his satire of hypocrisy to encompass soul-destroying divisions and bigotries within the church iself: the scene is one of several instances where Scotland offers *additional* scope for his interests, and opportunities – which she takes throughout – for Lochhead to elaborate freely on her original.

Molière's appropriateness for Scots translation, however, is a matter not only of morality and theme but in many ways of stage idiom – of modes and manners Molière might first have learned when his company shared a theatre with an Italian *commedia dell'arte* troupe permanently established in seventeenth-century Paris. A ragamuffin descendant of the classical Roman comedy of Plautus and Terence, *commedia* relies on improvisation around standard plots by stereotyped characters – young lovers thwarted by a doddering father or *pantalone*, for example; then triumphing with the help of wily servants, *zanni*. Drawing strength from its embodiment of deep psycho-sexual impulses of comedy – of the need for fertility to triumph over sterility; of new generations to replace the old – and enlivened by brilliant gags and routines, *lazzi*, *commedia* flourished in the sixteenth and seventeenth centuries as a form of broad, immediately-appealing entertainment which could be played anywhere by itinerant troupes. Its influence remains strongly apparent in *Tartuffe*. Dorine, for example, remains close to the wily, omnicompetent servants of commedia, though Orgon is a more particularised version of the *pantalone*: one of Molière's achievements for the European stage – like Carlo Goldoni's later in Italy – was his addition to familiar plots and people of the kind of characterisation and complexity which extended the appeal of this comedy for more sophisticated metropolitan audiences at the time.

However significant for continental Europe, such developments might seem scarcely relevant to the Scottish context, in which there is no record of influence from the commedia. For that matter, there is little record of substantial theatrical activity of any kind in Scotland between the seventeenth century and the twentieth, and some very bare patches even during this century. Scottish drama can hardly fail to seem comparatively successful after the Second World War, since it scarcely existed in earlier periods at all. Nevertheless, where specific forms of performance are concerned, the picture of Scottish theatrical tradition is much less sparse and bleak. One of these is the music-hall. As David Hutchison has shown, music-hall and variety have been *more* successful in twentieth-century Scotland than elsewhere, partly as a result of what he calls 'a fundamental dependence on a shared identity of experience between performer and audience.'[3] The famous 'Five Past Eight' productions in Glasgow's Alhambra Theatre were one of the longest surviving of the variety shows: though they finally expired some years ago, much of the tradition of music-hall and variety still survives in the form of Christmas pantomimes – the continuing strength of whose hold on the Scottish imagination is confirmed by their occupation of many a civic theatre virtually from November to March. Music-hall, variety and pantomime are of course far from identical either with Molière's theatre or the kind of commedia which nourished it, yet with pantomime especially there are a good many elements in common – breadth of appeal; reliance on stock situation, plots or characters; and on wit, improvisation, gags and *lazzi*. Scottish Theatre Company, at any rate, clearly appreciated the relevance of Molière in terms not only of theme or moral vision but also entertainment style: the star of that opening production of *Let Wives Tak Tent* was Rikki Fulton – doyen of a thousand pantomimes – who duly included in his performance a range of gags and routines which would have done credit to any commedia or variety company.

Recent Royal Lyceum productions – such as their 1992 *School for Wives* – have continued to emphasise this aspect of Molière. Liz Lochhead's *Tartuffe* also accentuated pantomime elements in the original, and even invented new ones of its own. Her stage directions suggest, for example, that while eavesdropping, 'Dorine, bent over at keyhole, falls into room' (II, i) when the door is snatched open by Orgon; later, she exits 'pantomiming as much as possible . . . to the entering Elmire, then trying to disguise it as an itch as Tartuffe catches her at it' (III, ii) – gags at most suggested rather than stipulated in Molière's original. Lochhead shows a similarly irreverent readiness to adapt or extend Molière's dialogue with added satiric cracks and one-liners. This is one of many points of difference from Christopher Hampton's translation of *Tartuffe* – interesting to compare with Lochhead's as it was written around the same time, for production by the Royal Shakespeare Company in 1983. For example, when Orgon returns from the country in Act I scene iv, Hampton has Cléante blandly ask his brother-in-law 'Nothing much out yet, is there, in the country?', directly following Molière's '*La campagne à présent n'est pas beaucoup fleurie.*' But in Lochhead's version, Cléante just asks 'How was the country? Green and stuff?' This is cheekier, funnier, closer to music-hall patter and exemplary of sceptical Scottish wit – even of the outlook of a people whose rugged landscape has never left much place for conventional pastoral sentiment.

So in approaching Molière in 1985, Lochhead was turning to material with a range of the cultural congruences necessary for worthwhile translation and with a proven record of success on the Scottish stage – a record well known to Ian Wooldridge, who had included *The Miser* in an earlier season at the Royal Lyceum, and encouraged Lochhead's initial interest in *Tartuffe*. Nevertheless, however much cultural consonance may be a precondition for worthwhile translations, their success obviously depends in still larger measure on the verbal medium a writer can create in a new language. And however proximate and promising for a Scottish audience Molière seems in other ways, his language remains formidably challenging for the translator. *Tartuffe* is written in rhyming Alexandrines, which offer limited scope for direct rendition in Scots or English, risking Alexander Pope's censure of the kind of six-stressed line 'that like a wounded snake, drags its slow length along'.[4] Translations of *Tartuffe* have usually opted either for prose or for the kind of rhymed iambic pentameter which appears, for example, in Richard Wilbur's standard translation for Methuen: Christopher Hampton offers another possibility in the blank verse he employs in his RSC version of *Tartuffe*. None of these solutions is ideal. Prose translation largely removes the rhythm and colour in the original language: Richard Wilbur's version on the other hand, is *so* regular in rhythm and rhyme that it eventually seems repetitive and trite. Hampton reasons that the Alexandrine, the measure of the golden age of French drama, is most naturally rendered in English in the blank verse used by English dramatists in *their* golden age, yet – probably just because it does have such strong associations with the grand visions of Jacobethan drama – Hampton's verse seems occasionally too sober and serious for some of the broader, even slapstick elements discussed above as an essential part of Molière's stage.

In her Introduction to *Tartuffe*, Liz Lochhead recalls basing her approach to Molière's verse on a decision that 'the really important part, the comic drive, came from the rhyming'. She explains that, accordingly, she

> set to, in rhyming couplets with a cavalier and rather idiosyncratic rhythm that I justified to myself by calling it 'the rhythm of spoken Scots'.

As she suggests, the rhythm of her lines seems either natural, imperceptible, or sometimes just missing, and it is the rhyme which creates her translation's most striking feature, and perhaps its most daring. Any sort of rhymed version of Molière is a considerable challenge for the translator. The commonness of inflected endings, regular participle forms and consistent verbs in French makes rhyme easier to sustain than in many another language, English included, and can strain severely even the rich resources of Scots vocabulary. As Christopher Hampton suggests, 'there have been a number of admirable rhyming translations of Molière; but the ingenuity they demand cannot avoid drawing attention to itself'.[5] One of Lochhead's best achievements in *Tartuffe*, however, is that she consistently makes a virtue and a source of comedy something which Hampton suggests is more likely to be a problem for the translator. Lochhead's rhymes draw a great deal of attention to themselves, but in ways which not only highlight her ingenuity, but contribute to the texture, satire and what her Introducton calls 'comic drive' of the piece as a whole.

At many points, first of all, rhymes provide an elegantly comic emphasis of moral imperatives or dilemmas. The language's precise closures help to focus with the concision of aphorism some of the dangers of moral narrowness and regimentation – for example, when Dorine warns that

> To live the virtuous life is awfy chancy
> When a lassie's merrit tae a man she disnae fancy.
>
> > (II, ii)

Secondly, audiences discovered a strong comic drive created by their continual expectation of rhyme's consecutive completion of successive lines – often heightened by delighted anticipation of exactly what this rhyme would be. In the Royal Lyceum production, this comic foresight was perhaps most apparent when in his closing speech the Officer reassured Orgon that

> Just men who love the Government needny fear the Law.
> Is a contract worth the paper that it's written oan? Nut at a'!
> Thank God Good Government's Sovereign Power can aye
> > arrange it
> That if a law isny servin' Justice, well . . . they can change it.
>
> > (V, vii)

By the middle of the last of these lines in Lyceum performances, through the audience's general laughing expectation of the conclusion several spectators could sometimes be heard actually speaking it for themselves. This sense of words fulfilling familiar patterns of their own contributed to the production's sense of language as performance – of the form as well as the content of what was said, the medium of the play as well as what it expresses, functioning as a comic element as powerful as any character or action.

The formal inevitability of the Officer's conclusion also helped

Lochhead to establish in her version particular elements of contemporary satire. The lines quoted are largely her addition to Molière, whose Officer speaks only of the king, who *'d'un souverain pouvoir . . . brise les liens/ Du contrat'* ('with sovereign power, breaks the bonds of the contract'). Lochhead's version also converts the king into the aloof, all-powerful, slightly sinister figure of 'Mr Prince'. This deletion of monarchical government, along with the production's twentieth-century setting, the emendation of the Officer's speech, and the glib, suave certitude with which he delivers it, all contribute to the last scene an aspect of up-to-date political commentary – of mockery of the status quo and the complacent confidence with which it sustains itself and rewards its agents and favourites. Molière obviously directs his satire principally against the kind of contemporary religious hypocrisy represented by Tartuffe – a point he stressed to the king, Louis XIV, when defending his play against the controversy it aroused at the time.[6] Though Lochhead, of course, highlights the threat of Tartuffe's hypocrisy as much as Molière, she also directs a particular shaft of knowing laughter against the facility with which the moneyed classes can close ranks with the government against any threat to their affluence, casually assuming ownership of the laws of the land and manipulating them in favour of their interests. Lochhead talks in her Introduction of finding in Molière 'an ending of quite explicit political satire which bland English translations totally lost'. However firmly this is actually present in the original – Molière's ending seems more interested in flattering the king than in satire – Lochhead's version created or translated a political resonance unlikely to be lost by Scottish audiences in the eighties, generally suspicious of the government of the day and the affluent Toryism on which it depended.

In emphasising the form as well as the meaning of what her characters said, Lochhead's use of rhyme also highlights the flexible, unusual nature of the Scots vocabulary on which she sometimes hilariously, sometimes triumphantly relies for the completion of her lines. Though the Officer's suavely corrupt assurance of Government power provided a concluding comic climax, it was earlier surpassed in the Lyceum production by the audience's relish of the language Dorine employs to deal with Tartuffe in Act III scene ii. Suggesting that Dorine should cover up her 'whidjies', Tartuffe complains that

> It's evil sichts lik yon, I'm sure it is,
> That swall men's thochts wi' impurities.

Dorine replies:

> You must be awfy fashed wi' flesh tae fire
> Yir appetites sae quick wi' Base Desire.

> As fur masel', Ah'm no that easy steered.
> If you were barescud-nakit, aye and geared
> Up guid and proaper, staunin' hoat for houghmagandie
> I could lukk and lukk ett you, and no get randy.

An emphatic, terminal position in the line helps assert the gallus colloquialism of the term 'randy', but celebrates even more strongly the suggestively wild-sounding 'houghmagandie'. Once again, the peculiarity and particulars of language are installed as central elements of performance – as performers themselves, occupying the audience's attention as objects of relish and surprise.

Typically, too, feeling – or failing to feel – randy about potential 'houghmagandie' is linguistically more weird and wonderful than anything other translations manage; and even, once again, a slight expansion on Molière's original, in which Dorine remarks only:

> je ne suis point si prompte,
> Et je vous verrais nu du haut jusques en bas
> Que tout votre peau ne me tenterait pas

> (I am not so hasty:
> I could see you naked from head to foot
> And your whole body would not tempt me.)

In Hampton's version, the passage translates as:

> I'm not so easy to arouse:
> For instance, I could look at you stark naked
> and not be tempted by a single inch.

– more coldly lewd and verbally pallid than Lochhead's lines. In general, Hampton's sober blank verse avoids colloquialism or dialect almost altogether. Pernelle once pronouces herself 'discombobulated' (V, v), but this is unusual, leaving Hampton unable to match the vividness and verve Lochhead creates throughout. Hampton's Pernelle telling Flipote to 'come along, wake up, don't gawk at me!' is a pale shadow of Lochhead's Pernelle accusing the same servant of 'staunin' in a dwamm like a big daft dug' (I, i). The conclusion Hampton's Orgon reaches about religious people – 'in future I'll recoil from them in horror/ and never miss a chance to be their scourge' – likewise hardly compares with Lochhead's Orgon's explosive 'May God damn an' blast an pit a pox on pious folk/ Ah loathe and detest them they gie me the boke' (V, i).

Such passages and many others like them illustrate the richness and colloquial immediacy of Scots language which seemed in the Lyceum theatre the most fundamental strength of Lochhead's *Tartuffe*. Straight-forward as this strength seems, it is worth investigating in more detail – if only to emphasise the theatrical potentials involved – how and why Lochhead's language exercised the sway it did over those first audiences. No doubt a full answer ought to rehearse the whole debate about the power and effectiveness of Scots language in general: for the present, it might be enough just to return to MacDiarmid's conclusion in 'Gairmscoile' – that

> It's soon', no' sense, that faddoms the herts o' men
>   . . . the rouch auld Scots I ken
> E'en herts that ha'e nae Scots'll dirl rich thro'
> As nocht else could – for here's a language rings
> Wi' datchie sesames, and names for nameless things.

Lochhead's language hardly names nameless things, but flourishes instead in the names it finds. There are many other names for houghmagandie – after all a familiar and fundamental part of life – yet few of equal phonetic richness and strangeness: certainly not the simple, sombre translation in *The Concise Scots Dictionary* as 'fornication'. Such Scots vocabulary gives a sesame sense of rediscovery, of freshly imaginative fathoming even of the familiar. The richness of Scots soon, too, dirled in the hearts of audiences seduced partly through its idiosyncrasies into a peculiar sense of community with the stage; what David Hutchison might have called 'shared identity of experience between performers and audience'. Lochhead's Scots consummated the complicities between stage and spectators discussed earlier in moral, religious and political terms; her language inhabiting the imagination of audiences with an intimacy which annulled the boundary of the footlights and made the production's words and vision, unusually completely, the possession of the whole house. MacDiarmid demanded of the drama 'a distinctly Scottish form, the dramatic equivalent of the *differentiae* of the Scots psychology':[7] the language of *Tartuffe* showed clearly how this can be achieved on the modern stage, and the enormous effectiveness of the result.

And yet in one way at least this sense of shared experience and shared expression is artificial: probably not one person in ten in audiences of *Tartuffe* could have been familiar with words like 'houghmagandie'; perhaps not one in a hundred had spoken it that week. Lochhead's Scots is like MacDiarmid's, synthetic rather than always quotidian, colloquial or confined to the norms of any single dialect, as she explains in her Introduction:

> Actually it is a totally invented . . . theatrical Scots, full of
> anachronisms, demotic speech from various eras and areas: it's
> proverbial, slangy, couthy, clichéd, catch-phrasey, and vulgar; it's
> based on Byron, Burns, Stanley Holloway, Ogden Nash and
> George Formby . . . it's deliberately varied in register − most of
> the characters except Dorine are at least bilingual and consequently
> more or less 'two-faced'.

As Lochhead describes it, the language of *Tartuffe* might seem no more
than a deliberately vulgar mish-mash of speech and style: in fact, far
from diminishing its power, its insouciant eclecticism is one of its most
fruitful features. Communication of the *differentiae* of the Scots
psychology does not necessarily require an absolutely authentic, natural
or everyday language, merely a differentiated one; one able to create at
least the *impression* of a specifically Scots speech − which lacks in reality a
standard form and is in almost every mouth something of a dialectal
mish-mash anyway.

Moreover, Lochhead's shifting, variable registers and their mutual
tensions and frictions help direct and structure her satire of the
attitudes, assumptions and world-views which are characteristic of each
form of speech. Sometimes such tensions and frictions occur simply
between the speech-styles habitual to individual characters. Recommen-
dation of restraint, common sense and sweet reason, for example, is
made to seem amusingly ineffective throughout in the voice of Cléante,
whose standard English is constantly replete with wisdom but lacks the
kind of colloquial vitality which might communicate it effectively, and
which, ironically, flourishes in the remarks of almost all the characters
around him. More frequently, however, sharp contrasts in language
appear not *between* the register of individual characters, but *within* the
speech of each. Pernelle's second speech, for example − forming the
third and fourth lines in the play − runs:

> Wait, haud oan! I've had an ample sufficiency
> Of your good manners, there's no necessity . . .

The change in register from the exclamation in dialect to the anglicism
of 'ample sufficiency' separates the second sentence, as if setting it apart
in quotation marks within the context established by the first. This
creates another kind of language as performance, through which the
character enacts her affectations and social pretensions, exploiting the
kind of 'two-faced' bilingualism Lochhead identifies. Quotation marks
actually are present − at least in the printed text − at several points:
Orgon, for example, concludes his outburst against the pious people
who all of a sudden gie him the boke, by threatening 'Ah'll "In-the-

name-o'-the-faither-son-an'-Holy-Ghost" them!' (V,i). In one way, this
is just another example – though an unusually complex one – of the
bizarre predilection for creating verbs out of nouns in Scottish colloquial
speech recently identified by Billy Connolly. It also, however, shows
how the juxtaposition of different registers helps establish critical,
satiric distances between attitudes represented in each. Speeches of this
kind hold ideas and outlooks up as it were for separate inspection and
mutual interrogation, whether the words themselves are separated by
actual or imaginary quotation marks.

Such possibilities for the mutual illumination of speech and attitude
add greatly to the comic, critical potential of Lochhead's translation,
enabling a satire sharper than Molière's locally, as well as more clearly
politically directed overall in the way discussed above. In related ways,
gradations of register in Scots colloquial speech help to incorporate into
the translation something less available to the original – the kind of
carnivalesque potential of language defined in the theories of Mikhail
Bakhtin. In studies such as *Rabelais and his World*, Bakhtin retraces
some of the fundaments of comedy to the medieval practices of carnival,
in which parodic, playful shows half-celebrated and half-mocked or
travestied the official culture of the time. Competing linguistc strata –
different social registers, forms and habits of speech, each figuring its
own set of attitudes – encapsulate and reproduce in texts such as *Tartuffe*
the same ludic, metamorphic energies of opposition as well as
engagement to official culture and its linguistic norms. Multiplication
of linguistic strata and of the carnivalesque energies they can realise is
obviously facilitated, in general, by the use of Scots – distinguished
from the official tones of standard English and the power of the media
which employ it – and particularly so by Lochhead's broad houghmagandie of intertwining dialects and styles.

This and other aspects of the success of *Tartuffe* offer several
conclusions to the contemporary Scottish theatre. Firstly, the linguistic
resourcefulness that Lochhead deploys suggests that – at least as Britain
is currently structured – Scots may be particularly adapted for political
satire, as has often been the case in the past. There is probably no real
reason why Greek tragedy – say – could not be perfectly adequately
translated into Scots, but it is harder to see what particular benefits
could be derived from the nature of the language itself. On the other
hand, as Lochhead herself remarks, there are in Scots possibilities for
political satire which in 'bland English' are 'totally lost'. Satire
obviously profits from a language that immediately declares its distance
from official culture; establishes at least an impression of solidarity and
familiarity for its audience; and in its various registers encapsulates and

allows to conflict a range of social, class and political identities. Though Greek Tragedy may await an ideal Scots version, Greek Comedy has often been successfully translated into Scots, several of Aristophanes's satiric plays appearing in Edinburgh Festivals in recent decades.[8]

Secondly, Lochhead's spectrum of registers – her free-range verbiage throughout *Tartuffe* – offers a straightforward, practical answer to the kind of question which troubled Alexander Reid in the fifties. While finding 'meaning and sincerity' regained by a return to Scots, Reid questioned

> whether a Scottish National Drama, if it comes to birth, will be written in Braid Scots or the speech, redeemed for literary purposes, of Argyle Street, Glasgow, or the Kirkgate, Leith.[9]

Lochhead's answer is to cease worrying about the question; freely appropriating, instead, whatever seems useful from any of the areas Reid mentions, and others as well. Like her irreverent, multi-faceted treatment of Mary Queen of Scots, Lochhead's language shows her belonging to a second generation of the renaissance in Scottish theatre since the war; a phase in which less importance is attached to questions of exactness and verisimilitude, whether in speech or history. Freedom from Reid's anxieties allows the kind of fruitful free play of speech discussed above: it may also free the Scottish theatre to carnivalise itself in areas other than language. Lochhead's own recent collaboration with Communicado on the production of *Jock Tamson's Bairns* which launched Glasgow's year of culture in 1990 – however successful in itself – at least showed the beginnings of this process; a free interchange of non-realistic and often physical performance styles allowing the verbal medium to fade into relative insignificance.

Communicado recently enjoyed a more assured success with Edwin Morgan's translation of Edmond Rostand's dramatisation of the life of Cyrano de Bergerac – incidentally a close friend of Molière's. As inventive, flexible and free as Lochhead's, Morgan's Scots contributed to a final lesson offered, after all, not only by *Tartuffe* but a good many other recent productions – the importance and potential of translation for the culture of a small country. A visit to a bookshop in any of the smaller nations of continental Europe will show how determined and accustomed they are to make available, to relive in their own voice, visions from elsewhere. Whatever the native powers and riches of Scottish culture, it has much to enjoy and appropriate from the wider European and indeed world theatre repertoire. Depending more firmly on the spoken word, the drama probably has more to offer in this way, more potential as a medium of translation than the novel or even poetry. Certain Scottish theatres have already shown their awareness of parts of this lesson: the Royal Lyceum, in particular, has persevered with translations of Molière by Hector MacMillan and others. And the Citizens' Theatre in Glasgow has in the past twenty years staged translations of Proust, Tolstoy, Goethe, Goldoni, Karl Kraus, Schiller, von Hoffmannsthal, Ernst Toller, Rolf Hochhuth, de Musset, Genet, and de Sade. Though almost invariably in standard English, Robert David MacDonald's translations of this material for the Citizens have at least helped to demonstrate its appeal for domestic audiences and confirmed the natural alignment of Scottish imagination and theatrical development with some of the wider contours of the European repertoire. The domestic scene can hardly fail to gain from further awareness of its consonance with other cultures, as well as of significant *differentiae*. So vivid and varied in its oral powers, Scots language should provide, as Liz Lochhead and others have shown, the necessary medium for the integration within the Scots imagination of the strengths or subtleties derived from this intercourse with other cultures. That 'houghmagandie' of style and speech in the Royal Lyceum in January 1986 not only offered the Scottish stage a complete comic achievement: it confirmed a potential whose fullest realisation may be yet to come.

NOTES

1 Alexander Reid, Introduction to *Two Scots Plays* (London: Collins, 1958).

2 Liz Lochhead, Introduction to *Tartuffe: A Translation into Scots from the Original by Molière* (Edinburgh and Glasgow: Polygon and Third Eye Centre, 1985). References are to this edition.

3 David Hutchison, 'Scottish Drama 1900–1950', in Cairns Craig, ed., *The History of Scottish Literature*, vol. 4, *Twentieth Century* (Aberdeen University Press, 1987), 164.

4 Alexander Pope, 'An Essay on Criticism', l. 357.

5 Christopher Hampton, 'A Note on the Translation', in Christopher Hampton, trans., *Molière's Tartuffe or The Impostor* (London: Faber and Faber, 1984), 8. References to Hampton's translation are to this edition.

6 The Church found the play irreligious: Louis XIV thought it funny and defended it. In Molière's 'Premier Placet: présenté au roi, sur la comédie du *Tartuffe*' (1664) he stresses his intention to attack the vices of his century in general, and, in particular, one of the most common, hypocrisy, in *Tartuffe*. The 'Placet' is reproduced in Molière, *Le Tartuffe ou L'Imposteur* (Paris: Nouveau Classiques illustrés Hachette), the source of the French quotations in this essay.

7 Hugh MacDiarmid, 'R. F. Pollock and the Art of the Theatre', in *Contemporary Scottish Studies* (London: Leonard Parsons, 1926), 186.

8 Of *The Puddocks*, Douglas Young's translation of Aristophanes's *The Frogs*, T. S. Eliot remarked that 'Aristophanes seems to fit extra-

ordinarily well into the Scots language'. Another of Young's translations from Aristophanes, *The Burdies*, was the Royal Lyceum Theatre's first-ever contribution to the Edinburgh Festival, in August 1966. Directed by Tom Fleming and starring Fulton Mackay and Duncan Macrae, the production emphasised, according to critics, pantomime and carnival aspects in the original. See Douglas Young, *Scots Burds and the Edinburgh Reviewers* (Edinburgh: Macdonald, 1966), from which the above quotation is taken (p. 35). Aristophanes has also been more recently produced in Scots versions on the Festival by 7:84.

9 Alexander Reid, op. cit., (note 1).

I am very grateful to Sarah Carpenter and Roger Savage for help and advice in preparing this essay, and to Ian Wooldridge of the Royal Lyceum Theatre for his recollections of directing the first production of *Tartuffe* in 1986.

Eight

Putting New Twists to Old Stories:[1] Feminism and Lochhead's Drama

Jan McDonald and Jennifer Harvie

In this chapter we shall examine Liz Lochhead's three published plays: *Blood and Ice*, *Dracula* and *Mary Queen of Scots Got Her Head Chopped Off*. Part One, entitled Revision: The Reconfiguration of Myths, is primarily the work of Jan McDonald. Part Two, Metatextuality, is largely by Jennifer Harvie. In choosing not to homogenise our individual critical approaches and arguments, we hope to demonstrate that a variety of feminist approaches may be rewardingly employed in examining Lochhead's drama.

REVISION: THE RECONFIGURATION OF MYTHS

'Oh, everyone thinks they know the story', says Lord Byron in Lochhead's first full length stage play *Blood and Ice* (*PW*, 111). He is referring to Mary Shelley's novel *Frankenstein*, but his remark is equally applicable to the subjects identified in the titles of Lochhead's other plays, *Dracula* and *Mary Queen of Scots Got Her Head Chopped Off*. Although based on historical events, involving 'real' characters, and/or on myths that have become part of common cultural currency, Lochhead's plays do not simply repeat and thus reify 'official' versions of myths and legends or their subversions promulgated, and accepted, by popular culture. Rather, Lochhead's work reconfigures each story, both thematically and structurally, from a feminist standpoint. The plays are thus re-visions as described by Adrienne Rich in her essay, 'When We Dead Awaken: Writing as Revision':

> Re-vision — the art of looking back, of seeing with fresh eyes, of entering an old text from a new critical direction — is for women more than a chapter in cultural history: it is an act of survival. . . .
> We need to know the writing of the past, and know it differently

than we have ever known it; not to pass on a tradition but to break
its hold over us.[2]
Lochhead's plays re-examine the myths, roles, and images which
historically have limited the signifying possibilities of 'women' — and
hence the roles open to women.

Blood and Ice

In *Blood and Ice*, Mary Shelley is presented, not only as the reluctant
author of *Frankenstein*, a novel which critics have interpreted as
autobiographical, but as the even more reluctant author of her own
'story'. In order to take control of the latter, she must deconstruct and
reconfigure the various mythologies that she (and co-incidentally the
audience) has inherited, not least the myths of her celebrated parents,
William Godwin and Mary Wollstonecraft. Lord Byron aptly sums up
her 'undeconstructed' state in his lines, 'Poor Mary — Mary. Wearing
her mother round her neck and her father on her sleeve' (*PW*, 94). The
miniature portrait of her mother who died giving birth to her is both a
decoration and an albatross.

'Hearts' rather than 'fathers' are worn on sleeves. Despite Mary's
passionate loyalty to William Godwin whose approval she tirelessly
sought, after whom she named both her son and the fictional child in
her book, and to whom she dedicated that 'hideous progeny,' her novel,
she must cease to be 'Godwin's daughter wishing to convince us — and
her papa — that she has her *head* in the right place' (*PW*, 95).

The protagonist's self-realisation in the course of the play, which
Lochhead suggests is set entirely in the consciousness of Mary Shelley
(*PW*, 118), is marked by the success she has in gaining ownership of her
intellectual and emotional development. She moves to being the subject
and narrator of her own story.

At the outset, Mary believes that even her personal relationship with
Shelley is the result of her parentage. Shelley 'was half in love with Mary
before [he] even met her' because he 'worshipped Godwin, his politics,
his reason'. He wanted Godwin as *his* father and his relationship with
Mary would make him a surrogate son of his idol. But this relationship
would make Mary his sister. 'Mary is my soul's sister', he rejoices. Yet
they are also lovers, and Mary's half-sister, Claire, voices the commonly
held view that the progeny of a brother and sister are 'Imbeciles.
Monsters. The rotten fruit of incest' (*PW*, 93). Of course Mary and
Shelley are only metaphorical siblings, and their children are not
literally monsters. But what might be monstrous about their 'incest' is
the way it exploits Mary as an object of exchange or conduit of desire for
Shelley's and Godwin's male homosocial relationship.[3]

Shelley met Mary at her father's house, but Mary was quick to remove
him to her mother's territory, the graveyard where Mary Wollstonecraft
was buried and where the lovers held their meetings, 'a sacred place'

where they played like children at blowing bubbles and sailing paper boats (*PW*, 93). Shelley woos her as her father's daughter. She woos him as her mother's child. The blood spilt at Mary's birth is thematically and symbolically linked both to her own menstrual blood and to the blood she sheds on her miscarriage.

> CLAIRE   Your mama died! I heard Maria tell Cook your mama died giving birth to you. Rivers of blood she said.

Mary turns away upset, gathering at her skirt. Claire points to Mary's shift.

> CLAIRE   Mary! Mary! What's the matter? Mary, you're bleeding, your shift is all covered, what is it?
>
> MARY   (*coldly fascinated*) Great . . . gouts and spatters . . . crimson trickle, tickling . . . a thin dark red line running . . . scribbling as if a quill was dipped in blood and scribbled . . .
>
> CLAIRE   What is it? Mary! Mama! Mama! Come quick, Mary's bleeding. Mary's dying!
>
> (*PW*, 88)

Noting the reference to the 'quill scribbling in blood' as both Marys sought to confront gender issues in their writing, albeit in contrasting ways, one must recognise the paradox of 'blood' as both life-giving and life-threatening, a paradox to be further developed in *Dracula*. While Mary Wollstonecraft bled to death giving birth to her daughter, Mary Shelley's bleeding was stopped and her life saved by her immersion in the bath of ice. Her child, however, was aborted. Mary is the survivor both of the bleeding which killed her mother and of that which led to the death of her child. Both 'daughter' and 'mother' roles are shed as she establishes herself as subject.

In the play, Mary's liberation from both her living father and her dead mother is effected in parallel scenes by the intervention of two characters, Lord Byron and Mary's maid, Elise. Byron verbalises her growing doubts about previous certainties and Elise's actions expose to questioning much of her parents' teaching.

Political Justice is to Byron 'euphoric bombast' (*PW*, 94) and in his role-playing experiment with the maid, Elise, who frankly admits that in a life-threatening fire she would save herself rather than her neighbour, however philosophically gifted that neighbour might be, he exposes to Mary the false rhetoric of her father's elitist intellectual position.

Lochhead highlights through Byron the state of Mary's progress to self-awareness in the following exchange, which precedes his questioning of Elise.

BYRON   And do you know who Godwin is, Elise?

ELISE   He is Mrs Shelley's father, sir.

BYRON   Indeed. Mary Godwin's famous father.

(PW, 95)

Byron underlines the point that Mary is still her father's creature intellectually by calling her 'Mary Godwin'.

The character of Elise, whose silent, pervasive presence on stage throughout large sections of the play is a reminder to Mary and the play's audience of the class which is ignored by the philosophers and poets, is used by Lochhead to free Mary from the myth which she has created around her mother. Elise has been taught to read and write by Mary who sees it as a 'duty to educate her, enlighten her' (*PW*, 96) – an attitude viewed sceptically by Byron in whose opinion this benevolence is nothing less than cultural imperialism ('I won't tyrannise the world,' he says, 'by force-feeding it freedom' [*PW*,96]). Elise has read *A Vindication of the Rights of Woman* and when she is dismissed by Mary and told sharply that a mere maid cannot understand such sentiments as are enunciated in the book, she responds violently:

ELISE   . . . Even though I was only a maidservant. Indeed I understood it very well. The Rights of Woman. The marvellous Mary Wollstonecraft was very keen on freedom for Woman. At least freedom for the woman with six hundred a year and a mill-owning husband to support her – and a bevy of maidservants sweeping and starching and giving suck to her squalling infants – not to speak of her rutting husband.

Mary slaps her hard. Elise and Mary looking at each other . . .

Don't you think we are sisters? Are we not somewhat alike?

(PW, 107)

As Mary plays with the doll which Elise made for William, the puppet which is on one side herself and on the other Elise, a toy that made William 'screech and laugh – to see his mama, and how under her skirt she was but a maid' (*PW*, 114), she realises that she must expand and develop her mother's assertions of equality, as she links the servitude of all women with the demeaning status of their maids.

> MARY   To be born poor is to be born a slave. To be born a woman
>   is to be born a slave. Poor Elise, you were a slave's slave —
>   and that's a jumbled up collection of wood and wires!
>
> (*PW*, 114)

As Mary comes close to acknowledging her 'sisterhood in slavery' with Elise, she casts off Claire, the half-sister imposed on her by William Godwin's second marriage whom her 'papa had told her to love' (*PW*, 88). The 'mirror' scene in which Claire and Mary '*brush out their long hair slowly with silver hairbrushes, each other's image*' (*PW*, 86), shows Claire seeking to establish the similarities between them, while Mary, resistant, stresses the differences. Prophetically, as it turns out, Claire complains, 'Lord, Mary, I think you love Elise better than your own sister. But then I'm not your sister, you do keep reminding me' (*PW*, 88).

Despite Mary's constant assertion that there is no tie of 'blood' between her and Claire, she has to go further and exorcise once and for all this inherited 'false' sister whose spurious claims on her jeopardise her relationship with Shelley, contribute to the deaths of her own children, and deny her the chance to foster Harriet's.

The final exorcism takes place in the dream that she recounts to Shelley near the end of the play (*PW*, 114). Elise, with the help of instructions from 'Mary Wollstonecraft's Pattern Book' is sewing a life size puppet, identified initially as Claire because of the flounces it is wearing, but when these are pulled back by Shelley in a sexual frenzy, it is revealed to be Mary herself. This 'doll' thus links Mary and Claire in the same way that the toy made for William linked Mary and Elise. It is also the female monster in her novel to whom Frankenstein (and Mary as Frankenstein's creator) denied life. The dream ends with a cry. 'Elise, I should not have sent you away. Claire, I should have sent you away long ago' (*PW*, 115). Mary must learn to reexamine and redefine 'sisterhood' – the ways in which women are and, importantly, are not the same.

Mary Shelley finds the spark of life that she and others have denied her in her own *Frankenstein*. 'Read that story,' advises Byron as he sacrilegiously flicks her mother's pendant. In the first published version of *Blood and Ice*, Lochhead expressly links each of the characters to one of the fictional roles in *Frankenstein*: Shelley is Frankenstein; Byron, the Monster; Claire, Frankenstein's betrothed, Elizabeth; and Elise, Justine, the maid falsely accused of the murder of Frankenstein's young brother, William. This doubling underlines the interpretation that Mary was drawing directly on her personal experiences and relationships in her creative fiction. The 1985 text discards this overt role-playing device and draws the parallels more subtly. For example in Act 2, scene 3, Mary rehearses her story aloud:

> But the creature went out into the world. A child called William was killed. And a maid unjustly accused.

> (*PW*, 106)

The next scene shows Mary mourning over *her* dead children, Clara and William, and spurning the sympathetic overtures of the maid, Elise, whom she blames for encouraging her to take the ailing children on the trip that precipitated their deaths. There is then a 'timechange/ flashback' to the 'real' version of the scene, in which it is Elise who emphasises the children's ill-health and pleads with Mary not to travel. Back in the present time, Mary curtly dismisses her maid, 'unjustly accused'. Theatrically, the second version is less cumbersome and the point that Mary Shelley chooses to 'kill' the fictitious William (who closely resembled descriptions of her own child) before she becomes in part responsible for the death of the real William, is more subtly made.

In addition, this change in the second version means the focus is much more on Mary. The characters in her novel are not representations of her companions, but are facets of herself. This is made clear in her last speech:

> I thought: I am Frankenstein, the creator who loves creation and hates its results.

(A reference both to her children and to 'the hideous progeny' of the novel.)

> Then I thought: no, I am the monster, poor misunderstood creature feared and hated by all mankind.

(A reference, perhaps, to her ostracisation by society after her flight with Shelley [*PW*, 108], her disaffection from her father, her uneasy relations with her half-sister and the disintegration of her partnership with Shelley.)

> And then I thought: it is worse, worse than that, I am the female monster, gross, gashed, ten times more hideous than my male counterpart, denied life, tied to the monster bed for ever.

(A 'monster' created by her parents' idealism coupled by their inadvertent or deliberate desertion of her, 'gross and gashed' by pregnancy and childbirth, 'denied life' both in the sense that her children died and that she was frustrated in self-fulfilment, tied to a 'monster' [or dead man's] bed, not only as Shelley's widow, but even as his wife.)

But now I see who I am in my book. I am Captain Walton,
explorer. Survivor. My own cool narrator.

(PW, 115)

The last image of Mary is of her sitting down to write. The question as
to whether or not she will heed the call of Frankenstein to Walton 'to
endure the cold' or withdraw to 'the warm firesides of the withdrawing
rooms of England' (*PW*, 116) remains unanswered.

Dracula

Although vampire myths are rooted in world cultural history extending
in time as far back as Lilith and in location from Mongolia to Europe,
Lochhead uses as her primary source Bram Stoker's novel *Dracula*
(1898), a work that is very much in the nineteenth-century Romantic
tradition. The Romantic model for the vampire which reached its
apotheosis in Stoker's *Dracula* was that of a Byronic hero.[4] The victim is
almost invariably a young woman of good family and high moral
principles who is simultaneously attracted to and repelled by her
attacker.

Contemporary reviews of Stoker's novel attributed to it none of the
post-Freudian overtones that were to accrue to it in the twentieth
century. Hindsight, and a re-evaluation of Victorian social, and
particularly sexual, values, have led critics to interpret Dracula's female
victims as repressed women who, unable to acknowledge their own
sexual drive, conjure up a fiendish 'other' who forces them into a
physical relationship which they loath but also partly enjoy. The result
of unleashing their sexual desire is bodily weakness and usually death.
In the Romantic vampire tradition, female sexuality is inextricably
linked to evil, 'unnatural,' and self-destructive forces which could not
be accepted as part of a woman's being and which, therefore, had to be
attributed to a 'spell' or bewitching laid upon her by an outsider.

Nina Auerbach, while admitting that '[i]t is fashionable to perceive
and portray Dracula as an emanation of Victorian sexual repression',
puts forward the alternative view that, 'it seems plausible to read the
novel as a *fin de siècle* myth of newly-empowered womanhood, whose two
heroines are violently transformed from victims to instigators of their
story'.[5] This may not be a particularly apt interpretation of Stoker's
novel, but it provides a useful starting point for an examination of how
Lochhead reconfigures the Romantic version of the vampire myth in her
play.

The nineteenth-century male writer's view that a fiendish vampire
preyed on young women, awakening in them desires that were best left
dormant, is replaced by a twentieth-century female writer's view that
Dracula liberated his victims from their sexual and psychological
repressions induced by a patriarchal culture and its dominant religion,
Christianity.

One of the sources of the play was *The Wise Wound* by Penelope Shuttle and Peter Redgrove. In the chapter entitled 'The Mirror of Dracula,' the authors speculate on the 'benefits' bestowed by Dracula on his women.

> Before they were bitten, they were chlorotic weak creatures with the vapours, dressed in stiff constricting corseted garments, who spoke in faint genteel voices expressing deep frustration. After their blood had been shed for the vampire though (and it is always from the *neck*; as we say the neck or cervix of the womb) and they suffered their first death into their new lives as vampires – why, what creatures they became! The corsets were replaced by practical white unhampering shrouds, very free and easy. . . . Their eyes shone, they spoke energy with every glance, and their smiles, full of bright teeth with handsome canines, were flashing and free.[6]

Lochhead, both in the play and in a poem in *Bagpipe Muzak* entitled 'Lucy's Diary', represents Lucy as anorexic.

> This gross flesh I will confine
> in the whalebone of my very own
> hunger.
>
> ('Lucy's Diary' *BM*, 62)

She describes herself as 'crazy Lucy, mad sleepwalking skinny Lucy with her migraines and her over-vivid imagination' (*MQD*, 85). In common with many anorexics, she suffers from amenorrhea.

> All term
> I would not bleed
> for Matron, Mama, Mademoiselle
> nor my sister, Mina.
>
> ('Lucy's Diary' *BM*, 62)

On the one hand, then, the audience sees Lucy as immature, an undeveloped child, not a woman. On the other, Lochhead, using her favourite device of doubling, represents Lucy as the vampire in Castle Dracula who tempts Jonathan Harker into 'languorous ecstasy' and to whom he surrenders the key that would allow him to escape and return to Mina (*MQD*, 100). In this role, Lucy tells Jonathan, 'I am thousands of years old, I'm not just a little girl' (*MQD*, 128).

The advent of Dracula on the safe shores of England is coincidental with the recommencement of Lucy's periods and the beginning of her sexual maturity. The power of Dracula is linked to the waxing and waning of the moon which is also temporally and symbolically linked to the rhythm of women's menstruation. 'I've got a visitor . . . Must have come in the night . . .', says Lucy, 'My friend, my bloody friend.' 'The curse', replies Mina, with clear dramatic irony. A curse and a secret that 'No gentlemen need ever know', the bleeding from the womb and from the neck being both the promise of life and the prefiguring of death (*MQD*, 105). So, as in *Blood and Ice*, blood has both negative and positive connotations. Yet Lucy's fiancé still treats her not as a woman, but as a sick child. He shaves off her hair, thus constructing her as a prepubertal youth rather than a mature woman. His professional medical (male) ethics will not allow him to spend the night in her room, thus leaving the way clear for the entry of her 'real' lover, Dracula.

When Lucy appears to her fiancé and his friends as a vampire, she is described as 'lovely and terrifying and ethereal' (*MQD*, 134). She is accompanied by two children, a boy and a girl, each holding her by the hand. She speaks: 'Come, come with me Arthur. Come to me, my arms are hungry for you. Leave those others and come to me, my husband, come' (*MQD*, 134). This image of Lucy transformed into a mature woman, initiating sexual union with her chosen partner, contrasts with Stoker's transformation of his virginal heroine into a creature of pure evil: 'They were Lucy's eyes in form and colour; but Lucy's eyes unclean and full of hell-fire instead of the pure gentle others we knew . . . the lips were crimson with fresh blood . . . the stream trickled over her chin and stained the purity of her lawn death robe.'[7] Stoker's Dracula condemns Lucy to spiritual damnation: Lochhead's Dracula gives her sexuality. But in the society of which she is a member, to be a sexualised woman is also to be demonic. Arthur Seward acknowledges his own, and his masculine culture's, responsibility for such travesty in the scene in which, totally avoiding the sensationalisation of Stoker's novel, he '*performs the ritual of staking* Lucy'. 'Lucy, my darling, forgive me . . . I failed you' (*MQD*, 141–2).

Mina in Lochhead's play is Lucy's sister, rather than her impecunious friend, as in the novel. The dramatist's fascination with 'sisterhood' as witnessed in the Mary/Claire, Mary/Elise relationships in *Blood and Ice* and that of the 'sister' queens, Mary and Elizabeth, in *Mary Queen of Scots*, probably motivated this alteration to Stoker's text as much as dramaturgical economy. These sisters, however, are as different as 'chalk and cheese' to Jonathan, and 'night and day' to Dracula. Dramatically, Mina is more akin to Mary Shelley, with whom she shares the same ambivalent relationship to female servants, intellectually seeking to view them as equals and friends, while emotionally perpetuating feelings of ownership over their bodies and minds. Like Mary Shelley, she is, in many ways, a conventional woman, disturbed by behaviour that does not fit in with the social codes of her class, and, like Mary, she sees her 'sister' as the embodiment of disruptive or disturbing forces that threaten to wreck or challenge her own relationship with her sexual partner.

Lochhead's Mina is not, like Stoker's, the epitome of ideal Victorian womanhood. Yet, true to the source, Jonathan in the play consciously determines to distance his fiancée from the predatory women of Castle Dracula. In a composite setting, representing on stage, Heartwood, the asylum, and the Castle, Jonathan screams, 'Those . . . women . . . My God. Help me, I . . . Mina! Mina has nothing in common with them.' The ensuing stage direction ironically comments:

> But as we see Mina, in her underwear and barefoot and in her indolence and impotence, wander round Heartwood, we might momentarily see her as a very recently powdered one of them?

(MQD, 101)

And 'one of them' she becomes. Condemned to impotence by her male colleagues, who seek to 'protect' her, sexually challenged by Jonathan's confessed attraction to her silly little sister, Mina admits Dracula, who makes with her a deeper and more profound pact than he had with Lucy. He promises his mate:

> Oh, and you will be revenged on them. Not one of them but shall minister to your needs. You will love me for all the love they all shall spill for you.

(MQD, 137)

Mina's awakening by Dracula is not to sexual maturity, but to other forms of power. The brute force of the men cannot move the gates of the vampire's castle, but one word from Mina and '[t]he gates fly open wide', revealing 'Mina, wrapped in furs and deathly pale, blindfolded, reaching out straight ahead of her' (MQD, 143–4). Iconically reconfigured as Nemesis/Justice, Mina is implacable. This is the gift of Dracula – it was what she wanted.

In general, feminists have eschewed vampire mythology, disliking the image it presented of women either as victims or predators. By expanding the mythology to include the idea of women being transformed by the exposure of a transgressive impulse, Lochhead has added a new dimension to the legend. It is important to her that Dracula cannot enter unless first invited. Lochhead's women subconsciously desire his intrusion. Terrifying as it may be, it signals liberation, empowerment, which the women effect for themselves.

Mary Queen of Scots Got Her Head Chopped Off

In this play, Lochhead once again turns to an amalgam of history and popular myth for her source. Historically, Mary, dubbed by her English royal cousin 'the daughter of debate', remains the 'enigma' that Ian B. Cowan sought to explicate:

> The enigma of Mary Stuart extends over every aspect of the queen's life. . . . Friend and foe alike, however, attest to her charms, and this coupled to the tragic story of her downfall, captivity and the halo of martyrdom which accompanied her execution, has undoubtedly swayed the judgements of many historians who might otherwise have condemned her. And in the realms of literature, it has rendered her position impregnable.[8]

In her selection of historical facts, Lochhead chooses those which present a sympathetic portrait of Mary, reinforcing her legendary status as victim, of Elizabeth, of John Knox, and of her husband, Darnley, and his band of unruly noblemen. Lochhead does not, as she might well have done, go so far as to foreground historical sources that undermine the romantic image of the martyr Queen and present Mary as a highly political woman who comes to grief because of the power of the forces ranged against her rather than as a result of her own inadequacies. Lochhead offers the audience not a re-vision of the historical Mary, but a re-vision of the myth that popular culture has built up around her.

If the piece is indeed 'iconoclastic' as an early critic labelled it,[9] it is so in form rather than content. The historical characters open the play as 'snarling' and 'posing' circus animals in a tawdry and grotesque parade, controlled by the whip of La Corbie, a ragged, ironic commentator on the action (*MQD*, 11–12). They close it as twentieth-century children, no less brutish and bigoted in their street games.

Within this framework the actors are called upon to assume several roles. Although 'Mary' occupies the title role, the actress representing her also plays Elizabeth's maid, Marion, and Mairn, the youthful whore who attracts John Knox. Likewise, the Elizabeth actor plays Mary's maid, Bessie, and Mairn's street companion, Leezie. As in *Blood and Ice* and *Dracula*, mistresses and maids are thematically and structurally intertwined. As Bothwell flirts with Bessie/Elizabeth, Mary acknowledges the sexual *frisson* (*MQD*, 29). As Marion/Mary urges Elizabeth to 'follow her heart' in legalising her union with Leicester, the English Queen proposes a union between Leicester and Mary, who would be willing to marry *her* if she were a man, but who, in fact, weds her creature, Darnley. The judicious use of doubling (and trebling) fragments individual characterisation preventing continuous identification by the audience with the plight of any one dramatic character.

Mary does not stand alone centre-stage as a heroine. From the outset, she and Elizabeth are thrown into juxtaposition. La Corbie parades both queens in the bestial circus procession which opens the action, stressing the similarities of their regal status, but highlighting the contrasting material conditions of each kingdom.

Mary and Elizabeth, or the actors representing them, are both present on stage throughout much of the action. In parallel scenes, both women grieve for the loss of their respective mothers in their early childhood years. In Elizabeth's dream sequence, her 'father' tosses away the headless doll that represents her mother, as childishly she calls for her 'Mam.' Mary recounts to Darnley how she 'grat full sore' when *her* mother sent her to France with religious icons sewn into her clothes. Mary additionally, suffers the loss of her namesake, Mary, virgin mother of God, whom she is forbidden to worship publicly in Scotland. Paradoxically, 'widow' Mary is a virgin, while Elizabeth, the so-called Virgin Queen, is certainly married 'in the eyes of God,' if not by the letter of the law. Both women are presented with the same string of foreign suitors. Both prefer a liaison with one of their subjects, but Elizabeth has a vision of Leicester stealing her crown and resolves that he will never master her. Mary will not share her regal status with Darnley in any way but in name, yet she turns to Bothwell in 'despair' and 'black joy,' thus losing her kingdom and ultimately her life. In the penultimate scene, Mary is represented as '*on her knees caught in her tight spot and at the other side of the stage, balancing her, is Elizabeth in (quite literally) her tight spot. All alone too*' (MQD, 63).

Rather than focus solely on the plight of Mary as a closed historical character, Lochhead, using cross-cutting and role-playing techniques which highlight the similarities and contrasts in the choices open to the two women and in the decisions they take, investigates the conflicting personal and public demands made on women.

METATEXTUALITY

Lochhead's plays resist and challenge traditional representations of femininity by re-configuring cultural stories and myths with women characters, problematising traditional feminine signifiers, and foregrounding the material conditions which may affect women's cultural construction. But beyond problematising already existent representations, Lochhead's plays further encourage their audiences to rethink the entire notion of representation, and particularly the notion of representing women. Through a persistent metatextuality – a representational emphasis on representation itself – Lochhead's plays increase audience awareness of, and focus audience attention on, the ways in which meaning, including what women may 'mean,' is textually produced and controlled.

Representation and performance are thematically emphasised throughout Lochhead's plays (in the imagery of, for instance, mirrors and pictures), initiating a metatextuality that is developed through foregrounding each play's own narrative construction, and explicit quoting from other texts. Highlighting the textual production of meaning, not least by changing the meanings of other texts by changing their contexts, Lochhead's plays indicate that no representation is ever a mimetic reflection of the 'real', but is always the product of ideologically influenced context and choice. The plays' audiences are thus encouraged to think critically about how other texts , have represented, or more precisely constructed, women and femininity, and to engage actively in producing new meanings.

Metatextuality thus acts as one of several alienation devices evident in Lochhead's plays, each device estranging the audience from a complacent acceptance of the 'reality' presented in each play, and encouraging scepticism about any notion of reality as 'true,' fixed, and therefore unchangeable. From *Blood and Ice*, to *Dracula*, to *Mary Queen of Scots God Her Head Chopped Off*, elements which might contribute to audience alienation increase, so that the audience's fixity of perspective is likewise increasingly problematised. The plays' audiences are presented with increasingly unresolved and unresolvable texts, thus suggesting that the process of creating meaning may be more significant than any final stable product. Actively representing women rather than providing static representations, Lochhead's plays encourage fluid, adaptable understandings of 'women' and 'femininity', resisting appropriation into a stable and therefore potentially reductive model.

Textual self-referentiality and self-problematisation begin in Lochhead's plays with repeated emphases through imagery and plot on representations and acts of representation. In *Blood and Ice* Mary and Claire, and Mary and Elise are linked through their mimetic representation as dolls and in mirrors. As Mary emphasises, however, there are many ways in which the three are not 'somewhat alike', Claire and Elise are and are not Mary, and the implicit contradiction between each mimetic representation and each woman's differences problematises the 'truth' of mimetic 'reflection'. What destabilising mimesis specifically puts at stake here is a notion of women's experience as universal, a notion of a sisterhood which transcends cultural and material conditions. Women may share the physical characteristics of our sex − we may look 'the same' − but we may not share the same experiences − our genders may be variously socially constructed and inscribed.

In the opening scene of *Dracula*, Lucy with her mirror is prepared for (re)presentation to Jonathan. Being costumed before the audience, Lucy says, 'The day they put me in stays and made me wear my hair up I swore blind if I was to be pinched and skewered then I was to have the thinnest thinnest waist and the highest highest hair' (*MQD*, 73). 'They' are unnamed, but Lucy is obviously fashioned according to some cultural imperatives determined not by herself but by others more powerful. The maid in *Dracula*, Florrie, similarly represents not, in a way, herself, but others' expectations of what she should be. First befriended and then bullied by her mistresses, Florrie tells herself, 'Better pinch yourself, Florrie my girl, look in the mirror, pinch yourself to see if you're real' (*MQD*, 98). Fulfilling the roles dictated by her employers, however contradictory those roles are, Florrie is not a 'reality' but a function of what others expect.

Using picture imagery, Lochhead's plays suggest that through their representation, subjects, particularly women, may be appropriated or controlled as objects. Jonathan in *Dracula* proudly carries photographs of his fiancée Mina, Lucy, and Florrie. Admiring the photographs, Dracula comments,

> Is very wonderful thing this photography. Although I am sure that portrait painters do not agree with us! Each common clerk can keep his last duchess in sepia inside his pigskin wallet.

(*MQD*, 91)

With an intertextual aside to Browning's 'My Last Duchess', the play emphasises how representation may reinforce women's cultural commodification, as they can be shown off, objectified in absentia. In *Mary Queen of Scots Got Her Head Chopped Off*, Mary says hopefully, 'They say [Elizabeth] wears my portrait I sent her in that wee jewelled case hangin' fae her girdle.' (The likelihood that Elizabeth does wear the portrait is suggested in La Corbie's ironically dangling comment, 'Oh aye . . .!' [*MQD*, 16].) Significantly, however, as it is Elizabeth who may or may not choose to wear the locket – who controls Mary's 'representation' – it is Elizabeth who controls Mary's fate. Repeatedly, imagery of mirrors, pictures, and presentation in Lochhead's plays suggests that representation potentially means a falsification of similarities, objectification, and appropriation.

Combined with this pervasive metatextual imagery is a consistent foregrounding of narrative construction, both the constructions of the plays themselves and of the characters' individual stories within the plays. With the plays' metatextual imagery working primarily to focus audience attention on the appropriative potentials of representation, this narrative metatextuality focuses attention more specifically on the purposes of that appropriation; in other words, *why* representations, including narratives, are controlled the way they are, and *who* controls them.

In *Blood and Ice*, for instance, the emphasis on narrative provided by Byron's commands ('Write that story!' [*PW*, 101] and 'Read your story' [*PW*, 111]) and indeed the play's entire construction, which parallels Mary's life with her reading from her 'story', highlight the play as Mary's narrative construction, formulated according to her beliefs, her biases, and importantly, her often contradictory feelings. Of course, the play is not literally Mary's construction but Liz Lochhead's, with Lochhead imagining/image-ing Mary's perspective. But Lochhead even implicitly problematizes her own narrative authority in appropriating Mary's perspective by problematising Mary's narrative authority in relation to the characters in *her* fiction, *Frankenstein*.

In *Dracula*, narrative construction is foregrounded particularly through stage directions which cue an overt theatricality or non-naturalistic performance style. At Dracula's first entrance, which does not occur until scene seven, stage directions and Dracula's opening line may be read as self-reflexive, acknowledging the narrative importance of the arrival of the play's title character and antagonist. '*At last, arms open in welcome, out of us, out of auditorium in a sweep, Dracula himself*', read the stage directions, themselves rhetorically reinforcing the suspense of Dracula's anticipated entrance by withholding his name until the final phrase. 'At last,' reiterates the Count, 'I am Dracula' (*MQD*, 89).

Scene ten offers a composite crisis: Jonathan escapes Castle Dracula, Mina breaks down over her wedding dress ('Oh, Lucy, I don't think I'll ever wear it' [*MQD*, 103].), Lucy sleep walks, and Dracula's ship lands at Whitby. '*The storm Renfield and Dracula have been brewing up*' (*MQD*, 103) develops and breaks. The storm is intensely theatrical: '*A sudden streak of lightning and the wind bashes the window open. Noise.*' . . . '*Storm starts in earnest. . . . Thunder, lightning, wind. And louder*' (*MQD*, 104). And the fact that it is constructed by our antagonists emphasises not only Dracula's and Renfield's 'authorship' of the other characters' crises, but specifically emphasises the play's construction of its own crisis, its own turning point – its admission of Dracula to the protagonists' world. The 'threat' posed by Dracula is complex, but, among other things, he imperils Mina's and Jonathan's marriage and Lucy's sanity and life – what might also be read as conservative, capitalist, heterosexist notions of coupling and female behaviour. Foregrounding the construction of these threats, Lochhead's *Dracula* brings an angle of irony to them, so that the audience may wonder if what Dracula precipitates, released female sexuality and power, really is a threat, and if so, for whom.

In *Mary Queen of Scots Got Her Head Chopped Off*, the metatheatricality already evident in Lochhead's earlier plays goes several steps further. Of the three plays under discussion here, *Mary Queen of Scots* requires the most consistent non-naturalistic performance style, with considerable doubling of roles (where character switching often occurs on stage, before the audience), and numerous non-naturalistically explained songs and dances, all contained within the narrative provided by the ever-present La Corbie. Stressing the performance of *Mary Queen of Scots Got Her Head Chopped Off* precisely as a performative and therefore an interpretative act, the play emphasises that representation does not neutrally reflect, but actively interprets.

This play also includes the most overt example of a metadramatic scene, with its play within the play, the mummers' scene. This scene shows how performative representation constructs people and situations according to its own prerogatives, as the mummers cast Mary as King, Darnley as Salome, and an unsuspecting Riccio as the sacrificial victim, John the Baptist. This situation resembles the scene in *Blood and Ice* where Byron, as 'director,' controls the 'performance' in which Elise plays another victim, and Mary, the male philosopher. And as Mary Shelley resisted the role thrust on her by Byron, Mary Queen of Scots resists the role of King Herod assigned her by the mummers. The mummers give the cue,' – Herod said!' '*And they force a bit of paper on* MARY, *forcing her to read Herod's part*', repeating '*more forcefully*', 'Herod said! –' (*MQD*, 54). Manipulated by the mummers as Mary Shelley and Elise were manipulated by Byron, Mary Stuart complies, but not without a hesitation that makes clear her resistance to fulfilling the role. Superficially, it may appear that both Marys are empowered by being assigned the roles of a male philosopher and a king. But both roles are assigned by the male characters with a healthy dose of ill-disguised irony and both roles lead to a loss of power for the women: Mary Shelley's beliefs are mocked and undermined, her charge Elise is humiliated, and Mary Stuart's 'maist special servant wha [she] loved richt well' (*MQD*, 56), is murdered before her eyes, the shock of the scene further endangering herself and her unborn child.[10] The power lies not with the subject of representation, but with who controls that representation. And again, while the subject of representation ostensibly may be empowered women, Lochhead frames this more specifically as women whose power is undermined through their objectification by men who control the representation. Both Marys must try to achieve control over their own representation. The plays' audiences must gauge who controls representation and how.

One final important technique employed by Lochhead in foregrounding narrative construction is her use of language. Although she uses language which is primarily naturalistic, poetic language repeatedly asserts itself in her plays, showing language as potentially having more than one level of meaning beyond naturalistic referents. The monologues which frame Mary Shelley's flashbacks, for instance, use language as more associative than directly referential. Of the moonlight, Mary says,

> My element. I swim in it and I do not drown. I dream in it.
> Swimming, dwamming, dreaming . . . drowning. Sleeping in a
> dead man's bed. Not yet thirty and I'm sleeping in a dead man's
> bed.
>
> (*PW*, 83)

The moonlight becomes, among other things, an emblem of Mary's isolation and yet also her power (she does not drown). Her meaning is polyvalent and non-prescriptive, emphasising that it need not, indeed it does not, mean simply one thing.

Similarly, La Corbie's framing narrative in *Mary Queen of Scots* is self-consciously rhythmic, imagistic, and, precisely as La Corbie points out, it is *her* narrative, inscribed with choices and emphases specific to 'her' perspective.

> Country: Scotland. Whit like is it?
> It's a peatbog, it's a daurk forest.
> It's a cauldron o' lye, a saltpan or a coal mine
> If you're gey lucky it's a bricht bere meadow or a park o' kye.
> Or mibbe . . . it's a field o' stanes.
> . . .
>
> It depends. It depends . . . Ah dinna ken whit like
> *your* Scotland is.
> Here's mines.
>
> (*MQD*, 11)

La Corbie's language is stylised, bearing the influence of her sardonic, irreverent character, and framing the play as an irreverent reading of history as narrative. Juxtaposed with naturalistic language, these examples of poetic language and others like them in Lochhead's plays denaturalise the apparently real referentiality of naturalistic language, showing that all language is constructed and ideologically inscribed. La Corbie, for instance, does not hide her ironic attitude to the story she is re-telling, and in so doing, she problematizes the neutrality of other tellings of history.

In a technique similar to the juxtaposing of naturalistic and poetic language, Lochhead's plays juxtapose their own narratives with other writers' narratives, 'making strange' those narratives and highlighting some of their assumptions. Mary in *Blood and Ice* quotes portions of Coleridge's 'The Rime of the Ancient Mariner', re-contextualising them and testing some of the Romantic inscriptions of femininity. '"Is that a Death? And are there two? Is Death that woman's mate?"' Mary recites, continuing,

> 'Her lips were red, her looks were free,
> Her locks were yellow as gold;
> Her skin was as white as leprosy,
> The Nightmare Life in Death was she,
> Who thicks man's blood with cold.'
>
> (*PW*, 98–9; cf. Coleridge, 'The Rime of the
> Ancient Mariner', II. 188–94)

'*Shelley has a fit of hysterics and hallucination, screams*' and describes Mary, as Byron points out, as 'The Lamia! Eyes in breasts, like a vision from Coleridge's Christabel!' (*PW*, 99).[11]

In both 'The Ancient Mariner' and 'Christabel', the sexualised woman ('Her lips were red, her looks were free') is constructed as demonic, heralding trial and torture for the Mariner and a loss of innocence for the Romantic idealist, Shelley. Ironically, it is Mary not Shelley who must live the torture of 'life in death', living on after the deaths of her husband and children, deaths which might have been prevented were it not for Shelley's idealism, and Mary's idealism, learned from Shelley. Feminist literary critic Anne K. Mellor suggests that 'Mary Shelley was profoundly disturbed by what she saw to be a powerful egotism at the core of romantic ideology'.[12] And Lochhead's Mary certainly expresses a profoundly ironic attitude to her husband's idealism:

> I wonder what it is like to drown? Did he expect to breathe easy in a brand new element, plunge straight in, embracing it, I would not put it past him. What bobbed up at him from the lone and level sands of the sea bottom?
>
> Nymphs? Nereids? Mermaids? All the flimsy impossible women, glittering hermaphrodites, did they tangle with him, did he clasp his sweet ideal at last?
>
> (*PW*, 115)

Regarding 'his sweet ideal', Shelley had earlier told his wife, 'Mary, Woman is the door to all life. I sink to my knees and worship at her –' and Mary replied, 'God save all women from men who worship

"Woman"' (*PW*, 113). Re-contextualising the romantic classic 'The Rime of the Ancient Mariner', *Blood and Ice* shows how male Romantic writers, including the professedly free-thinking Shelley, discursively constructed sexualised women as dangerous and transgressive, leaving virtually the only other representation for women an impossible, ever innocent, idealised 'Woman'. In Romantic ideology, Mary concludes, there is no space for a 'flesh and blood Mary' (*PW*, 115).

Lochhead's *Dracula* quotes from another text rife with images of sexualised women as the particularly horrible 'life in death', Stoker's *Dracula*. Re-contextualising Stoker's demonic representations of women as vampires, Lochhead's *Dracula* reveals Stoker's Victorian bias against female sexuality. In a scene in Castle Dracula,

> VAMPIRE 3 '*goes on her knees and bends over [Jonathan], fairly gloating. There is a deliberate voluptuousness which is both thrilling and repulsive and as she arches her neck she actually licks her lips like an animal till he can see in the moonlight the moisture shining on the scarlet lips and on the red tongue as it laps the white sharp teeth . . .*'
>
> (*MQD*, 100).[13]

And so on. As this is a stage direction, its power to alienate will depend particularly on the way it is performed. But given the extremely descriptive language employed in the passage, it might be performed non-naturalistically, historicising itself and encouraging its audience to see it, not as true, but as an ideologically inscribed representation of women, one with an investment in portraying a sexualised, assertive woman as evil and demonic.

In *Mary Queen of Scots Got Her Head Chopped Off*, Lochhead offers not a direct quotation from John Knox's *The First Blast of the Trumpet Against the Monstrous Regiment of Women*, but an extrapolated précis. In '*a parodic public parade . . . Knox, in bowler hat and with umbrella . . . is ranting:*'

> I, John Knox, do preach the evangel of Jesus Christ crucified, by repentance and faith. And justification by faith alone. Moved by my God and in humble obedience to him wha is abane us a', I hae been commandit to blaw the first blast o' the trumpet against the monstrous regiment o' women, an abomination against nature and before God; and to disclose unto this my realm the vanity and iniquity of the papistical religion in all its pestilent manifestations in Sodom priesthooses and poxetten nunneries.
>
> (*MQD*, 19)[14]

During this speech, '*Two men, stamping, sway a big sheet like a blank banner behind [Knox, and] swagger on the spot with exaggerated Orangeman's gait. Music and hoochs and ugly skirls*' (*MQD*, 19).

Framed as part of a 'parodic', 'exaggerated', 'ugly', Orangeman's parade, Knox's speech reeks of a sectarianism dangerous in its intolerance. This might not seem an entirely new or particularly feminist construction of Knox's *First Blast*, especially since the vehemence of his title alone may sensitise contemporary readers to expect sexism if not misogyny in the tract.[15] But rather than meeting Knox at his own polemicism and rejecting him grandly as a sexist and religious bigot, Lochhead chooses instead to touch sensitively on what forms the basis of his, or indeed anyone's, opinions: subjective perspective, however constructed. Mary suggests that Knox's reading of the scriptures is just that, a reading, an interpretation, not a transcendent hot line to the truth.

> MARY   And do you no interpret as suits you?
>
> KNOX   I believe only what God plainly speaks in his word.
>
> MARY   And yet the same words sound different to my ears!
>
> (*MQD*, 21)

As the 'Knox and Mary' scene closes, the audience is left with a much more sympathetic representation of Mary than that of Knox which began the scene, but Mary, after all, has spoken of 'guid tolerance', and Knox of 'the Siren song o' toleration' (*MQD*, 22), casting Mary, interestingly, as an archetypal siren, a temptress. Subtly, rather than broadly, Lochhead delineates the misogyny of Knox's perspective. The play hints at Knox's choice to blame women (as sirens) for men's desires (as *he* stirs with what is '*perhaps lust*' [*MQD*, 22] when Mary begins to sob) and shows how Knox's church rejected the female figurehead and, for Mary and La Corbie, the positive images of women of Mary's Catholic church.

> MARY   Then the Protestants dinna love oor Blessed Virgin?
>
> LA CORBIE   Knox has torn the Mother of God from oot the sky o' Scotland and has trampit her celestial blue goon amang the muck and mire and has blotted oot every name by which ye praise her – Stella Maris, Star of the Sea, Holy Mother, Notre Dame. Oor Lady o' Perpetual Succour.
>
> MARY   But if he hae torn her frae the blue sky what has he left in her place?
>
> LA CORBIE   A black hole, a jaggit gash, *naethin'*.
>
> (*MQD*, 23)

His ideas reframed, what Knox seems to lack most, for Lochhead, is poetry. While he begins the scene with a marching, abusive catalogue of the evils of women and Catholicism, La Corbie ends the scene with this poetic tribute to Mary's spiritual 'mother'.

All of the metatextual elements of Lochhead's work discussed thus far alienate the plays' audiences from passive acceptance of representation as true. The audiences are encouraged to see the plays and other forms of representation as representational apparatus which do not merely reflect but construct meaning, and to analyse how that meaning may be ideologically inscribed in ways which denigrate or circumscribe women. Lochhead's plays are replete with other alienation techniques, which we shall identify briefly here, and which continue to 'denaturalize and defamiliarize what [dominant] ideology makes seem normal, acceptable, inescapable'.[16]

Of the three plays, *Blood and Ice* is perhaps the most consistently naturalistic. The play seemingly allows its audience to identify with a unified subject, Mary, an opportunity which may be empowering for a female audience, since it offers the positive role model of a woman who challenges the ideologies and gender inscriptions of her society. But the construction of a unified subject might also limit women's power since it may suggest identity as stable, fixed in gender codings which limit what women and men can be. Mary may also be seen as non-unified, however, particularly as she identifies herself in the final scene as many different characters. She accepts each stable identity, allowing each to empower her, but she also acknowledges each as a fiction, a construct, so that the concept of stable identity is rendered provisional in *Blood and Ice*. The play's audience thus does not identify with the stable 'Woman' Shelley idealised, but with a woman in process, a much more politically viable configuration.

Dracula de-stabilises its own naturalism using many more techniques, including the use of an often 'camp' style, bold cutting between disparate scenes which denaturalises the setting of any scene, and the use of polyvalent imagery and language which do not limit but multiply meaning. To focus on language, the play is filled with puns which broach single meaning, denaturalising the truth of language which we, as inheritors of a tradition of naturalistic language, normally accept.

For instance, puns on food and eating run throughout the play, and their deployment suggests some interesting ironies about how women are constructed through language as food. On Mina's first entrance, she is described as '*a peach*', and she also happens to be '*eating out*'. Using a familiar turn of phrase, Lucy says, 'You look good enough to eat'

(*MQD*, 73). But because the play is *Dracula*, this line is heavily ironic – Mina and Lucy will, of course, literally be 'eaten' later in the play. Florrie, described as '*very young, very pretty*', is serving chicken and asks, 'Leg or breast, Mr Jonathan?' Having trouble separating his sexual appetite from his appetite for lunch, Jonathan replies, 'Pardon?' then, 'Breast. No. Leg. Breast . . . I think . . . emm . . . could I have a little piece of each please, Florrie?' (*MQD*, 83–4). Repeatedly, the play configures women as food and indicates how this configuration objectifies women as commodities for consumption, usually by men.

Polyvalent imagery in *Dracula* suggests how turning the tables, with men fulfilling women's sexual appetites, is unacceptable in the characters' Victorian society. In a sort of Brechtian *Gestus*, when Dracula tries to leave Mina after their scene of mutual vamping, '*She grasps at his cloak. Very ambiguous. Almost like an embrace, but also to detain him.*' Her gesture signifies both sexual desire for him and fear of him, detaining him so that he may be destroyed. Her husband is disgusted. He accuses Mina, 'You wanted him!' and '*turns away from her*' (*MQD*, 137). Mina's gesture liberates a desire which is, for her society, transgressive, and implicitly asks why that must be so. Her gesture is not, however, unequivocal, and it thus further liberates imagery and gesture themselves from their teleological binds to single meaning.

To interrupt the linear, naturalising flow of its own narrative and thus the cultural narrative on Mary Stuart, *Mary Queen of Scots Got Her Head Chopped Off* uses a variety of performance styles, from naturalistic to the heightened theatricality of the songs and dances; a narrator, La Corbie, who provides ironic and disjunctive commentary; and anachronistic detailing, including Knox's bowler hat, the Polaroid of baby James, and the whole final scene, '*Jock Thamson's Bairns*', where the characters are stripped of all dignity and historicity (*MQD*, 63).

With its 'history' highlighted as culturally constructed narrative, *Mary Queen of Scots* again demonstrates how women are culturally constructed, and invites its audience to examine its own practice of narrativising and constructing the present. The final scene suggests how historical patterns of socially constructed gender and religious difference have, for instance, become institutionalised, contributing to 'present day' school yard bullying. The play further interrupts narrative teleology by 'giving it all away' in the play's title (we *know* Mary gets her head chopped off) and through the use of scene titles, which could be displayed to the audience as signs. Denied the suspense of not knowing what will happen to Mary, the suspense which realist narrative uses to control its audience's passive engagement, *Mary Queen of Scots*'s audience is freed to engage actively rather than passively in a critical relationship with the play, freed to ask not *what* will happen to Mary but *how* this will happen, who will control her fate, and so on. As with *Blood and Ice* and *Dracula, Mary Queen of Scots*'s audience is invited consciously to put new twists to old stories.

NOTES

1 We borrow our title from Lochhead's poem, 'In the Cutting Room' (*DF*, 34–5).

2 Adrienne Rich, *On Lies, Secrets, Silence* (London: Virago, 1980), 35.

3 For a thorough discussion of male homosocial desire, see Eve Kosofsky Sedgwick, *Between Men: English Literature and Male Homosocial Desire* (New York: Columbia University Press, 1985).

4 Coincidentally, the originator of this aristocratic vampire was none other than Dr John Polidori, a member of Shelley's circle in Geneva. The occasion of the writing of Polidori's tale, *The Vampyre*, was that same literary competition organised to relieve the group's boredom in the wet summer weather, that incited Mary Shelley to write *Frankenstein*. The model for Polidori's new-style vampire was Lord Byron, the character whom Lochhead, in the 1982 version of *Blood and Ice*, doubled as Frankenstein's monster.

5 Nina Auerbach, *Woman and the Demon: The Life of a Victorian Myth* (Cambridge, MA: Harvard University Press, 1982), 24.

6 Penelope Shuttle and Peter Redgrove, *The Wise Wound* (London: Penguin, 1980), 267.

7 Bram Stoker, *Dracula* (Toronto; 1897 and New York: Bantam, 1981), 252–3.

8 Ian B. Cowan, *The Enigma of Mary Stuart* (London: Victor Gollancz, 1971), 35.

9 See back cover blurb.

10 Importantly, the mummers' scene is preceded by a similarly metadramatic scene involving Elizabeth. In Elizabeth's dream, a *'shadowy figure (Dad) puts something – not a crown but an improvised and very clear representation of one – on Fiddler's head'*, the fiddler representing Elizabeth. *'All the men throw Fiddler . . . kissing her'*, they blindfold and cajole her, she is mock married, and then the man she 'married' steals her crown (*MQD*, 23–5). The dream acts out how Elizabeth anticipates she would be manipulated by 'all the men' were she to marry. Going to bed a queen, she would awaken recast as 'plain . . . Mistress Dudley' (*MQD*, 24).

11 In Coleridge's 'Christabel', the 'lovely lady, Christabel' (l. 23) is literally entranced by the mysterious Geraldine. Geraldine sexually initiates Christabel, demonically instigating the fall of 'holy Christabel' (l. 228) from innocence to experience. The collision of innocence with sexuality is captured in these lines, (which also tie in to Shelley's vision of Mary's breasts) in which Geraldine has just removed her robe: 'Behold! her bosom and half her side/ A sight to

dream of not to tell!/ O shield her! shield sweet Christabel!' (ll. 252–54).

12 Anne K. Mellor, 'Why Women Didn't Like Romanticism: The Views of Jane Austen and Mary Shelley' in Gene W. Ruoff, ed., *The Romantics and Us: Essays on Literature and Culture* (New Brunswick and London: Rutgers University Press, 1990), 284.

13 See also Stoker, 39–40.

14 For a recent edition of Knox's *The First Blast of the Trumpet Against the Monstrous Regiment of Women* (1588), with modernised spelling and punctuation, see Martin A. Breslow, ed., *The Political Writings of John Knox* (Washington and London: Associated University Presses, 1985), 37–80.

15 The London-based women's theatre company Monstrous Regiment takes its name from Knox's tract, 'reclaiming' the appellation by refusing its formerly pejorative connotations and taking the meaning of 'monster' as 'divine portent, warning, prodigy, marvel'. See Gillian Hanna, selector and compiler, *Monstrous Regiment: Four Plays and a Collective Celebration* (London: Nick Hern, 1991), viii.

16 Elin Diamond, 'Brechtian Theory/Feminist Theory: Toward a Gestic Feminist Criticism,' *Tulane Drama Review* 32.1 (Spring 1988), 85.

Nine

Scripts and Performances

Anne Varty

'Boy or girl, what are you gonny go as?' asks one of the unborn company
of children at the start of the pantomime-farce *Same Difference* written for
Wildcat in 1984. 'What do you want to dress up as? What do you want
to play at?', they continue, girded only in their babygrows. A sense of
play governs Lochhead's approach to the exploration of role, just as an
experimental urge governs her selection of dramatic form. Although her
subject matter has remained relatively constant over the last decade, the
form in which she presents it has not. Her drama is marked by a
versatility of approach and method. She writes for radio, television and
the stage; she writes singspiel, children's theatre, agit-prop; she
translates, devises, collaborates; has adapted a novel for the stage, and,
with *Blood and Ice*, has adapted her own stage play for both radio and
television. This urgent, exploratory attitude to the resources of
theatrical expression, incurring failure as well as success, has been
fortified by her colleagues: Gerry Mulgrew's confidence, for instance,
that 'we can do anything, you know, talking crows, *anything*'.[1] It is a
style which relies heavily on, but also fosters, the collaborative venture
of theatre work. And just as a sense of ensemble and mutual
responsibility is often required of a company performing new and
evolving work, so too is it elicited from the audience: her experimental
method finally and cumulatively reinforces the thematic exploration of
social identity.

Lochhead shares a collaborative approach to composing for the stage
with many of her fellow women writers. Caryl Churchill, Pam Gems,
Timberlake Wertenbaker, Sarah Daniels, have often arrived at scripts
after an intensive period of workshopping with a company. Certainly,
one explanation here is simply that during the seventies and eighties in
Britain this was a fashionable and stimulating method of generating
new writing, by both women and men. But, as Michelene Wandor

points out, the difficulties experienced by women in taking sole authorial control of a theatre script are conspicuous in what is still a largely male professional field (and Joyce Deans and Marilyn Imrie are the only women to first direct new work by Lochhead).[2] Coming to the theatre from the more solitary and verbal crafts of poetry, dramatic monologue and even revue, Lochhead has allowed herself to learn from colleagues schooled longer in the more diverse and visual medium of theatre. Churchill writes about her own development that '[w]orking with companies for the first time, while before I had always worked very much alone, made the year [1977] almost as much of a watershed as 1972',[3] so too Lochhead has taken advantage of the opportunities afforded by collaboration to make the transition from poet to playwright.

Even so, prejudices also have to be overcome in the field of critical reception. There is a marked difference between the reception met by *Shanghaied*, a script workshopped by Lochhead with Borderline (and announced as such in their press release for the first production) and *Blood and Ice*, her first solo composition, which is not simply due to the relative quality of the work. Mary Brennan writes of *Shanghaied*, 'the dialogue is spot-on and superbly funny with it, performances – like the writing – are pitched just right . . .' (*Glasgow Herald*, 8 May 1984); Mary Brennan on *Blood and Ice*: 'with . . . her first full-length play, Liz Lochhead comes distressingly unstuck. I have ransacked my first impressions . . . to find points to commend simply because I know Ms Lochhead to be a writer of talent and integrity' (*Glasgow Herald*, 20 August 1982). Confident about the collective work, she is anxious about the solo piece. Alternatively, Cordelia Oliver, writing for *The Guardian* (27 August 1982) introduces the play by saying that it is 'also by a woman, . . . about another woman, Mary Godwin/Shelley, and her problem in dealing with the Frankenstein in the home'. Although Oliver is more generous about the play, its salient feature is the gender of the author, closely followed by her proper reflections on a domestic environment. It is disappointing that both critics (themselves women) retreat first into what they know about about Lochhead before they can address the work that crosses the boundary from poetry to drama. While this concessionary attitude may seem to marginalise, there is also a sense in which a woman writing for the stage has novelty value that wins commissions: this too, Lochhead has turned to her advantage.

As a dramatist conspicuously concerned with the socially constructed nature of role, relationship and identity, Lochhead began composing for the stage with a play about the relationship between the specifically female creator and her creation/creativity. It is a fundamental issue, and one which, given the constant revision to which *Blood and Ice* has been subject, remains unsettled and fruitfully unsettling for Lochhead. Before Michael Boyd's first version of the play, titled *Mary and the Monster*, opened at the Belgrade in Coventry in March 1981, Lochhead was wrestling with the problems of apparently unacceptable creativity and wrote to Emma Tennant (author of *The Bad Sister*) in January 1980:

> What exactly is the relationship of self to others and image in a woman; the problem of the Female Muse for the female writer, or do we have to discover, or re-discover some 'male principle' within ourselves to be whole, can we have a Male Muse? . . . or must we squabble with parts of ourselves, live with our Bad Sisters . . .[4]

This knot marks the completion of *Grimm Sisters*, and heralds the play about 'dreaming Frankenstein'. Written for three actors, the play extends the prevailing dramatic monologue form of that poetry collection. It takes place entirely within Mary Shelley's consciousness, so that reminiscence and imagination operate on the same plane of theatrical reality and Shelley has as much life as the monster, while Mary the ultimate creator is the most monstrous of all. The 'man' and 'woman' who accompany Mary on stage play all the other roles; and together they portray the monster, indicating the androgynous aspect of female creativity alluded to in the letter to Tennant, for example:

> *Man and woman begin, behind Mary's back and without her turning round to see them, to transform themselves into the monster. They should 'couple' acrobatically, suggesting (subtly) various sexual positions en route to donning the monster's shrunken looking black suit and mask, woman on man's shoulders to become the giant, the monster.*[5]

Mary and the Monster was not a critical success. Lochhead calls it 'fumbling' (*PW*, 117), while Gareth Lloyd-Evans wrote in the *Guardian* that it was a 'desperately worthy but boring brew of animated lecture and choric lamentation' (13 April 1981). Even so, some features of this early version emerge again later, as, for instance, the visual allusions to Karloff films, or the dialogue of seduction between Byron and Mary, and the sisterly scene between Mary and Claire.

The first version of the play to carry the title *Blood and Ice* was written for the Traverse Theatre and directed there by Kenny Ireland for the Edinburgh Festival, 1982. This met with a more cordial reception in the press, although Lochhead herself remained critical: 'it still didn't work. . . . despite the passion and intelligence of Gerda Stevenson [Mary] . . . what she had to do disintegrated in its imagery at the level of my writing before the long difficult monologue ending of the play', and 'the casting of that production had not gelled' (*PW*, 117). Despite anxieties about fluency, the script itself affords easy progress, compounded (if not complicated) by the doubling of roles required from the cast of five actors. Mary Shelley remains herself throughout; Percy Shelley becomes Frankenstein; Byron becomes the Monster (and also the Accuser, in an inserted scene from the novel); Claire Claremont becomes Elizabeth Lavenza Frankenstein (from the novel); Elise, the Shelleys' maid, becomes Frankenstein's maid and also plays the 'female monster'. It is a two act play, the monster is conceived between the acts, the transition from I to II is neatly, if derivatively, made. In the last scene of Act I (I. vii) Mary soliloquises her vision, 'my imagination, unbidden, possessed me', while the stage direction reads '*Sinister music and sexual breathing noises*', blatantly linking artistic creation with sexual reproduction. Act II opens on '*Mary writing. Thunder and lightning. Door flashes open she shuts it, etc. Out of the cupboard comes Frankenstein and the monster strapped to his bed.*' Frankenstein speaks to the monster, 'I sweated blood to make you'. A lengthy dumb show follows, as the creature stirs, at the end of which:

> *Frankenstein . . . reacts horrified into a panic start, rushing helter skelter across the stage to where Mary Shelley is sitting writing 'Frankenstein', her novel. By the time he reaches her he is Shelley.*[6]

These images of Shelley-Frankenstein, Byron-Monster and both, ultimately, as male and monstrous aspects of Mary, illustrate directly the 'relationship of self to others and image' in the female writer that Lochhead was grappling with.

Although it is difficult to see why Irving Wardle, writing for *The Times* (1 September 1982), classes the play initially as a 'Byron play', given that the focus is so clearly on Mary, in the light of the stage directions and Kenny Ireland's production which, Wardle states, 'relies heavily on nightmare transformation of the sunny villa into a midnight castle with doors blown open and the cries of lost souls', it is obvious why he believed that Lochhead had 'come along to put the old Gothic view'. In this version Lochhead capitalises on Karloff clichés (for example, '*very slowly the classic monster-movement it sits up and opens its eyes*') and on the overt and over-emphatic theatricality that this entails (for example, '*Music crescendoes, ground-ice groans, a total gothic version of the trad. panto transformation scene, . . . total visual, sensual, scarey excitement . . .*'.[7] In the light of her concern with the controlling effects of cliché, the deployment of these familiar images and huge theatrical climaxes challenges with the possibility for reflex audience dismissal of what Mary is wrestling with. But it is a risk, obliterating the more interesting purpose of the play which is to scrutinise the burden of female creativity. And Mary is just as subject to recoil from her creativity as both her household and auditorium audiences. The stage directions reveal the writer's uncertainty about how to achieve a theatrical effect without giving way to parody.

Lochhead remains clear about the problems for women in confronting their own artistic creativity: 'a lot of women poets write as if ink were blood. But it's not. Ink is ink — and I would like to celebrate it for itself.'[8] The difficulty lies in finding artistic expression for this view that is sufficienlty controlled for it to gain acceptance. In the 1981 version of the play, Mary herself seemed to be a victim of this confusion as she describes her first period, ' here, scribbling down my thigh, as if it is being written by a quill dipped in blood, spills this little crimson trickle . . .'.[9] While Mary's naivety is authorially placed by the knowing puns which follow, 'Jane was hysterical, she screamed, 'Fanny! Fanny! Come quickly . . .' the monologue betrays a poet's handling of situation, and not that of a playwright. In her choice of subject matter, title, and earliest treatment, Lochhead, with *Blood and Ice*, tackles the difficulty directly, but not clearly enough.

She states that the main problem with the 1982 version lay in the disintegrating imagery of the script. Wardle's review, however, points to its cohesive power: 'Suspense is thrown away in favour of imagery and recurring motif'. Others were less convinced. Allen Wright stated 'luxuriating in language instead of using it [to] drive the drama, Ms Lochhead makes things difficult for her actors' (*Scotsman*, 21 August 1982). Subsequent revisions to the script develop the polyvalent imagery of blood and ice with skill. What impedes the narrative flow of the 1982 script is the juxtapositioned inclusion of scenes from the novel, while the thematic and metaphoric flow is confused by the delayed introduction of Frankenstein and the monster. In all subsequent versions, enactments from the novel are cut, taken simply as 'given' facts in the background, while the monster is omnipresent from the start. Suspense is of no interest and the play is not a dramatising of the novel but, as the subtitle (introduced for the 1986 Winged Horse production and kept for radio) indicates, it is 'A Tale of the Creation of Frankenstein'. However, the 1982 script does not yet command the successful blending of the interior drama of monologue with an epic, Brechtian style of narration where the contours of the story are known in advance and interest is focused on how the burden of creativity is borne by the protagonist. Subsequent versions of the play do exhibit these features, as Lochhead can be seen moving further from the concerns and techniques of naturalist drama which offers explanations, towards a more demonstrative, playfully serious style, which has at its heart the abstract issue of compromised female creativity merely illustrated by the case of Mary Shelley.

When Howard Brenton came to write about the Byron/Shelley circle in 1984, with *Bloody Poetry* for the Foco Novo Theatre Company, his concern was to salute the 'Utopian aspirations' of the group in a 'celebration of a magnificent failure.'[10] For Brenton too, these lives were to illustrate an abstract political principle. When, as in *Blood and Ice*, Shelley rushes in convulsions from the stage, Polidori explains that Shelley saw his wife 'with eyes in her nipples. . . . Is there no end to their fantasms? To the indulgence of these revolutionary apostles . . .?'[11] When Lochhead deploys this biographical incident, it is Shelley himself who says, 'Eyes, Mary, you have eyes for nipples . . . the eyes in your breasts are staring me down' (*PW*, 99), the husband asserting the monstrous in his wife, punning neatly on the ice (eyes) in her breast that freezes her too with her own vision and compulsive revision. The trained poet makes her point more obliquely than the trained playwright, but by now no less effectively.

Lochhead revised the script for Pepper's Ghost Theatre Company to perform in February 1984 at New Merlin's Cave, London. The 'gothic' effects were deleted. Instead the play is set in a *'ghostly nursery'*, expressionist style heightened by the presence of *'bleached-out . . . unreal toys, perhaps a bit out of scale'* (*PW*, 83). One of these dolls becomes a major device which replaces the shooting monster of 1982. Seven of the nine scenes of this two act play open with Mary alone on stage and the other characters exist more clearly in her consciousness. A careful mirroring is established between the three women of the piece, (taking up 'The Other Woman' (*DF*, 92)), as Claire and Elise are shown to represent facets of Mary's self-understanding. The first signs of this are when:

> *Mary and Claire alone together by the fire and candlelight. As if under a spell they begin to brush out their long hair slowly with silver hairbrushes, each other's image.*
>
> (*PW*, 86)

The link between Elise and Claire, in Mary's mind, occurs in Act II scene iv, when Mary dismisses Elise because of her illegitimate pregnancy and Elise accuses Mary of hypocrisy: *'Mary slaps her hard. Elise and Mary looking at each other. Echoing the Claire/Mary mirror scene in Act One'* (107). The merging identities are confirmed verbally by Mary in the penultimate scene of the play (II.vii, 114). As in the 1982 version, Lochhead has found theatrical expression for the manner in which women have internalised views of themselves promulgated by a masculine hegemony. In 1984 this is taken to the point of denying, or 'sending away' apparently unacceptable aspects of themselves. The mirrors and the dolls, carefully integrated with action and dialogue, are means of visual, theatrical, expression that are much less open to misinterpretation than the earlier deployment of filmic cliché. No characters or events from *Frankenstein* are recreated in the 1984 version; the novel remains submerged, there to be pieced together like the monster, forcing the audience to participate in the act of creation. Similarly, no adequate explanations are offered as to how the experience of Mary Shelley's life could give rise to the novel. It is a mystery which expresses her predicament rather than something which her predicament explains.

In 1986 the play was again rewritten for a touring production by Winged Horse, directed by John Carnegie, choreographed by Peter Darrell, and it opened on 11 September 1986 at the Harbour Arts Centre in Irvine, before touring from Cumbria to Shetland. The 'creature' (no longer the 'monster') is introduced as a 'thankfully ungrotesque' character in his own right (Mary Brennan, *Glasgow Herald*, 24 September 1986), making a cast of six with no doubling. The nursery and doll have been deleted. The setting of the play is emphatically in a region of Mary's imaginative memory, while the opening and closing words of the play are spoken by the 'Creature'. He begins (addressing Mary): 'Why did you make me. Frankenstein?' These are disembodied words, which break out of the thunder and lightning that accompany the evocative opening tableau:

> *Bare floor. Coffin like, or square crates, rough nailed. . . . Irregular hanging slats. Dirty sail-coloured canvas dust-cloths . . . almost seaweedy tatters of lace. An oval mirror frame (no mirror in) on a stand. Can be tilted. A single . . . drab chaise-long. A hugely ot of scale, unrealistic skeletal rockinghorse with a skullhead but bulging blank marble-eyes − the head of the* Fuseli *'Nightmare' from his famous painting. . . . On the chaise-long, asleep in a classic nightmare pose (also from the* Fuseli*) is* Mary Shelley. *She has fallen asleep with her own book open on her chest (where* Fuseli's *. . . homunculus lies in the painting . . .). It is dark. A stormy night. In the flash of lightning we see − behind and through the broken slats of the irregular and incomplete hung canvas strips and slats − flashes of something? Someone? Moving, not moving again. Did a hand stretch through and set the nightmare rockinghorse a-rock? Certainly it is moving. . . . Two notes. . . . Lightning. . . .Nothing. . . . The rip of thunder as the woman, sleeping so still she might be dead, sits up to an unmistakeable-cry. . . .*[12]

A speaking picture, this teases with familiar images of Romantic nightmare, making strange (blending Shelley and Brecht) and making domestic by substituting a/the book *Frankenstein* for the 'grim homunculus' on Mary's chest, while she, like the monster of 1982, rises as from the dead. These are stage directions which accommodate an interpreting reader, while suggesting the effects and connotations their enactment could have on an audience. The deployment of cliché, including the link, implicit in the allusion to Fuseli's paintings, between sex and artistic creation, is more controlled than in 1982. In fact these directions were not followed by Carnegie whose production opened on Mary writing at her desk in a sea-green room, populated only by frozen figures who one after another surprise both Mary and the audience by animation, and it was Shelley who lay shrouded on the chaise-long, rising from the dead into a tablecloth for scene two. The Creature assumes a carefully integrated shadow identity throughout the play, at first as just a limb, then a voice, eventually a fully assembled and importunate being, his manifestations accompanied by 'creature music' composed by Richard Pettigrew and used again for the radio adaptation. Throughout Act I he was kept in a state of unbeing, on the boundaries of Mary's consciousness, pressing for admittance to the stage, and his utterances, like the music, were recorded and broadcast on the sound system. Not acknowledged until Act II, he then became a permanent stage presence:

> *The* creature *appears suddenly, wrapped in a strange cloak – a cloak with a frame in it such as turkish shepherds and goatherds use (one cowers down in it and it becomes a tent). It is made of the same material as the backdrop so he can sometimes almost emerge out of it, or almost disappear, by merely turning.*[13]

Throughout this act he is in quest of affection and a mate: 'Men recoil from This, they are afraid. . . . Men love. This cannot love'.[14] His helpless desire for love is demonstrated rather than stated when, marginalised and monstrous as women's artistic endeavour, 'on the edge of the stage [he] cries like a baby'.[15] His cries are projected into the centre of attention, because throughout II.ii, the Creature makes the noises of the imaginary baby William (represented by the folded shroud/tablecloth), who is comforted by Claire or Mary. It is an economic device which conjures the child into the women's arms, animating the cloth, while it also implies the distorting analogy between reproduction and artistic creation. Throughout Act II the Creature facilitates the progress of the drama, a kind of symbolic stage hand. His last job is to carry on the drowned Shelley, as if to finalise the distinction between art and life.[16] 'But,' Mary concludes, 'you would not die' and the Creature's closing rejoinder, 'Come, pursue This, chase This, till This shall catch you. . . .' supplies a last threatening invitation to write.[17]

The radio version of *Blood and Ice*, first broadcast on Radio 4 on 11 June 1990 and repeated on 2 August 1992, directed by Marilyn Imrie, with Gerda Stevenson again playing Mary, transposes some of the successful visual imagery into auditory effects. The play opens with Mary's inarticulate cries; the creature's echoing voice asks the first coherent question, 'Why did you make me? [pause] Frankenstein?' A window rattles in a storm, Mary shuts it forcefully and states 'Nothing' as the Creature whispers insistently 'Frankenstein . . . Frankenstein' and Mary begins to sing 'we'll go no more a roving' to blot him out. Alternatively, when Mary weeps for her dead baby Clara, the creature's whimpering blends with her own cries. But the general effect of this transposition is to push the play into psychological realism, a narrative of emotion recollected in tranquility where only the imagery of the dialogue carries the weight of metaphoric meaning; background sounds of birdsong, storm, or waves breaking indicate what is perceived as real location, just as careful attention to the characters' pronunciation locates their class and background.

The most recent broadcast of the play in autumn 1992, twenty-four minutes long, *The Story of 'Frankenstein'*, made for Yorkshire Television, directed by Jenny Wilkes, takes its unlikely place as one in a series of science fiction programmes and is introduced by Tom Baker who states that *Frankenstein* is 'the most powerful piece of science fiction ever written'. Peter Kelly, who played the Creature for the radio, again supplies the monstrous voice. The film opens on the child Mary listening to Coleridge read in a firelit room of her parental home, flashes to Mary and Shelley kissing on her mother's grave, the camera pauses on the gravestone, then to the graveyard empty against a dusky sky, with a delayed Miltonic voice-over by the Creature 'Did I request thee Maker, from my clay, to mold me man?' and the title appears against Mary sitting alone in the dusky graveyard.

While this just preserves the sense that Mary is telling the story, the economy of televisual narration which prefers to deal literally with flashback, utterly transforms the stage play. (The film of *Death of a Salesman* failed, for similar reasons, to render the 'mobile concurrency of past and present' of Miller's play.) A larger cast, of thirteen, is required to accommodate the past; two generations of children are needed (Mary, Claire and William); Mrs Godwin (Claire's mother), Humphry Davy, Polidori and Coleridge are introduced. A powerful new scene of confrontation between Mary and her father about her relationship with the married atheist Shelley is brought in. The acting style is naturalistic, and the plotting, although it jumbles chronology, emphasises Mary's lifelong exposure to scientific experiment, from Polidori's galvanising machine to Humphry Davy demonstrating the effects of electricity on frogs' legs in her childhood home. The naïve confidence of Shelley's, 'the truths of our new science will have transforming effects', operates ironically on the impressionable imagination of Mary. But early in the film, the pastoral image of Mary playing with her bare-bottomed baby on a meadow, accompanied by her shockingly disjunctive voice-over 'how did I, a young girl not nineteen years old, come to conceive of so very hideous an idea?', makes the naturalistic, explanatory thrust of the film clear. The Creature is not allowed to have the last word. His 'come, pursue this, chase this, Mary Shelley, describe what haunts you' (significantly not concluding with 'till this shall catch you' – to Lochhead's dissatisfaction – of 1986 and the radio) is taken as a simple injunction and Mary, writing at her desk, speaks the opening lines of the novel as the last lines of the film.

During this long span of metamorphosis, Lochhead wrote both TV and radio plays which exploit without compromise the realism and the visual or auditory narrative techniques of these media. *Sweet Nothings* is directed by Ian Knox for the series 'The End of the Line' about unemployment in the west of Scotland, broadcast on BBC1 in 1984. Set in Irvine, it concerns a strike by the workers, mainly women, against the threatened closure of their underwear factory, 'Brevity'. Lochhead's choice of factory product is an ingenious device to suggest the intimate link between the public and the private domains of women's lives. Knox's film teases with a documentary style, lengthy shots of factory machines, ferociously manufacturing bras or lying idle; strike meetings, press involvement, are set against domestic scenes. Given this, the happy end, of continuing jobs for the girls, seems unlikely. But two thematic points are more important than the story. The first of these is the transformation of Charlotte (Eileen McCallum) the main character and shop steward, from a self-effacing housewife working for pin money to a competent and forthright strike leader. She is driven both by a sense of justice and by the need of a wife/mother to provide for her family since her husband is a recent Ravenscraig 'redundancy'. Whether or not the strike achieves its objectives, Charlotte is irreversibly empowered by the social pressures that challenge her, and her family structure changes with her. A fine bedroom scene between Charlotte and her husband epitomises the change. She returns late at night fourteen weeks into the strike to find her husband in bed; the tone balances, will they row, or not? We, like Charlotte, are teased by her husband who could play on her conscience, guilty of domestic neglect, before, very gradually, his pleasure and her relief in the complete role reversal that has taken place between them emerges.

The second overriding theme is that the strike is not simply about the right to work, but about the need for 'sweet nothings', leaven in the lump of grim working-class life. For Lochhead, the same feminism that stands on women's right to work must also accommodate pleasure. Conspiratorial glee overwhelms the office girls as orders come to the newly opened factory, one from 'Bitten Cherry Sex Shops . . . a new range in mouth-watering colours – says he's got backing'. Interviewed after their victory by a solemn English lady from the *Guardian* Women's Page, Charlotte is asked, 'and did you find a commitment to feminism as such through all this?':

CHARLOTTE: Oh, ah'm not . . . I'd never call myself a feminist. No . . . I'm not. Listen, as far as everybody here is concerned, all this is very simple. We're here, fighting for our jobs. And some of us have our men on our side, and some of us huvnae.

JOURNALIST: But you won.

CHARLOTTE: Aye. And what have we won back? Jobs that are boring, badly paid, what a lot of us used tae think of as pin money. And what we make, are just pricey wee bits o' flimsy lace that lassies wear tae try perk up their sex life. The little sweet nothings tae counteract the brewer's droop if they're lucky. We know all that, but we need the work . . . Some of us are our own worst enemies. We don't like tae see a man at a sink, you know, it doesn't look right tae us . . . We're changing . . . We huv tae change. And so will they. But first, we're gonny save this factory . . . Nothin's guaranteed, eh girls?

Fancy You Minding That, directed by Marilyn Imrie, broadcast on Radio 4, 30 November 1986, for a cast of six women (three generations of one family), concerns their relationship with their absent men and explores the intimacies which arise, or fail to arise, between them to fill the gap. It opens and closes with a song, the refrain, 'Daddy, my heart still belongs to you'. Ina, the grandmother in her 'douce Glasgow suburb' bungalow, is recently bereaved, and her daughter Valerie and grandaughter Kate are visiting from North Finchley. It is an intimate drama, set almost exclusively in domestic interiors, retreating finally to telephone conversations between Valerie and her mother. Even the one excursion taken by Ina and Kate is to another woman's home, the Glasgow Tenement House Museum in Garnethill, once the home of Miss Agnes Toward. Valerie leaves Kate behind, ostensibly to keep her mother company, but actually to shield Kate from the departure of her present partner ('a father figure to Kate') and, more accurately, to give herself the privacy to cope with his loss. Kate is not told of Ray's departure, and Valerie never hears that Kate was reunited with her real father while in Glasgow. These secrets are shared with girlfriends.

This careful editing of events to suit the speaker's view of the listener is underlined by the nightmare which Valerie recounts to her friend Anna. Valerie, who works for TV, dreams that she is in the cutting room at work and has speedily to edit a film, about her own family picnic at which her father was present. Angry in the dream that it was fiction, when she played the film back, it was blank. As Lochhead states in 'In The Cutting Room' (*DF*, 35), 'a heart is not/an editing machine – we can cut/out nothing'. Valerie's subconscious superimposition of one grief upon another (simultaneous loss of father and lover), which leaves her empty or blank, is matched in the dialogue by the patently inadequate platitudes which the women peddle to each other in an effort to edit out the pain of loss: 'Men don't have the inner resources', 'He'll be the one that suffers, Val, in the long run', 'She had a good job . . . and friends'. It is symbolically significant that Kate, reunited with her father, discovers that he works as a 'restorer'. But life on the desolation of the telephone lines, does not look so optimistic for the older generations as the play closes. As with Imrie's production of *Blood and Ice*, locations are precisely placed by background sounds and accent carefully labels the social status and regional belonging of the characters.

Quelques Fleurs, which began as a revue monlogue for the character Verena (*TCNC*, 9), becoming an extended monologue in *Bagpipe Muzak* (37–51) and further developed as a stage play performed by Lochhead herself with Stuart Hepburn as Verena's husband Derek, directed by Joyce Deans at the Edinburgh Festival in 1991 and revived for the Glasgow Mayfest 1992, has been adapted for radio with the same cast, directed by Marilyn Imrie, broadcast on Radio 4, 8 May 1993. As John Linklater writes, the transition from revue to play is 'carefully plotted in the 11 linked pieces which form a kind of diary of progressive despair, and a minor part of the process is achieved by letting us see, for the first time, the fatuous chauvinist to whom she is married' (*Glasgow Herald*, 12 August 1991). Derek's monlogues span from his arrival in Glasgow Queen Street, mid-evening on 23 December 1991 back to his departure from Aberdeen earlier that afternoon. Verena's appearances, which open and close the play, cross-cut against Derek's, take place from 23 December 1990 until 23 December 1991. The play therefore ends with a physical separation to match their emotional distance, yet their occupation of the same stage space, painfully emphasises what should be their married proximity. But as Joyce McMillan has observed, their alienation from one another and society at large is implicit throughout: 'Derek's despair surfaces only under the influence of drink, Verena's is held at bay by a continuous, garrulous babble of hilarious and beautifully observed talk about catalogues and glitter-wrap . . .; but in the end, it bursts to the surface in a stunningly bleak conclusion' (*Guardian*, 17 December 1991).

Lochhead states that she wrote Derek's five monologues 'hearing the voice of, and seeing the actor Stuart Hepburn, regardless of whether he would actually do it . . . imagining helped me get it down in black and white. Because in no way was I as confident of getting right inside this male character, knowing him better than he knows himself, as I had been of being under the skin of Verena' (*Guardian*, 29 August 1991). For radio (with title music, Wayne Nutt's '28 Days On An Offshore Rig' – in full bad sub-country 'n' western), the monologues are hardly altered, but the visual gag that accompanies the inverse chronology of Derek's journey south is lost. On stage he appears first beside a great pyramid of empty lager cans which gets smaller as he gets more sober towards the start of his travels. On radio, this increasing sobriety has to be conveyed by his voice alone, while the purely auditory medium draws out Verena's isolation most powerfully. Her crass materialism and casual viciousness retain the power to disturb as to raise laughter in both media, and the work has met with generous critical praise. Joyce McMillan writes, 'through its willingness to look unblinkingly at the trivial detail of our culture [the play] achieves a depth and truthfulness other writers can only envy' (*Guardian*, 17 December 1991).

These excursions into naturalism are not typical of Lochhead's dramatic work during the mid-eighties, nor do they bear resemblance to the roots of her involvement in theatre, which peaked in 1987 when she worked with Communicado Theatre Company to produce *Mary Queen of Scots*. Attracted by their 'whole expressionistic, epic, storytelling, anachronistic, *non* "fourth wall" direct-to-the-audience style of *presentation* (rather than "acting")',[18] which built on techniques she had used with Borderline for *Shanghaied* (1983) and Wildcat for *Same Difference* (1984), she agreed to Mulgrew's commission to mark 400 years since Mary's beheading.[19] Both of these scripts evolved after workshop with the actors, and in both adults play the parts of children. *Shanghaied* (to shanghai: to drug or otherwise render insensible, and ship on board a vessel wanting hands, OED) shows '3 tenement waifs from Clydebank', evacuated in 1939 to 'a posh country house in Ayrshire', where they meet eight-year old Emily, their upper class hostess, and set out, through game playing to conquer the alien.[20] The children are shanghaied by evacuation, but also by the propaganda that accompanied the war effort, for example, Emily's 'careless talk costs lives', or her 'we've to eat lots of carrots so we can see in the dark'.[21] The Clydebank children are less cowed and are sceptical of all that Emily stands for. Eventually they do succeed in making a new community, indicated at the level of dialogue by the cross-fertilization of linguistic mannerisms. Morag begins to use Emily's 'actually' tag, while Emily begins to use 'dead' as an intensifier and even changes her RP into Clydebank, for example, 'You were dead lucky, Hughie. Nae kiddin''.[22] Where *Shanghaied* shows children's games as a way of creating a new community that has overcome prejudice, *Mary Queen of Scots* shows adults as children, playing to confirm their prejudices against the outsider. And Lochhead credits the 'memory of a wee childhood game with dandelion heads, "Mary Queen of Scots Got Her Head Chopped off, Mary Queen of Scots got her head chopped OFF"', as one starting point for the play.[23]

The record of the first workshopped scenes with Communicado, dated May 1987, indicate that it was with this game that the company started work, and also that this was originally envisaged as the start of the play:

> Sc. I. *The black court, a Glasgow tenement* 1953. *The actors are all kids,* Joan Eardley *street brats in this scene.* Betty *and* Margaret *have got a reluctant* Wee Henry *cawing their rope for them. One skips and both sing.*[24]

Although the opening stage directions of the printed text differ, particularly in the omission of reference to Eardley, the scene which follows, apart from some more elaborate rhymes chanted by the children, is almost exactly that of *Jock Tamson's Bairns* (*MQD*, 63–7). This early concentration on childhood ritual, innocently knowing of religious prejudice, victimisation, and sex, indicates the motive force of these issues for the developing play. Lochhead confirms this in her statement that it was Mulgrew's faith that 'the story *must* still be alive for the Scots today when a Male, Irish-Catholic city Scot (him) and a Female, Proddy, rural Lanarkshire Scot (me) had been taught such different versions' that 'got the play made'.[25] Joyce McMillan, reviewing the 1987 premier at the Edinburgh Festival, notes the importance of this scene: 'all its most important insights – from Mary's suicidal rush into the arms of Bothwell, through her defeat, imprisonment, execution and enduring significance in the street culture of Scotland – are concentrated into a devastating whirlwind of a 10-minute finale' (*Guardian*, 14 August 1987). As a finale, the scene comments grimly on 'the legacy of those battles' (Lochhead, *Time Out*,

16–23 August 1987) and on the childishness they induce. As a prelude in earliest conception, the scene functions as a nightmare premonition by Mary. After the games (in the ms.), deserted by her friends, Marie sobs, a receding voice calls 'Ma-rie . . . Marie . . . Ma-rie'. She calms herself, *'Becoming* Mary. *Alone. Dignified. Afraid.* La Corbie *hops on'*, already the fully fledged creature of the printed text, *'No cute panto talking creature this'* and delivers a virtually complete version of what became the actual opening speech of the production and printed text (*MQD,* 11).[26]

Communicado rehearsed the play until July, toured in Scotland before opening at the Edinburgh Festival where the play won the 'Fringe First Award' and continued the tour south, via Derby, to the Donmar Warehouse in London. They revived the production for tour in 1988 and the play was subsequently produced south of the border by the Contact Theatre Company in Manchester, directed by Brigid Larmour in 1991. The script remains relatively stable throughout. The most conspicuous change is the gradual elision of the role of Leicester. In 1987 he discussed with Elizabeth at length the politics of their potential marriage after his wife's suicide (included in I.v, 'Repressed Loves'). His appearance is cut in 1988 to the briefest of sex scenes, called 'Elizabeth's Nightmare', appended to I.iii ('Queens and Maids') after Marian advises her queen to marry Leicester and avoid scandal. The actor who played this part doubled as Darnley. By the time of publication, in 1989, the role had been cut altogether and Leicester exists only in Elizabeth's conversation and nightmare which taughtens the narrative and emphasises her self-denying resolution. Other changes, at the level of dialogue, also represent moves towards greater clarity and streamlining. The powerful conclusion of II.vi (*MQD,* 63), where Elizabeth plots Mary's death and states 'Would have to trick me. Trick me. Trick me!', turning a conditional verb into an imperative to absolve herself of responsibility, appears in 1987 in embryonic form, as part of an appended 'Extra Speech for Elizabeth' which ends with the much weaker 'And my so-called "wise advisors" would have to trick me before I would consent to sign a warrant for her death.' In 1988 this speech, fully incorporated into the script, concludes, 'They would have to trick me. Trick me! Tell them they'll have to trick me first' with the last sentence deleted.[27]

Exhaustively researched, it is emphatically not a history play, but instead, Lochhead insists, it is 'a metaphor for the Scots today' (*Time Out,* 16–23 September 1987). La Corbie, cracking her whip at the assembling guisers and animals who enter the circus ring, is the first signal to the audience that the play is spectacle, its characters lifted out of the 'tights and ruffs' solemnity of historical recreation. The production and performance style of the company compounds the contemporaneous message of the script. A beating drum and the constant stage presence of the fiddler (Anne Wood) set pace and an often ironical atmosphere ('mad tango music', for instance, accompanies 'The Suitors' (I.ii)), while the dancer (Frank McConnell) acts as a kind of voiceless chorus, complementing La Corbie. The sheer versatility of the actors permits the meaningful doubling (initially a practical constraint) that allowed Elizabeth to act out alternative roles, and 'the whore confronted by Knox on the street turns into Queen Mary by a mere stiffening of the neck' (Michael Ratcliffe, *Observer*, 16 August 1987). Elizabeth (Alison Peebles), with pink hair, Ray-bans, leopard skin stole and kneelength coctail dress, Knox with his bowler, Darnley/Leicester 'blazered and faintly Bridesheadish' (Martin Hoyle, *Financial Times*, 24 August 1987), catch contemporary resonances, while Mary (Anne Lacey), dressed in a dark ankle-length and narrow gown, with siren-long hair, was set apart by costume as by role.

When Contact staged the play in Manchester they set it in the mist-swept ruins of a Gothic cathedral choir, thereby altering the circus element, but they retained, necessarily, the energetic physical aspect of performance style, and anachronistic costuming and props. Elizabeth 'wears what would be the classic Gloriana portrait gown except that it is bright crimson and sliced into a flounced mini-skirt. . . . This conception of Elizabeth as a scarlet woman forced to play the part of Virgin Queen is a brilliant, and finally affecting notion' (Jeffrey Wainright, *Independent*, 28 September 1991). Critics also noted that 'there is no handbag but author and actress clearly have Thatcher in mind' (Alan Hulme, *Manchester Evening News*, 28 September 1991), picking up a quality of the characterisation which Lochhead admitted during composition, 'she's somebody you love to hate, and so it was easy to compare her with the Thatcher monster' (*Time Out*, 16–23 September 1987). Like Communicado, Contact's work met with wide-ranging critical praise, the only qualification being the equally universal cry that the language of the play was difficult for English ears to understand. Lochhead had anticipated such criticism in 1987: 'This can't be made into Mary Queen of Surbiton. If people can't hear what's being said, I suggest that they're not listening' (*Guardian*, 22 September 1987).

In October 1989 Lochhead extended her collaboration with Communicado to devise *Jock Tamson's Bairns*, an iconoclastic celebration of Burns Night which opened at the Tramway Theatre in Glasgow on 25 January 1990 at the start of the city's 'year of culture'. Many of the

emerging themes from *Mary Queen of Scots* were re-addressed, and
Lochhead's exploration of female androgyneity and its compromises
there became focused as a way of understanding the Scots' sense of
national identity. 'The English, she suggests, are like men – nonchalant
and unquestioning about existing. By contrast, "Scotland is like a
woman; the Scots know they are perceived from the outside"' (interview
with John Cunningham, *Guardian*, 8 February 1990). The show,
critically very well received, was an attack on the isolating nostalgic
wares of Scottish nationhood: the drunk man, haggis, tartan, poverty,
chauvinism, features of Scottish culture which Lochhead regards as
'comforting like drugs are comforting'.[28] Joyce McMillan states that
Lochhead's 'script is central to the mood of the piece' because 'its ironic
and self-critical tone is relentless, shattering what's left of the Scots
language into parodic fragments, mercilessly sending up the clichés and
cant of traditional Scottish speech', while it also 'takes these fragments
and blends them into a mosaic of such wit and colour that it affirms the
possibilities of the language and the people much more positively than
any reverent reconstruction' (*Guardian*, 29 January 1990). Lochhead
herself remains cool about her role in the ten-week-long devising
process which incorporated paintings by Keith McIntyre and music by
Karen Wimhurst to support the intensely physical theatre of the finished
product. It was not, in Lochhead's view, writer's theatre with
developing narrative and intellectual debate, but much more the theatre
of physical presence, carried by the dance, movement and ritual of the
performers.

A more satisfactory, if lighter, exercise in collaboration and devising
the year before had led to the production of *The Big Picture* at Dundee
Rep. in 1988. Commissioned and directed by Alan Lyddiard, designed
by Neil Murray, choreographed by Tamara McLorg, with music
directed by Iain Johnstone, it is a memory play, the shared reminiscence
of girlhood to womanhood of two school friends, Dorothy and Deanna.
The opening and closing frames of the two act play are set in the
present, when the two meet after long separation at Dorothy's mother's
funeral. The drama in between is largely flashback, set in the fifties (and
like many of the pieces in *True Confessions*, exhibits a wry nostalgia for
the popular culture of that era), where song triggers the memory and
keeps it in motion as the adult women act out their lives as ten-year-olds
and onwards.

> *Although they are wearing their grown-up funeral clothes they imagine
> each other as they were. Dorothy's outer clothes tended to the Clarks shoes,
> hairy knee socks, kilt and Fairisle jumper look. . . . Today Deanna is*

wearing the *American-dress-out-of-a-parcel. Very fancy. . . . They're*
'dressed' now.[29]

They are assisted by the device of two alter-ego dancers:

> *Our Deanna twirls, a little girl of ten, clumsy. But magically, in a*
> *beautiful swirl, Dorothy and Deanna's* image *of Deanna-in-the-*
> *American dress lights up behind them as dancer 'Deanna' twirls and spins*
> *while an alterego 'Dorothy' looks on, quite still. . . . They never look at*
> *these 'old selves' directly, these absolutely spot-on, precisely dated and clad*
> *dancers.*[30]

Dedicated to the memory of Anita Loos (author of *Gentlemen Prefer*
Blondes), the play explores the broken dreams of youth and it is set in 'a
symbolic cinema, backed by a broken proscenium arch and a giant
Technicolour cloudscape' (Tony Paterson, *Glasgow Herald*, 4 May
1988). Youthful fantasy is juxtaposed with assuredly naturalistic
dialogue as the adult women come to recognise the divisions within and
between themselves that have shaped their lives.

Lochhead's fondness for incorporating music in her work comes to the
fore in two short plays: *Patter Merchants* (1989), which uses contemporary popular music, and *Mozart and Salieri* (1990), written to incorporate
as many Mozart (and Salieri) arias as possible. *Patter Merchants* extends
Lochhead's work with Molière; it is derived from his 1658 curtain
raiser, a satire on affectation in the salons where linguistic pretentiousness and extravagant manners were rife, *Les Precieuses Ridicules*. As one in
a double bill called *Professional Pretenders*, it was premiered at the
Lyceum Studio, Edinburgh on 21 August 1989. Commissioned and
directed by John Carnegie for Winged Horse, the play is set in
contemporary Glasgow. Faithful to the spirit of Molière, it picks up
many of Lochhead's favourite themes of adolescent female friendship,
class differences, English versus Scots, courtship and fashion rituals, and
it clinches with political satire her perceptions of eighties' yuppydom,
epitomised locally by some of the gaudier extravagances of the 1990
Culture City. 'In these bluestocking-ingenues, ridiculously piqued
suitors and bemused above-it-alls, I found . . . a beating heart of a
situation which cries out to be translated into a particular familiar social
set and setting', Lochhead writes in a note to the script.[31] The play tells
how two snobbish Surrey girlfriends are gulled by their vanity into
entertaining the (disguised) Glaswegian lads they had previously
shunned. Music from Jive Bunny's then current chart hit of fifties
songs to a beat rhythm, selected by Carnegie, set the tempo and tone of
the always new old story. The pleasure of the piece lies in the way the
lads, patter merchants extraordinaire, spin out the duping of the girls
by outdoing their trend-setting predilections. Their disguise is

suddenly rumbled and the play comes to a perfunctory but goodhu-
moured conclusion as the girls, brought down to earth, speak in unison,
'I dinnae fancy the yin you're getting'.

Mozart and Salieri was written specially for the students at the Royal
Scottish Academy of Music and Drama where it was performed in
February 1990, directed by Joyce Deans, in a double bill with Rimsky
Korsakoff's setting of Pushkin's identically named piece. Lochhead's
play is a party. Held in the garden behind the Theater auf der Wieden
in Vienna on 30 September 1791, it is the celebration after the first
performance of *The Magic Flute*, which took place less than three months
before Mozart's death. Jealousies between lovers are at a peak, and
Salieri's cold-blooded hatred of his rival is fuelled by the evening's
success. These undercurrents form the dramatic substance of the play,
while the occasion provides an excuse for impromptu singing from
operas by both composers present. The atmosphere is deeply ironic, as
more and more characters enter still half-costumed for their parts in an
opera which celebrates love, to find themselves participating in their
own and other people's quarrels (all historically documented). A golden
brown autumnal stage, set with lanterns hanging from the trees,
suggests the rich sadness of the situation, while the witty rhyming
couplets of the dialogue impell the effervescent action forwards. Play
has really been incorporated in the script: on several occasions the
characters toss for it to settle who shall sing which aria, and in each case
Lochhead supplies a version for either outcome. But then, as Salieri
says,

> There's the earnest blue-stocking getting analytic,
> The *fan*, the free-loader, the hanger-on, the *critic*
> Who doesn't know a note from a sparrow fart.
> 'Darling it was wonderful, but was it art?'[32]

This chapter offers by no means an exhaustive survey of Lochhead's
dramatic work (major pieces, *Dracula* and *Tartuffe* have not been
mentioned, nor has the adaptation of the *York Mystery Cycle*),[33] yet
something of its extent and range beyond the few published pieces has
been indicated, and some of her favoured techniques have emerged. Her
early training in the visual arts is reflected in stage directions which
often refer to painters or films to evoke the stage picture, a habit – like
her early tendency to let poetic language do the dramatic work for her –
which to some extent she discards. But equally, a determined
accommodation of music hallmarks her style and signals a move towards
greater confidence in handling the non-verbal craft of the stage, as does
her scripted deployment of theatre games. Increasing skilled use of the

many dimensions of dramatic space and time, together with various devices to indicate multiple or split selves, confirm the ironic tone so often achieved by the dialogue. This physical and verbal irony of style lends subversive, discomfitting aspects to her comedy, while the seriousness of her observation strikes home through the disjunctive humour of its delivery.

CHRONOLOGY

(Excluding Revues):

1981   *Mary and the Monster* (Belgrade Theatre, Coventry, Dir. Michael Boyd)

1982   *Blood and Ice* (Traverse Theatre, Edinburgh, Dir. Kenny Ireland)
Disgusting Objects (Scottish Youth Theatre)

1983   *A Bunch of Fives* (co-written with Dave MacLennan, Dave Anderson, Tom Leonard and Sean Hardie, for Wildcat Theatre Company)
Shanghaied (Borderline Theatre Co., Dir. Paul Elkins)

1984   *Sweet Nothings* (BBC Scotland, Dir. Ian Knox)
Same Difference (Wildcat, Dir. Hugh Hodgart)

1985   *Dracula* (Traverse Theatre, Dir. Hugh Hodgart and Ian Wooldridge)

1986   *Tartuffe* (Royal Lyceum Theatre, Edinburgh, Dir. Ian Wooldridge and Colin MacNeil)
Fancy You Minding That (Radio 4, Dir. Marilyn Imrie)

1987   *Mary Queen of Scots Got Her Head Chopped Off* (Communicado Theatre Co., Dir. Gerry Mulgrew)

1988   *The Big Picture* (Dundee Rep Theatre Co., Dir. Alan Lyddiard)

1989   *Them Through The Wall* (with Agnes Owens, Cumbernauld Theatre, Dir. Robert Robson)
Patter Merchants (Winged Horse, Dir. John Carnegie)

1990   *Jock Tamson's Bairns* (Communicado, Dir. Gerry Mulgrew)
Mozart and Salieri (RSAMD, Dir. Joyce Deans)

1991   *Quelques Fleurs* (Nippy Sweeties, Dir. Joyce Deans)

1992   *The York Mystery Cycle* (Theatre Royal, York, Dir. Ian Forrest)

NOTES

1 Lochhead, 'Rough Magic', Perth Theatre Programme Notes for *Mary Queen of Scots Got Her Head Chopped Off* (September 1992).
2 Michelene Wandor, *Carry On, Understudies. Theatre & Sexual Politics* (London: Routledge & Kegan Paul, 1986), 121–9.
3 Caryl Churchill, *Plays: One* (London and New York: Methuen, 1985), xii.

4 To Emma Tennant, 28 January 1980, held in the National Library of
   Scotland, Manuscripts, Acc. No. 9870.

5 Typescript title page reads: 'Mary and the Monster. The story of
   Frankenstein & Mary Shelley. . . . "A free woman in an unfree
   society will be a monster." This is not a "historical" play', 46. The
   script was kindly lent to me by John Carnegie, copyright Liz
   Lochhead.

6 These quotations are taken from the Traverse Theatre script of *Blood
   and Ice*, held in the Scottish Theatre Archive, Glasgow University
   Library, STA H.O. Box 10/2, 37–8. Copyright Liz Lochhead.

7 Ibid., 38; 63–4.

8 Radio 4 interview with Peggy Reynolds, Kaleidoscope, 30 May
   1992.

9 'Mary And The Monster', ts., 7(a).

10 Howard Brenton, *Plays: Two* (London: Methuen, 1989), xiv.

11 Ibid., 270.

12 *Blood and Ice. A Tale of the Creation of Frankenstein*. Typescript of the
   1986 version staged by Winged Horse Touring Productions, held at
   the Scottish Theatre Archive, Glasgow, STA H.O. Box 10/2, 2. Text
   copyright Liz Lochhead. Production copyright John Carnegie and
   Peter Darrell. A version of this script has been published in the
   second edition of *Plays by Women, Vol.* 4; edited by Michelene
   Wandor (London: Methuen, 1987).

13 Ibid., 50.

14 Ibid., 50.

15 Ibid., 53.

16 Ibid., 82.

17 Ibid., 85.

18 'Rough Magic', Perth Theatre Programme Notes, 1992.

19 Gerard Mulgrew had worked for both of these companies and played
   the part of the dog in *Same Difference*.

20 *Shanghaied*, Borderline Theatre Programme Notes, 1984, held by the
   Tron Theatre, Glasgow.

21 *Shanghaied*, script, Scottish Theatre Archive, Glasgow University
   Library, 33, 42.

22 Ibid., 41.

23 'Rough Magic', Perth Theatre Programme Notes, 1992.

24 Manuscript at the National Library of Scotland, Acc. 10176 No. 2.

25 'Rough Magic', Perth Theatre Programme Notes, 1992.

26 National Library, Acc. 10176 No. 2, 14.

27 Typescripts of the play, held by Communicado Theatre Co.,
   Edinburgh.

28 In an interview on *The South Bank Show* (ITV), broadcast January
   1990, a programme dedicated to *Jock Tamson's Bairns*.

29 Typescript, Dundee Rep., 9.

30 Ibid., 11.

31 *Patter Merchants*, typescript and programme, Scottish Theatre
   Archive, Glasgow University Library.

32 Type/manuscript, RSAMD, Glasgow, 2.

33 For a most illuminating study of the first production o Dracula, see Jan McDonald, '"The Devil is Beautiful": *Dracula* – Freudian Novel and Feminist Drama' in Peter Reynolds, ed., *Novel Images* (London: Routledge, 1993), 80–104, *Tartuffe* has been discussed in this volume; the *Mystery Plays* were the subject of Radio 4 debate on Kaleidoscope, 30 June 1992.

Ten

Liz Lochhead: A Checklist

Compiled by Hamish Whyte

The usual disclaimer of incompleteness applies here. Time and circumstances have prevented this checklist from being as full as it could be. It is offered as a representative coverage of Liz Lochhead's work over the twenty-one years from her early success as a poet (*Memo for Spring* sold 1500 copies in a few months) to recent acclaim as a playwright (the award-winning *Mary Queen Of Scots Got Her Head Chopped Off*, etc.).

Given that Liz Lochhead has not been prolific in print – she is an indefatigable public performer and most of her scripts are still unpublished – the value of the checklist is necessarily limited. It concentrates on published work; it does not include radio and television broadcasts or performances of revues and plays. What remains is enough I hope to provide a guide (a hearing aid?) to the variety of Liz Lochhead's voices.

The checklist is arranged in sections as follows:

- A: Books, pamphlets, etc. by Liz Lochhead.
- B: Contributions to books, including anthologies.
- C: Contributions to periodicals and newspapers.
- D: Interviews.
- E: Ephemera.
- F: Manuscripts.
- G: Recordings.
- H: Critical and biographical.

The entries in all sections are generally arranged chronologically. Section A is a list of Liz Lochhead's separately published collections of poems, plays and performance pieces. Place, publisher, date and contents of each are given, with brief notes and an indication of press and magazine review coverage. Printed plays rarely get reviewed, so a few reviews of performances are included as evidence of critical response. All publications are paperback except where indicated.

Section B consists mainly of poems contributed to anthologies. As in A, place, publisher and date are given, with occasional notes. In Section C, volume and part number of each periodical, date and page references are listed. The interviews listed in Section D are usually in the form of articles based on interview; there are a few exceptions of the Q and A style, such as those with Rebecca Wilson and Emily Todd. The other sections are self-explanatory. Where titles are given without quotation marks or italics they should be assumed to be of individual poems or songs. Titles of prose pieces (articles, monologues, etc.) are put in quotation marks.

I should like to thank Barbara Benjamin, Robert Crawford, Ewan McVicar, Hazel Miller, Edwin Morgan and Winifred Whyte for their help in putting the checklist together. I am most grateful to Gordon Wright (Reprographia), Jane Pickett (Penguin Books) and Kathryn MacLean (Polygon) for kindly supplying publication details. The errors are my own; I should be pleased to receive any corrections, omissions and comments.

A BOOKS AND PAMPHLETS

A1   *Memo for Spring*. Edinburgh: Reprographia, 1972. *Contents*: Revelation – Poem for other poor fools – How have I been since you last saw me? – On Midsummer Common – Fragmentary – The Visit – After a Warrant Sale – Phoenix – Daft Annie on our village mainstreet – Obituary – Morning After – Inventory – Grandfather's Room – For my Grandmother knitting – Poem for my sister – Local Colour [Something I'm not] – Poem on a Daytrip – Overheard by a young waitress – Notes on the inadequacy of a sketch – Letter from New England – Getting Back – Box Room – Song for coming home – George Square – Man on a Bench – Carnival – Cloakroom – The Choosing – Homilies from hospital – Object – Wedding March – Riddle-Me-Ree – Memo to myself for Spring (5–48).

Notes: Published 15 May 1972 in an edition of 1500 copies which sold out in a few months. Reprinted the same year (3400 copies) and sold out in 1977. 125 review and promotional copies distributed. Cover photograph of Liz Lochhead taken by the publisher, Gordon Wright, on Blackford Hill, Edinburgh.

Reviews

Stewart Conn. *Glasgow Herald* 19 August 1972, Saturday Extra, II.

Robert Garioch. *Scottish International* 5:6, August 1972, 35.

Philip Hobsbaum. *Lines Review* 42/43, September 1972–February 1973, 148–9.

Alexander Scott. *Studies in Scottish Literature* XI:1 & 2, July–October 1973, 20.

A2   *islands*. Glasgow: Print Studio Press, 1978.

Contents: Outer (I. Another life – II. And so we go to Callanish to see the stones – III. And when the butter wouldn't churn – IV. Wind hurts – V. Golden Harvest – VI. Laura has gone in a clean white blouse) – Inner (I. make a change – II. the birds – III. mail comes) – Laundrette – The Bargain – In the Francis Bacon Room at the Tate.

Notes: Published September 1978. 600 copies, of which 26 are lettered A–Z, signed by the author and printed on Chariot cream cartridge paper. Stapled pamphlet.

Reviews

G. Mangan. *Words* 8, [1979], 64–5.

A3   *Liz Lochhead*. Glasgow and London: National Book League, 1978. (Writers in Brief No. 1)

Contents: ['I was born in Central Lanarkshire . . .']; Revelation – Poem for Other Poor fools – The Grim Sisters – Poem for my Sister – My Rival's House – The Last Hag.

Notes: Card 20.2 cm × 43.5 cm folded (3 times) to 20.2 cm × 11 cm (8 pages). Includes photograph of Liz Lochhead on p. [1].

A4   (a) *The Grimm Sisters*. London: Next Editions in association with Faber and Faber, 1981 (Next Editions 2).

Contents: *The Grimm Sisters*: The Storyteller Poems (I: Storyteller – II: The Father – III: The Mother) – The Grim Sisters – The Furies (I: Harridan – II: Spinster – III: Bawd) – My Rival's House – Three Twists (I: Rapunzstiltskin – II: Beauty & The – III: After Leaving the Castle) – Tam Lin's Lady – Six Disenchantments – *The Beltane Bride*: The Beltane Bride – Song of Solomon – Stooge Song – Midsummer Night – Blueshirt – The Hickie – The Other Woman – Last Supper – *Hags and Maidens*: Everybody's Mother – The Ariadne Version – Poem for

My Sister – My Mother's Suitors – Girl's Song – The Cailleach –
Poppies – The Last Hag (11–53).

Notes: Published January 1981. Card covers, spiral bound. Book
edited by Emma Tennant. Book design by Julian Rothenstein.
Cover drawing by Hiang Kee. Epigraph from Robert Graves,
The Greek Myths: 'The moon's three phases . . . Selene,
Aphrodite, Hecate.'

Reviews
Alan Bold. *Weekend Scotsman* 7 February 1981, 3.
James Campbell. *Times Literary Supplement* 15 May 1981, 553.
Paul Mills. *Cencrastus* 8, Spring 1982, 45.
Neil Philip. *Aquarius* 13/14, 1981/1982, 157.
Scottish Review 23, August 1981, 55 [bad review].
Anne Simpson. *Glasgow Herald* 22 January 1981, 4 (Photograph
of Liz Lochhead).
Val Warner. *Logos* 6, 1981, pp. 17–19.

(b) *A Selection from The Grimm Sisters*. Designed and illustrated by
Ingebjorg Smith. Glasgow: Printed at Glasgow School of Art,
1983.
Contents: Spinster – Poem for My Sister – After Leaving the
Castle – Blueshirt – Song of Solomon – Bawd.

Notes: Six A4 sheets within folder.

A5   *Blood and Ice*. Edinburgh: The Salamander Press, 1982 (The
Traverse Plays 5).

Notes: First published June 1982. Cover design by June Redfern.
Stapled pamphlet. 34pp. Programme for first run at Traverse
Theatre, Edinburgh, 19 August–11 September 1982, inserted
between pp. 18 and 19.

Reviews
Mary Brennan. *Glasgow Herald* 20 August 1982, 4 (perfor-
mance).
Cordelia Oliver. *Guardian* 27 August 1982, 8 (performance).
Allen Wright. *Scotsman* 21 August 1982, 7 (performance).

A6   *Dreaming Frankenstein & Collected Poems*. Edinburgh: Polygon
Books, 1984.
Contents: *Dreaming Frankenstein*: What The Pool Said, On
Midsummer's Day – An Abortion – 1. Dreaming Frankenstein

(*for Lys Hansen, Jacki Parry and June Redfern*) – 2. What The
Creature Said – 3. Smirnoff For Karloff (*for Marilyn Bowering and
Bessie Smith*) – Smuggler – Page from a Biography – The People's
Poet (*for Edwin Morgan*) – Construction For A Site: Library On
An Old Croquet Lawn, St. Andrews: Nine Approaches – Fourth
of July Fireworks – The Carnival Horses – Ontario October
Going West – Near Qu'Appelle (*for Liz Allen*) – In Alberta – 1.
Sailing Past Liberty (*for Rick Shaine*) – 2. Two Birds – 3. My
House – 4. Inter-City – 5. In The Cutting Room – Ships (*for
John Oughton*) – Hafiz On Danforth Avenue – A Gift – Reading
The Signs – Flitting – A Giveaway – Heartbreak Hotel – China
Song (*for Janice and John Gow, 1980*) – Why I Gave You The
Chinese Plate (*for Kenny Storrie*) – Old Notebooks – Fin – That
Summer – West Kensington – The Empty Song [Today] –
Noises In The Dark – A Letter – Sunday song – The Legend Of
The Sword & The Stone – Rainbow – The Dollhouse Convention
– 1. In The Dreamschool – 2. The Teachers – 3. The Prize – The
Offering – Legendary – Fetch On The First Of January – Mirror's
Song (*for Sally Potter*) (7–68) – *The Grimm Sisters* (69–104) –
Islands (105–121) – *Memo For Spring* (123–59).

Notes: Published May 1984. Foreword by Edwin Morgan, p. [5].
Cover design by James Hutcheson. Photograph of Liz Lochhead
by Tony Martin on back cover. Each collection in the text is
prefaced by an illustration by a different artist: Lys Hansen
(*Dreaming Frankenstein*), Ingebjorg Smith (*The Grimm Sisters*),
Calum Mackenzie (*Islands*), Alasdair Gray (*Memo for Spring*).
Reprinted 1985 (3000 copies), 1987 (2000 copies) and 1989
(3000 copies) with corrections to text (mainly typos) and revised
blurb and new photograph (by Gunnie Moberg) on back cover.

Reviews
Kristine Furniss-Sander. *Radical Scotland* 10, August/September
1984, 28.
Kathleen Jamie. *Weekend Scotsman* 16 June 1984, 3.
Mario Relich. *Lines Review* 91, December 1984, 40–2.
Alan Riach. *Chapman* VIII: 4, No. 40, Spring 1985, 75–6.
Trevor Royle. *Books in Scotland* 16, Autumn 1984, 16.
Roderick Watson. *Studies in Scottish Literature* XXI, 1986,
254–6.
Roger D. Webster. *The Green Book* 2:4, [Autumn 1986], 53.

A7   *Tartuffe: A translation into Scots from the original by Molière.*
Glasgow and Edinburgh: Third Eye Centre and Polygon, 1986.
Contents: 'Introduction' ([v]); cast ([1]); 'Opening' ([2]); text (3–
63).

Notes: Edition of 1750. Cover design by James Hutcheson.

Reviews
Mary Brennan. *Glasgow Herald* 27 January 1986, 4 (perfor-
mance).
Allen Wright. *Scotsman* 27 January 1986, 4 (performance).

A8   *True Confessions & New Clichés.* Edinburgh: Polygon Books,
1985.
Contents: SUGAR AND SPITE and TRUE CONFESSIONS.
['Introduction']; True Confessions (*Rap*) – Open with the Closing
(*Song*) – 'Mrs Abernethy: Burns the hero' (*Monologue*); Scotch Mist
(The Scotsport Song); 'Verena: Security' (*Monologue*); Fat Girl's
Confession (*Rap*) Look At Us (*Song*); 'Phyllis Marlowe: Only
Diamonds Are Forever' (*Monologue*); The Suzanne Valadon Story
(*Rap*) – Vymura: The Shade Card Poem – Franglais (*Rap*) –
Cowboys and Priests (*Song*); 'Six Men Monologues' (No. 1:
Annemarie. No. 2: 'Pamela'. No. 3: Judith. No. 4: Kimberley.
No. 5: Mo. No. 6: Bette.) – Mean Mr Love (*Song*) – Maintenance
Man (*Song*) – Mae: Come Up and See Me Sometime (*Monologue*) –
Liz Lochhead's Lady Writer Talkin' Blues (*Rap*) – Page Three
Dollies (*Rap*) – Feminine Advice (*Rap*); 'Sharon: Incest'
(*Monologue*); Telephone Song – Alarm Clock Song – Clover (*Rap*)
– Meal-ticket Song – Gentlemen Prefer Blonds – Curtains (*Song*)
– What-I'm-Not Song (*Finale rap*) (1–56); TEAM EFFORTS
AND ASSORTED REVUES: ['Introduction']; *Tickly Mince and
The Pie of Damocles*: Calderpark Zoo Song; 'Verena: Anklebiters'
(*Monologue*); Sometimes It's Hard to be a Woman (*Parody*); 'The
Suitor' (*Sketch*); Encore for the Arts (*Rap for three*); 'Mullicking
Tyre: The Incomers Take the High Road' (*Sketch*); Country and
Western in Kyle (*Parody*) – Hillhead Election Song (*Rap for three*)
– West End Blues (*Song*); *A Bunch of Fives*: Interference Song –
Sincerely Yours (*Song*) – Promises (*Song*); *Red Hot Shoes*: Apple Pie
– A Mother Worries; 'Usherette Scene'; *Same Difference*: The
Babygrow Song (The Naked Truth) – It's a Dog's Life (*Song*) –
That's Why the Princess is a Puke (*Song*) – A Bit of the Other
(*Song*) – Change of Life (The Usual) (*Song*) – Midsummer Night's
Dog (*Song*) – The Sins of the Fathers (*Song*) – The Life of Mrs

Riley (*Song*) – Bazz's Serial Monogamy Song – Trish's Serial Monogamy Song – Who's Screwing Who – Who's Paying For All This? (pp. 57–110); NEW CLICHÉS: ['Introduction'] I Wouldn't Thank You for a Valentine (*Rap*) – St Valentine's Day Heart Catalogue (*Rap*) – How Do I Love Thee, Let me Count The . . . (*Rap*) – Adultery Song – Bluejohn Pockets – Plenty (*Rap*) – Favourite Shade (*Rap*); 'Donkey' (*Monologue*); 'Mrs Rintoul: Standard English' (*Monologue*); 'Mrs Abernethy: Festive fayre' (*Monologue*); 'Verena: Castaways' (*Monologue*); Postcard Us When the Wean Says Bananas (*The Greeting Card Song*) – Men Talk (*Rap*) (111–35).

Notes: Published July 1985 in an edition of 3671. Cover design by James Hutcheson. Revised and reprinted 1986 (2,250 copies), with press comments added to blurb on back cover, and 1989 (3,000 copies).

Reviews
James Aitchison. *Glasgow Herald* 10 August, 11.
George Mackay Brown. *Weekend Scotsman* 27 July 1985, 3.
William Reid. *Books in Scotland* 19, Autumn 1985, 14–15.
Roderick Watson. *Studies in Scottish Literature* XXIII, 1988, 262–3.

A9   *Liz Lochhead*. Glasgow and London: National Book League, 1986. (Writers in Brief No. 21)
Contents: ['The sequence of poems "For Bram Stoker" . . . comes from a play "Dracula" . . .']; For Bram Stoker (Count Vlad in his Castle – Lucy's Diary: Six Entries – Florrie's Advice – Nurse's Song – Renfield's Ravings).

Notes: Card 20.2 × 43.5 cm folded (3 times) to 20.2 × 11 cm (8 pages). Photograph of Liz Lochhead by Angela Catlin on p. [1].

A10 *Mary Queen Of Scots Got Her Head Chopped Off and Dracula*. London: Penguin Books, 1989.
Contents: 'Acknowledgements' ([6]); *Mary Queen Of Scots Got Her Head Chopped Off* ([7]–67); *Dracula* ([69]–147).

Notes: Published August 1989 in an edition of 3000. Reprinted December 1990 (2500 copies) and August 1992 (3000 copies). Cover photograph by Ginnie Atkinson of scene from Communicado production of *Mary*. Photograph of Liz Lochhead by Ed Heath on back cover.

Reviews

Mary Brennan. *Glasgow Herald* 18 March 1985, 4 (performance of *Dracula*).

Hamish Lennox. *Times* 9 September 1989, 39 (book).

Melanie Reid. *Scotsman* 16 March 1985, 2 (performance of *Dracula*).

Trevor Royle. *Glasgow Herald* 14 August 1987, 5 (performance of *Mary*).

P. H. Scott. *Scotsman* 12 August 1987, 9 (performance of *Mary*).

A11   *Bagpipe Muzak*. London: Penguin Books, 1991.

Contents: I. *Recitations*: Almost Miss Scotland – Sexual Etiquette – Advice to Old Lovers – The Complete Alternative History of the World, Part One – Con-densation – The Garden Festival, Glasgow 1988 – Festival City: Yon Time Again – Prologue for 'School For Scandal' – Bagpipe Muzak, Glasgow 1990 (3–[26]); II. *Characters*: 'Glasgow's No Different'; 'Meeting Norma Nimmo'; The Redneck; 'Quelques Fleurs (A Tale of Two Sisters)' (129–[51]); III. *Poems*: After the War (*for Susanne Ehrhardt*) – View of Scotland / Love Poem – Neckties – Lucy's Diary: Six Entries – Renfield's Nurse – The Bride – Papermaker (*for Jacki Parry at Gallowgate Studios*) – Good Wood – Tupalik – Five Berlin Poems (5th April 1990 – aquarium 1 – aquarium 2 – three visits – Almost-Christmas at the Writers' House) (55–[84]).

Notes: Published August 1991 in an edition of 3500. Reprinted December 1991 (2500 copies) and June 1993 (2500 copies). Cover portrait of Liz Lochhead by Claudia Petretti.

Reviews

James Aitchison. *Glasgow Herald* 28 September 1991, 22.

Kate Clanchy. *Weekend Scotsman* 12 October 1991, 8.

Emily Todd. *Scottish Literary Journal*, Supplement 35, Winter 1991, 37–9.

B   CONTRIBUTIONS TO BOOKS INCLUDING ANTHOLOGIES

B1   *Scottish Poetry 6*. Edited by George Bruce, Maurice Lindsay and Edwin Morgan (Edinburgh: Edinburgh University Press, [1972]).

Revelation (55).

B2   *Seven New Voices*. Edited and introduced by John Schofield. ([Edinburgh:] Garret Arts, 1972).

The Ballad of Melvin – Letter from New England – Wedding March (28–34).

Reviewed by P. Hobsbaum, *Lines Review* 42/43, September 1972–February 1973, 148.

B3 *Made in Scotland: an anthology of poems.* Edited by Robert Garioch (Cheadle Hume: Carcanet Press, 1974).

Rainbow – Laundrette – Three Women – Fourth of July Fireworks (84–91).

B4 *Scottish Poetry 7.* Edited by Maurice Lindsay, Alexander Scott, Roderick Watson (Glasgow: University of Glasgow Press, 1974).

Fourth of July Fireworks (34–6).

B5 *Contemporary Poets.* Second Edition. With a Preface by C. Day Lewis. Edited by James Vinson with Associate Editor, D. L. Kirkpatrick (London & New York: St James Press, 1975).

'I want my poems to be clear . . .' (926).
Reprinted in 3rd edition, 1980 (929); 4th edition, 1985 (507); and 5th edition, 1991 (571).

B6 *Scottish Love Poems: A Personal Anthology.* Edited by Antonia Fraser (Edinburgh: Canongate Publishing, 1975).

Today (210).
Paperback edition published by Penguin Books, 1976 (poem on 212).

B7 *Scottish Poetry 8.* Edited by Maurice Lindsay, Alexander Scott, Roderick Watson (Cheadle Hume: Carcanet Press, 1975).

Noises in the Dark (Anatolia, April 74) – Her Place (46–8).

B8 *Trees: an anthology.* Devised by Angus Ogilvy (Stirling: The Stirling Gallery, 1975).

Good Wood – Churchyard Song (Nos 7 and 8).

B9 *Modern Scottish Poetry: an anthology of the Scottish Renaissance 1925– 1975.* Edited by Maurice Lindsay (Manchester: Carcanet Press, 1976).

Her Place – Today – Poem for My Sister – Noises in the Dark (246–8).

B10 *Scottish Poetry Nine.* Edited by Maurice Lindsay, Alexander Scott, Roderick Watson (Manchester: Carcanet Press / Scottish Arts Council, 1976).

A Letter – Widow (42–4).

B11 *Birds: An anthology of new poems.* Edited by Angus Ogilvy, George Sutherland, Roderick Watson. Illustrations by children from Central Regional Schools (Stirling: The Stirling Gallery, [1977]).

Postcard from an Island [the birds *from* Islands] (59).

B12 *Jock Tamson's Bairns: Essays on a Scots Childhood.* Edited by Trevor Royle (London: Hamish Hamilton, 1977).

'A Protestant Girlhood' (112–26).

B13 *A Sense of Belonging: Six Scottish Poets of the Seventies.* Compiled by Brian Murray and Sydney Smyth (Glasgow: Blackie, 1977).

Lady of Shalott – Bawd – Song – My Rival's House – Bluejohn Pockets – Spinster – The Offering – Local Colour [Something I'm not] – Obituary (27–37).

The other five poets are: Stewart Conn, Douglas Dunn, Tom Leonard, William McIlvanney and Edwin Morgan.

B14 *New Poems 1977–78:* A P. E. N. Anthology of Contemporary Poetry. Edited by Gavin Ewart (London: Hutchinson, 1977).

Six Disenchantments (105–6).

B15 *The Lost Poets* ([Edinburgh:] Spineless Publications, 1978).

Tam Lin's Lady – Six Disenchantments – After Leaving the Castle – The Ariadne Version – The Last Hag ([9–16]).

The Lost Poets were: Ron Butlin, Liz Lochhead, Andrew Greig and Brian McCabe.

B16 *Identities: An Anthology of West of Scotland Poetry, Prose and Drama.* Edited by Geddes Thomson. Introduction by Edwin Morgan (London: Heinemann Educational, 1981).

'My Primary School'; Poem for my Sister – Poem on a Day Trip; 'Freedom'; The Choosing – For my Grandmother Knitting – Lady of Shalott (4–8, 26, 93, 130–2, 137–8, 156–7, 198–200). The prose extracts are from 'A Protestant Girlhood' (B12).

B17 *Akros Verse 1965–1982: An Anthology from 'Akros' Nos 1–49.* Edited by Duncan Glen (Nottingham: Akros Publications, October 1982).

My Rival's House (25).

B18 *Scotch Passion: An Anthology of Scottish Erotic Poetry.* Compiled by Alexander Scott (London: Hale, 1982).

Song of Solomon (162).

B19   *Noise and Smoky Breath: An Illustrated Anthology of Glasgow Poems 1900–1983*. Edited by Hamish Whyte (Glasgow: Third Eye Centre / Glasgow District Libraries Publications Board, 1983).

Obituary – Something I'm not [Local Colour] – The Bargain – Fetch on the First of January (88–9, 101–2, 137–8, 140–1, 155–6).

B20   *Glasgow: A Celebration*. Edited by Cliff Hanley. With photographs by Oscar Marzaroli (Edinburgh: Mainstream Publishing, 1984).

'Only Diamonds Are Forever (A Phyliss Marlowe Story)' (188–91).
In *TCNC* as 'Phyllis Marlowe: Only Diamonds Are Forever'.

B21   Angela Catlin, *Natural Light: Portraits of Scottish Writers*. Introduction by Trevor Royle (Edinburgh: Paul Harris Publishing / Waterfront, 1985).

What the Pool Said, On Midsummer's Day (44).
Photograph on p. 45.

B22   *Plays by Women Volume Four*. Edited and introduced by Michelene Wandor (London: Methuen, 1985). (A Methuen Theatrefile)

Blood and Ice; ['Afterword'] (81–116, 117–18).
Revision of the 1982 text.

B23   *The Other Side of the Clyde*. Edited by David Drever and Liam Stewart (Harmondsworth: Puffin Books, 1986).

Two Birds – Fat Girl's Confession – Vymura: the Shade Card Poem (57–8, 86–9, 140–1).

B24   *Twelve More Modern Scottish Poets*. Edited by Charles King and Iain Crichton Smith (London: Hodder and Stoughton, 1986).

['When I look back over the things I've written . . .']; What the Pool Said, on Midsummer's Day – In the Dreamschool – The Offering – Spinster – *from* Three Twists (I. Rapunzstiltskin) – My Mother's Suitors – Laundrette – Revelation – After a Warrant Sale (139–50).

B25   *Roadworks: Song Lyrics for Wildcat* by David Anderson and David MacLennan. Selected by Edwin Morgan (Glasgow: Third Eye Centre, 1987).

'Introduction' (1–2).

B26   *Voices of Our kind: An Anthology of Modern Scottish Poetry from 1920 to the Present*. Third Edition. Edited by Alexander Scott (Edinburgh: Chambers in association with The Saltire Society and the Scots Language Society, 1987).

Noises in the Dark – Poppies – Poem for my Sister (147–50).

B28   *The Best of Scottish Poetry: An Anthology of Contemporary Scottish Verse*. Edited by Robin Bell (Edinburgh: Chambers, 1989).

[Comment on poems]; What the Pool Said, on Midsummer's Day – My Rival's House (88–91).

B29   *The Hutchinson Book of Post-War British Poets*. Edited by Dannie Abse (London: Hutchinson, 1989).

Revelation – Song of Solomon (126–7).

B30   *Northern Lights*. Edited by Leslie Wheeler and Douglas Young (London: Unwin Hyman, 1989).

Poem For My Sister – The Teachers [not seen].

B31   *Streets of Gold: Contemporary Glasgow Stories*. Edited by Moira Burgess and Hamish Whyte (Edinburgh: Mainstream Publishing, 1989).

'Phyllis Marlowe: Only Diamonds Are Forever' (133–6).

B32   *Felt-Tipped Hosannas for Edwin Morgan on his 70th Birthday*. Edited by Susan Stewart and Hamish Whyte (Glasgow: Third Eye Centre, 5 May 1990).

5th April 1990 (9–10).

B33   *Sleeping with Monsters: Conversations with Scottish and Irish Women Poets*. Research and Interviews by Rebecca E. Wilson. Edited by Gillean Somerville-Arjat and Rebecca E. Wilson (Edinburgh: Polygon, 1990).

The Bride – Dreaming Frankenstein (14–17).

B34   *An Anthology of Scottish Women Poets*. Edited by Catherine Kerrigan (Edinburgh: Edinburgh University Press, 1991).

Dreaming Frankenstein – An Abortion – Revelation – Page from a Biography – St Valentine's Day Heart Catalogue – After a Warrant Sale (299–305).

B35   *Four Glasgow Writers*. Edited by Peter McLaren (Glasgow: Straight Line Publishing for Strathclyde Region Education Department, [1991]).

The Choosing – Poem for my Sister – Local Colour [Something I'm not] (12–15).

Accompanied by video.

B36   *New Approaches to Poetry.* Edited by Lois Keith (London: BBC, 1991).

'Some of the things Liz Lochhead says about poetry'; George Square – Laundrette – The Choosing – A Letter – Fat Girl's Confession (Rap) (5–8).

Booklet to accompany BBC Schools TV series English File (A Double Exposure Production).

B37   *100 Poems on the Underground.* Edited by Gerard Benson, Judith Chernaik, Cicely Herbert (London: Cassell, 1991).

Riddle-Me-Ree (53).

B38   *Meantime: Looking Forward to the Millenium.* Introduced by Janice Galloway (Edinburgh: Polygon In Association with Women 200, 1991).

'Women's Writing And The Millenium' (71–5).

B39   *The Literary Companion to Sex: An anthology of prose and poetry.* Collected by Fiona Pitt-Kethley (London: Sinclair-Stevenson, 1992).

Morning After (400–1).

B40   *Scotia Bar 1st of May Poetry Prize* (Glasgow: Taranis Books, 1992).

'Foreword' (iv).

Liz Lochhead was one of the judges.

B41   *The Faber Book of Twentieth-Century Scottish Poetry.* Edited by Douglas Dunn (London: Faber and Faber, 1992).

Dreaming Frankenstein – Heartbreak Hotel – Mirror's Song – The Grim Sisters – *from* The Furies (I: The Harridan) – My Mother's Suitors (344–52).

B42   *Three Scottish Poets.* Edited by Roderick Watson (Edinburgh: Canongate Press, 1992). (Scottish Classics 45)

Box Room – *from* Islands (Outer I – Outer V – Outer VI) – The Bargain – Hafiz on Danforth Avenue – The Empty Song – Fourth of July Fireworks – The Grim Sisters – Midsummer Night – Stooge Song – The Other Woman – *from* True Confessions ('Verena: Security') – Mirror's Song – Sorting Through (89–117).

The other two poets are Norman MacCaig and Edwin Morgan. Reviewed by 'Browser', *Scottish Book Collector* 3:8, December 1992–January 1993, 33.

B43 *The Virago Book of Wicked Verse.* Edited by Jill Dawson (London: Virago Press, 1992).

Favourite Shade – Everybody's Mother (124–5, 135–7).

C CONTRIBUTIONS TO PERIODICALS AND NEWSPAPERS

C1 Revelation – Obituary. *EMU* 1, 1971, 3, 8–9.

Glasgow University Extra Mural magazine. Both poems illustrated by Liz Lochhead.

C2 [untitled poem:] 'not the sunshine' – After a Warrant Sale – Quite a nice neighbourhood – Majestic – For my grandmother knitting. *Glasgow University Magazine* 82:3, [June] 1971, 9–11, 23, 29.

C3 ['My upbringing . . .']; Morning After – Revelation – Getting Back. *Scottish International* October 1971, 33–4.

C4 Object – Local Colour [Something I'm not]. *Scottish International* April 1972, 26–7.

C5 [Untitled poem:] 'miss' – Two games (1. Snakes and Ladders – 2. Patience). *Glasgow Review* III:1, Summer 1972, 17, 42.

c6 Fourth of July Fireworks – Laundrette. *Aquarius* 6, September 1973, 48–52.

C7 The Doll Museum: Elegy for Ethel Widness – Her Place – Today. *Akros* 9:25, August 1974, 10–13.

c8 Revelation. *The Literary Review* 18:3, Spring 1975, 296.

Published by Fairleigh Dickinson University, New Jersey.

C9 Pastoral (Derbyshire, August 74) – Noises in the Dark (Anatolia, April 74). *Akros* 9:27, April 1975, 98–9.

C10 Tam Lin – Lady of Shalott. *Words* 1, Autumn 1976, 45–7.

C11 The Changeling (*from* Speaking the woe). *Oasis* 1:4, [May 1976], 2–8.

Glasgow University magazine.

C12 Noises in the Dark. *Scottish Field* October 1976, 60.

Fourth in 'Scotland's Poets' series.

C13   Legendary. *Aquarius* 9, 1977, 36–40.

C14   The Bargain. *Asphalt Garden* 4, 1977, 7–8.

C15   'A Protestant Girlhood'. *Weekend Scotsman* 11 June 1977, 1.
        Reprinted from *Jock Tamson's Bairns* (published 23 June) (B12).

C16   [Review of Jane Wilson, *Ringing the Migrants*]. *Words* 4, Winter
        1977, 58–9.

C17   Monologue [Six Men Monologues No.1: Annemarie]. *Glasgow
        Herald* 3 April 1978, 4.

C18   Bluejohn Pockets. *Broadsheet* 30, June 1978.

C19   Midsummer Night – The People's Poet: Part II; [contribution to
        symposium] 'What it Feels Like to be a Scottish Poet'. *Aquarius*
        11, 1979, 41–4, 71.

C20   Old Notebooks – Colour Fields (for Tom Leonard Robert
        Rauschenberg & Barnett Newman) – Show of Presents. *Chapman*
        VI:3–4, Nos 27–8, Summer 1980, 111–2.
        'woven by women' issue.

C21   Poppies – The Cailleach. *Scottish Review* 19, August 1980, 9, 45.

C22   Inter-City – That Summer. *Cencrastus* 3, Summer 1980, 32.

C23   'Not waving but drowning.' *Glasgow Herald* 27 January 1982, 7.
        Diary-style article on life as a writer. 'Liz Lochhead will be on
        BBC Scotland tomorrow . . . discussing the New Wave.'

C24   Two new poems: How Do I Love Thee? – Thankless Valentine [I
        Wouldn't Thank You for a Valentine]. *Glasgow Herald* 12
        February 1982, 10. (Photograph)

C25   'Uncommon sense'. *Times Educational Supplement (Scotland)* 5
        March 1982, 72.
        On school uniform.

C26   'Making the words and Biro ink flow to put my slant on the
        world'. *Glasgow Herald* 13 October 1982, 9.
        Part of series 'From Scenes Like These: Scottish Writers Today'.
        (Photograph).

C27   Ode to a sonsie lass [Fat Girl's Confession]. *Glasgow Herald* 23
        September 1983, 10. (Photograph)

C28 In the dreamschool — What the Pool Said, On Midsummer's Day. *The Glasgow Magazine* 4, Spring 1984, 13–15.

C29 Six poems from 'Dreaming Frankenstein': What the Creature Said — Smirnoff for Karloff — Page from a Biography — The teachers — Why I Gave you the Chinese Plate — Fin. *Weekend Scotsman* 12 May 1984, 6.

C30 From *Tartuffe*: Act Two: the first appearance of Tartuffe. *Chapman VIII:6 & IX:1*, Nos 43–4, Spring 1986, 123–8.

Drawing of Liz Lochhead on p. 129.

C31 [Contribution to] 'Cultured views of Berlin'. *Scotland on Sunday* 18 December 1988, 38.

Reports on visit to Berlin by Stephen Mulrine, Jack Withers, Liz Lochhead and Edwin Morgan. Photograph.

C32 'Slightly demented in the City of Culture'. *Weekend Guardian* 1– 2 April 1989, 5.

Diary. Mostly on *Them Through the Wall*.

C33 'Moving Images'. *Scotland on Sunday Magazine* 21 January 1990, 7–8.

On cinema. Photograph.

C34 Bawd. *Scottish Poetry Library Newsletter* 17, August 1991, 7.

C35 'Once upon a Time in the West'. *Scotland on Sunday Magazine* 18 August 1991, 16–18, 20.

On experiences at Butlins, Ayr.

C36 Abraham and Isaac. *The Herald* 6 July 1992, 13.

Extract from Liz Lochhead's adaption of York Cycle of mystery plays.

C37 [Contributes to] 'The Great & The Good: Celebrities from the arts, sport, the church and politics recall their favourite books'. *Scotland on Sunday* 29 November 1992, 14.

Liz Lochhead's choice was Alasdair Gray, *Poor Things* and Alice Hoffman, *Seventh Heaven*.

D INTERVIEWS

D1 With Julie Davidson. 'Poet from the waste-lands'. *Weekend Scotsman* 10 June 1972, 1–2.

Photograph.

D2   With Anne Simpson. 'Liz Lochhead: Most of our men would secretly like to be Robert Burns, the romantic hero.' *Glasgow Herald* 3 April 1978, 4.

Article based on interview in series 'What the women of Scotland think about the men'.

Photograph.

D3   With Joyce McMillan. *Scottish Theatre News* August 1982, 3–6.

Mostly on BAI. Photograph on p. 2.

D4   With William Hunter. *Glasgow Herald* 10 May 1984, 10.

Article based on interview. Photograph.

D5   With Melanie Reid. 'The prime of Liz Lochhead'. *Weekend Scotsman* 12 May 1984, 6.

Photograph.

D6   With Ruth Wishart. 'Tales from a tartan duvet'. *Guardian* 24 July 1985, 8.

Article based on interview. Mostly on TC. Photograph.

D7   With Emilio Coia. *Scottish Field* April 1986, 36.

Portrait of Liz Lochhead by Coia on 37. In 'Caught by Coia' series.

D8   With Julie Morrice. 'Word play for friends and neighbours'. *Scotland on Sunday* 19 March 1989, 40.

Article based on interview. Liz Lochhead and Agnes Owens discuss their collaboration on the play *Them Through the Wall*. Photograph.

D9   'Poet's life one long paperchase'. *Scotsman Property Pull Out* 17 August 1989, Four.

Article based on interview about her flat in 'Our House' series.

Photograph.

D10   With Rebecca E. Wilson in *Sleeping With Monsters: Conversations with Scottish and Irish Women Poets*, research and interviews by Rebecca E. Wilson, edited by Gillean Somerville-Arjat and Rebecca E. Wilson (Edinburgh: Polygon, 1990), 8–14.

D11   With John Cunningham. 'Anima rights campaigner'. *Guardian* 8 February 1990, 37.

Photograph.

D12   *Marxism Today* September 1991, 48.

'Back Page' interview, with photograph.

D13   With Ajay Close. 'Almost Miss Scotland'. *Scotland on Sunday Spectrum* 8 September 1991, 33.

Photograph.

D14   With Emily B. Todd. *Verse* 8:3 & 9:1, Winter/Spring 1992, 83–95.

Published March 1992.

D15   With Ian Buchan. 'A degree of fun'. *Evening Times* 18 June 1992, 8.

On her honorary D. Litt from Glasgow University. Photograph.

D16   With Colin Nicholson. 'Knucklebones of Irony' in his *Poem, Purpose and Place: Shaping Identity in Contemporary Scottish Verse* (Edinburgh: Polygon, 1992), 203–23.

E   EPHEMERA

E1   *from* The Bargain. Glasgow: Third Eye Centre and Glasgow District Libraries Publications Board, 1983.

Art card, 15 × 20 cm, with photograph by Oscar Marzaroli, 'Paddy's Market, Glasgow 1969', on front. One of series of twelve, incorporating poems and visual images from *Noise and Smoky Breath*, ed. Hamish Whyte (Glasgow: Third Eye Centre / GDLPB, 1983).

E2   Mirror's Song. [Edinburgh: Polygon Books, 1984].

Yellow poster, 49 × 37 cm, printed in black and red, with illustration by Ingebjorg Smith. Published as publicity for *DF*.

F   MANUSCRIPTS

F1   Glasgow University Library

Typescripts of *Blood and Ice* and *Shanghaied*.
In Scottish Theatre Archive.

F2   John Rylands University Library of Manchester

Correspondence between Liz Lochhead and Michael Schmidt, 1980. Two letters each.
In Carcanet Press Archive.

F3   Mitchell Library, Glasgow

Five poems from *Islands*, [c. 1978]. (891291)

TS (photocopy) poem: 'The Last Hag' and two TS (photocopy) drafts and printed version of poem: 'Revelation', n.d. (891350)

Two letters to *Oasis* magazine, 1976. (MS. 201/1/35–6)

TS script: *Tickly Mince*, [1982]. Written with Tom Leonard and Alasdair Gray. (891284)

F4   National Library of Scotland, Edinburgh

Poems, [c. 1972–1980]. 37 items, autograph and typescript. (Acc. 7799)

G   RECORDINGS

G1   Readings from her work, 1971–1983, from BBC Radio 3 'Poetry Now' series. National Sound Archive, London.

G2   *Anthology of Contemporary Scottish Poetry: The Heretics*. Edinburgh: HEP Records, [c. 1980?]. 12 inch disc.

Includes Liz Lochhead reading poem 'Bawd'.

G3   *Men Talk* c/w *Smirnoff for Karloff*. Stretch Records, 1984. 7 inch disc. STR7–1.

With music by Alasdair Robertson.

G4   *Competent at Peever*. Glasgow: Book Trust Scotland, 1991. Audio cassette. GAL BT1

Liz Lochhead reads: Bagpipe Muzak; 'Security (Verena No. 1)'; 'Running into Norma Nimmo' ['Meeting Norma Nimmo']; Vymura (The Shade Card Poem) – Favourite Shade – Condensation; 'Anklebiters (Verena No. 2)'; Almost Miss Scotland – View of Scotland / Love Poem – After The War – The Choosing – Poem For My Sister – Page From A Biography – Poem For Other Poor Fools – My Rival's House – The Other Woman – The Hickey – Song Of Solomon – Ships – What The Pool Said On Midsummer's Day – Midsummer Night – A Giveaway – Smirnoff For Karloff.

Produced by Ewan McVicar.

H   CRITICAL AND BIOGRAPHICAL

H1   Edwin Morgan, [Essay] in *Contemporary Poets*, Second Edition, edited by James Vinson with D. L. Kirkpatrick (London & New York: St James Press, 1975), 925–6.

Reprinted in *Contemporary Poets*, Third Edition (London: Macmillan Press, 1980), 929; revised for *Contemporary Poets*, fourth edition (London and Chicago: St James Press, 1985), pp. 507–8; and revised again for *Contemporary Poets*, fifth edition (Chicago and London: St. James Press, 1991), 571. Brief biographical details and bibliography also included.

H2 Alexander Scott, 'Scottish Poetry in the Seventies'. *Akros* 10:28, August 1975, 112.

H3 Duncan Glen, 'Flourishing poetry in Glasgow and the west'. *Styx* (Glasgow College of Technology) Spring 1976.

H4 'Scotland's Poets: 4: Liz Lochhead'. *Scottish Field* October 1976, 60. Brief biographical note and photograph.

H5 Alasdair Gray, LIZ LOCHHEAD 1977.
Portrait of Liz Lochhead, in People's Palace Museum. Published as a postcard by Glasgow Museums & Art Galleries.

H6 'Marching on'. *Glasgow Herald* 11 September 1978, 6.
On *Sugar and Spite*.

H7 Lindsay Paterson, [Review of Wildcat's performance of *True Confessions*]. *Scotsman* 20 August 1982, 4.

H8 [Brief publicity piece on *Tickly Mince*, *True Confessions* and *Blood and Ice*, with photograph of cast of *True Confessions*]. *West End Times* 20 August 1982, 9.

H9 'Poet's fellowship'. *Glasgow Herald* 28 September 1982, 3.
On appointment as writer in residence at Tattenhall Centre, Chester.

H10 Ken Edward Smith, 'Scottish Poetry as I see it 1965–1981'. *Akros* 17:50, October 1982, 86–7.

H11 Alan Bold, *Modern Scottish Literature* (London and New York: Longman, 1983), 92–3.

H12 Glasgow Writers: Notes to accompany Book Four. Glasgow: National Book League (Scotland), 1985.
Channel Four TV Book Four programme featured Alasdair Gray, James Kelman, Liz Lochhead and Agnes Owens. First transmitted 10 April 1985.

H13 Jan Montefiore, *Feminism and Poetry: Language, Experience, Identity in Women's Writing* (London and New York: Pandora Press, 1987), 39, 41–2, 53–5.

Discusses GS in chapter 'Women and Tradition'.

H14   Joy Hendry, 'Twentieth-century Women's Writing: The Nest of
      Singing Birds' in *The History of Scottish Literature*, volume 4,
      edited by Cairns Craig (Aberdeen: Aberdeen University Press,
      1987), 306.

H15   Toni Pickering, 'Scottish Dance Theatre'. *Scotsman* 21 May
      1987, 4.
      Review of *Consuming Passions*.

H16   Robbie Dinwoodie, 'Women writers urged to break the rules'.
      Scotsman 19 August 1987, 8.
      Review of Meet the Author event at Edinburgh Book Festival.
      Liz Lochhead read 'The Bride'.

H17   Anthony Troon, 'Play dispute'. *Scotsman* 4 September 1987, 10.
      On SAC payments to playwrights. Liz Lochhead quoted.

H18   Catherine Lockerbie, 'Scottish parallels with Quebec'. *Scotsman* 7
      September 1987, 9.
      Liz Lochhead took part in conference on Quebec/Scotland at
      Stirling University.

H19   Joy Hendry, 'Channel 4 accused of London bias'. *Scotsman* 14
      September 1987, 8.
      Liz Lochhead contributed to arts conference organized by
      Richard Demarco.

H20   Lorn McIntyre, 'Feminist who puts poetry in motion'. *Observer
      Scotland* 23 October 1988, 7.
      In 'Reputations' series. Photograph.

H21   Gregg Ward, 'Enter a pioneering spirit'. *Scotland on Sunday
      Spectrum* 25 February 1990, 6.

H22   Keith Bruce, 'Baffling bag of in jokes will keep Jock at home'.
      Glasgow Herald 26 February 1990, 14.
      On *Jock Tamson's Bairns*.

H23   Julie Morrice, 'Blowing the whistle on Mozart's killer'. *Scotland
      on Sunday* 4 March 1990, 43.
      On script about *The Magic Flute* cast party.

H24   [Tour of Liz Lochhead's flat]. *Scam* August/September 1990, 11.
      [not seen]

H25 Ilona S. Koren-Deutsch, *Pam Gems and Liz Lochhead: British feminist approaches to the history play.* 1991.

Discusses *Mary Queen of Scots Got Her Head Chopped Off.* Submitted as M.A. thesis in Department of Theatre and Drama, Indiana University, May 1990. Copy of typescript (101 ff.) in Mitchell Library, Glasgow.

H26 Robert Crawford, 'The Gutter and the Dictionary: Some Contemporary Scots Poets'. *Verse* 8:2, Summer 1991, 74–5.

On Liz Lochhead's use of Scots in *T*.

H27 Marilyn Reizbaum, 'Canonical Double Cross: Scottish and Irish Women's Writing' in *Decolonising Tradition: New Views of Twentieth-Century 'British' Literary Canons*, edited by Karen R. Lawrence (Urbana & Chicago: University of Illinois Press, 1991), 181–4.

Mainly on *Mary Queen Of Scots Got Her Head Chopped Off.*

H28 Peter McLaren, ['Liz Lochhead'] in *Four Glasgow Writers* (Glasgow: Straight Line Publishing for Strathclyde Region Education Department, [1991]) 7, 15–16.

H29 Mario Relich, 'An Iconoclastic Storyteller' [and note on poem 'Bawd']; Angus Macneacail, 'I remember Liz Lochhead . . .'. *Scottish Poetry Library Newsletter* 17, August 1991, 6–7.

H30 Joseph Farrell, 'Rivalry which sent Mary for the chop'. *Scotsman* 9 January 1992, p. 13.

Report of conversation bwteen Liz Lochhead and Dacia Maraini on their plays about Mary Queen of Scots.

H31 Jackie McGlone, 'The Gospel according to Lochhead'. *The Herald* 6 July 1992, 13.

On Liz Lochhead's adaption of York cycle of mystery plays. Photograph.

H32 Roderick Watson, 'Liz Lochhead' in his *Three Scottish Poets* (Edinburgh: Canongate Press, 1992), 87–8.

About the Contributors

S. J. BOYD lectures in the Department of English at St Andrews University. His books include *The Novels of William Golding* (Second Edition, Harvester Wheatsheaf, 1990). He has also published work on Mary Shelley's *Frankenstein* and on Alasdair Gray.

JACKIE CLUNE lectures on Performance in the Department of Drama and Theatre Studies at Royal Holloway, University of London, and is a founder member of the Red Rag Women's Theatre Company. She has a wide-ranging interest in fringe theatre and feminist aesthetics.

ROBERT CRAWFORD's third collection of poems, *Talkies* (Chatto), was published in 1992, as was his critical book *Devolving English Literature* (OUP). He is Lecturer in Modern Scottish Literature in the English Department, University of St Andrews.

JENNIFER HARVIE is a graduate student in the Department of Drama and Theatre Studies, University of Glasgow, writing a doctoral thesis on the work of Liz Lochhead.

JAN McDONALD is Professor of Drama and Theatre Studies at the University of Glasgow. Her books include *The New Drama* (Macmillan, 1986) and amongst her articles is a study of Liz Lochhead's feminist revision of *Dracula*.

LYNDA MUGGLESTONE is Fellow in English at Pembroke College, Oxford. She publishes widely on the sociolinguistics of class, gender, and regional dialect, and is author of *Talking Proper* (OUP, 1993).

DOROTHY PORTER McMILLAN lectures in English Literature at Glasgow University, and is Secretary of the Association for Scottish Literary Studies. She has published extensively on modern Scottish women's writing.

ALISON SMITH is a Lecturer in English Literature at the University of Strathclyde. She has edited Synge's work for Everyman's Library, and is now working on Scottish Literature and Modernism.

RANDALL STEVENSON lectures in the Department of English Literature, University of Edinburgh. His most recent books are *Modernist Fiction: An Introduction* (1992) and *A Reader's Guide to the Twentieth-Century Novel in Britain* (1993), both published by Harvester Wheatsheaf.

ANNE VARTY is Lecturer in English and Drama at Royal Holloway, University of London. She writes on nineteenth- and twentieth-century English and Scottish literature, and is the British editor of *Lettres Européennes* (Hachette, 1992).

HAMISH WHYTE co-edited *About Edwin Morgan* (Edinburgh University Press, 1990). He is one of Scotland's leading bibliographers and runs the Department of Rare Books and Manuscripts at the Mitchell Library, Glasgow.

Index